P9-CRI-017

Key Concepts in International Relations

Series Editor: Paul Wilkinson

1

International Organizations

International Organizations

Clive Archer

University of Aberdeen

London
GEORGE ALLEN & UNWIN
Boston   Sydney

George Allen & Unwin (Publishers) Ltd,
40 Museum Street, London WC1 1LU, UK

George Allen & Unwin (Publishers) Ltd,
Park Lane, Hemel Hempstead, Herts HP2 4TE, UK

Allen & Unwin, Inc.,
9 Winchester Terrace, Winchester, Mass. 01890, USA

George Allen & Unwin Australia Pty Ltd,
8 Napier Street, North Sydney, NSW 2060, Australia

First published in 1983

British Library Cataloguing in Publication Data

Archer, Clive
    International organizations. – (Key concepts in international relations;
no. 1)
1. International agencies – History
I. Title   II. Series
341.2'09   JX1995
ISBN 0-04-320156-3
ISBN 0-04-320157-1 Pbk

Library of Congress Cataloging in Publication Data

Archer, Clive
    International organizations
(Key concepts in international relations; 1)
Bibliography: p.
Includes index.
1. International agencies.   I. Title.   II. Series.
JX1995.A72   1983   341.2   83-6329
ISBN 0-04-320156-3
ISBN 0-04-320157-1 (pbk.)

Set in 10 on 11 point Times by Fotographics (Bedford) Ltd
and printed in Great Britain
by Billing and Sons Ltd, London and Worcester

Contents

General Editor's Introduction

The word 'concept' is derived from a Latin root meaning literally gathering or bundling together. In any organized body of knowledge the major concepts developed and deployed by scholars are the vital instruments for organizing information and ideas; they are as indispensable for the tasks of gathering, classification and typology as they are in the more ambitious work of model and theory–building. And in any study of human history and society these key concepts inevitably constitute weapons and battlefields in the conflict of normative theories, ideologies and moral judgements. Every major concept of international relations has a very different connotation depending on the philosophical beliefs, ideology, or attitude of the beholder. Take the terms 'imperialism' and 'revolution': although liberal and Marxist writers frequently use these words the precise meanings and significance they attach to them will vary enormously, and even if a single author is perfectly consistent in usage in a single book, he may alter his usage, either consciously or unwittingly, over time. None of us is immune against this process of continual redefinition and reevaluation. This is one of the reasons why it is so important for us all, whether laymen or specialists, to become more aware, vigilant and critical of the problems and pitfalls of conceptualisation both for ourselves and others. The review and clarification of concepts should not be left to a small coterie of professional philosophers and linguistic analysts. It should be a regular part of our own mental preparation for study, reflection, writing, and the practical burdens of communicating and participating in a democratic society. Careful and informed use of the full range of major concepts developed in any field of knowledge, with due attention to clarity and consistency and the interrelatedness of concepts is also obviously a vital heuristic tool, a prerequisite for good scientific research. More than this, the refinement, modification and reevaluation involved in operationalising well-tried concepts often lead to the introduction of new concepts, fresh building–blocks in the development of knowledge, discovery and fuller understanding, whether of the physical universe, human history and society, or the nature and development of the individual human spirit, personality, and imagination.

If one examines the standard range of introductory texts on international relations used by universities in America and Western

Europe, one is struck by three features of their conceptual apparatus, aspects which are now so widespread that they can be said to typify the stock–in–trade of the discipline. First, there is the astonishingly wide consensus on the basic checklist of key organizing concepts in the subject, almost invariably reflected in the contents outline: international system, nation–state, sovereignty, power, balance of power, diplomacy, military strategy, nuclear deterrence, alliances, foreign policy–making, international law, international organization, trade, aid, and development. These are the almost ubiquitous repertoires. Other themes such as human rights, conflict resolution, ideology, and propaganda find inclusion in a minority of contents pages: almost invariably in the modern texts they will be mentioned only briefly at some point in the introductory survey course.

A second recurrent feature is the lack of attention to the origin and development of the concepts themselves. This characterises nearly all the well–known texts. It is almost as if the text–book writers wish to leave the student in innocence of the major historical developments of their subject. How many of the introductory texts, for example, even bother to mention such seminal contributions as those of Grotius in international law, Clausewitz in military strategy, or Mitrany in the field of international organization? Only rarely is attention given to problems of definition, to conflicting theories and approaches, and to the problems of conceptual obsolescence and innovation.

The third major weakness, in the editor's view, is the failure to adequately relate the key concepts of international relations to the real world thinking and activities of statesmen, officials, political parties, media publics, and other key participants in the international system. Yet the language of international relations we use as academic teachers, researchers, and students, is not the esoteric product of a research laboratory or seminar room: our major concepts are the very stuff of international diplomacy, foreign policy, and intercourse. True, on occasion, as in the case of the key concepts of nuclear deterrence and functionalist and neo–functionalist theories of integration, academicians and scientists serving or advising governments have also played a key role in developing new concepts. Yet the plain fact is that many of our newer concepts – in for example, military strategy, economic development and international organization, have been originated, modified, developed and debated mainly among politicians, diplomatists, civil servants, service chiefs, guerrilla leaders, and even journalists. And because we need to be closely in touch with the nuances and subtleties of the constant and evolution of ideas and assumptions of the main participants in the international system, narrowly–based surveys of conceptual usage and development in the scholarly literature would also be inadequate and distorting.

It is to remedy these grave deficiencies that this new series of individual monographs, each devoted to a thorough review of a major international relations concept, has been devised. The editor and publishers hope that the series will educate and illuminate at both the undergraduate and post–graduate teaching levels in all universities and colleges that offer courses in international relations. It is also hoped that the volumes will provide valuable background, sources, and stimulus to teachers and researchers, many of whom have long complained about the absence of such guides. Finally, the series should also be of value to officials, politicians, industrial executives and others whose professional work involves some degree of partici-pation in, and understanding of, international developments, trends, policy–making and problems. The series should also be of interest and value to students and specialists in cognate disciplines, such as history, economics, political science, and sociology.

It may help to recapitulate the brief given to each contributor in the series. It is intended that each volume will deal thoroughly with the following aspects:

The origins and evolution of the concept, including significant variations and changes in usage, and in relation to changes in usage, and in relation to changes in the international system and in the political systems of major powers; an attempt at an authoritative definition of the concept in order that it may be employed as a more effective tool in the analysis and theory of international relations; the identification of any important sub–concepts and typologies; a critical review of the ways in which the concept is utilized in major theories, models and approaches in the contemporary study of inter-national relations; the relationship of the concept to other key concepts in international relations; the relationship between the concept and the contemporary practice of international relations; the relationship between the concept and policy–making in inter-national relations; the future of the concept in international relations.

It should hardly be necessary to add that the publishers and the series academic editor have chosen the individual authors com-missioned to review each concept, with considerable care, taking into account not only their previous record of scholarly work in the field but also their experience as teachers and expositors. We hope and believe that the completed series will provide a boon to international relations teaching and research world–wide. We welcome suggestions, responses and even practical proposals for additional contributions to the series. Please correspond in the first instance with Michael Holdsworth of George Allen & Unwin at the address printed on the reverse of the title page.

*   *   *

In this learned and thoughtful contribution to the Key Concept Series Dr Clive Archer examines the concept of *International Organization*. His study brings out clearly the extent to which the development of the concept was stimulated by the experience of major international conflicts and by the desire of many statesmen, officials, and leaders of opinion to create fresh institutional structures in the hope that they would prevent similar large–scale conflicts breaking out again. He illustrates this theme by pointing to the proliferation of formal diplomatic machinery in the wake of the Congress of Vienna following the Napoleonic wars, the far more ambitious project of the League of Nations with its ideal of 'collective security' set up after the carnage of 1914–18, and the United Nations, the European Community, and the exponential growth of other international bodies after 1945.

But this was not the only important stimulus to ideas and theories of international organization. Dr Archer also explores the enormously significant role of the revolution in industrial technology, in international communications and in international trade and finance which made a whole range of new functional specialized institutions not merely helpful but essential to lubricate the wheels of international economic growth and development, uneven but in certain countries exponential. Again the new concepts of international organization can be explained as responses to, and manifestations of, deeper changes in the international system, and only rarely as creators or moulders of international behaviour in their own right. And in the central chapters of his book Dr Archer brilliantly characterises, classifies and compares these new international phenomena. With balance and realism he explores their difficulties, vulnerabilities and failures as well as their strengths, and evaluates the prospects for different models and techniques of international organization in the light of current conditions in the international system.

Many readers will be impressed not only by the author's erudition concerning the history and politics of so many international organizations, but also by the determined objectivity and realism of his assessments. Far too many general analysts of international organization became obsessed with favourite institutional structures of one kind or another as a panacea for the world problems. Clive Archer never allows his reader to fall into this trap. In this analysis the reader is constantly made aware of the sense of malaise that afflicts the work of almost all contemporary inter–governmental organizations: the public indifference or outright hostility displayed towards them in many countries; their apparent lack of adequate resources and powers to perform many of the tasks they were designed to achieve, leading to further crises of credibility; obstruction, suspicion and occasional efforts at manipulation on the part of certain governments – especially powerful ones and increasingly isolated and frustrated international civil servants struggling to cope with all these pressures.

A brief glimpse at these daunting problems of the typical inter-governmental organization (IGO) is in itself a reminder of some of the factors which sometimes cause the non–governmental organization (NGO) to enjoy greater dynamism and higher morale. What the NGO lacks in financial resources it can very often more than make up for in commitment, public support and imaginative innovation.

One of the major lessons of this book is that international organization is not a synonym for international cooperation: indeed, as so often demonstrated in European Community institutions, it may be used as a means of *preventing* greater cooperation. Dr Archer's study underlines the importance of relating international organization to its political, social, economic, and cultural contexts, and not least to the personalities and attitudes of its leaders. No international organization will be effective without political will, a minimum of support from member governments and publics, and a high quality of leadership. Any objective comparative study would have to admit that these conditions are even rarer among IGOs, than they are among governments.

Fortunately other means are to hand to compensate for some key weaknesses and failures of IGOs, and of the UN in particular, but these also have their intrinsic dangers. How long will the structure of nuclear deterrence which has kept a kind of nuclear peace between the major powers for thirty years, hold up? Not very long if generous, but misguided unilateralism succeeds in undermining nuclear defences on only one side, in the West. Industrial summits, the IMF and the possibilities of concerted action by governments of the industrial states, OPEC countries, and the Third World may provide informal agencies for radical reform and renewal of the international economy. The Brandt Commission and the poor Third World countries desperately hope so. But again there is no guarantee that ad hoc measures will be any more effective in achieving urgently needed changes than the UN and other well–established IGOs. Dr Archer makes clear why the most careful thought should be given to the possible role of existing IGOs in any project to launch a New International Economic Order. He also alerts us to the need to fully utilize the IGOs' expertise, experience and information resources: he is not a negative critic.

Finally, in looking ahead to the future of international organizations, the author argues that the elements of vision, imagination and idealism are badly needed if these projects for international cooperation are to succeed. They must capture and canalise confidence, energy and new loyalty. The old realist versus idealist debate in international relations is shown to be hopelessly outdated. No contemporary student of international relations of any standing advocates a return to policies of narrow nationalism and the chimera of total self–sufficiency and international isolation. The real divide is between the revolutionary internationalists who believe that the necessary changes in international power structures and economics will only be brought about by violent revolution, and the reformist internationalists who argue that radical improvements in the international system can be brought about by getting the essential support for peaceful change and voluntary cooperation by means of rational argument. Dr Archer skilfully explores the theories on both sides, and their possible international implications, and makes his own conclusions absolutely clear. The reader must make up his or her own mind. For some readers the idealism and radicalism implied even in the reformist position will come as something of a shock. Are the Brandt Commission's ideas too ambitious? Do they outstrip the practical possibilities of international politics? John Steinbeck once wrote in *Grapes of Wrath*:

> Man, unlike any other thing organic or inorganic in the universe, grows beyond his work, walks up the stairs of his concepts, emerges ahead of his accomplishments.

Given the scale of the problems and dangers confronted by the international community we may not have much choice or much time. However painful and difficult we may have to try to climb the stairs of our best concepts.

Paul Wilkinson
University of Aberdeen

Foreword

This book has been written as a result of over a decade's experience of teaching international relations at Aberdeen University. It is intended as a textbook for university and college students and as an introduction to the subject for those interested in international relations.

Chapter 1 provides a history of the growth of international organizations and a working definition. Chapter 2 examines the phenomenon and presents a classification of international organizations using the criteria of regional/universal attributes, aims and activities, and institutional framework. Chapter 3 deals with the major writings on the subject, including traditionalist approaches, modern Western views, Marxist ideas and Third World interpretations. Chapter 4 considers the roles and function of international organizations in the international system and the final chapter looks forward to the future of international organizations. A list of initials of certain organizations and their full titles, a full bibliography and index completes the book.

Except when attributed, the views expressed in this book are my own. Any mistakes are mine – I am only happy to have been able to remove those noticed by colleagues during the book's earlier stages of preparation. Indeed I am indebted to a number of people for the help they provided. In particular thanks are due to four colleagues who read draft chapters and offered useful advice: Professor Alan James, John Main, David Scrivener and Professor Paul Wilkinson. Further help and comments were received from Dr Patricia Birnie, Dr Jerome Davis, Peter Foot, Dr Dermot Healy, Michael Sheehan, Professor Harvey Starr and Michael Woodward. My thanks also to Helen Stuart for typing the final draft, to Margaret McRobb for secretarial help and to the staff of Aberdeen University library for their kind and able assistance.

1

Definitions and History

Definitions

Both words in the title of this book have been a source of puzzlement
for the student of international relations. It is worth examining them
more closely before turning to the realities they represent when
joined together. The term 'international', thought to be the creation
of Jeremy Bentham, is often seen as a misnomer. Instead, it is
claimed, the term 'interstate' or 'intergovernmental' should be used
when describing an activity – war, diplomacy, relations of any kind –
conducted between two sovereign states and their governmental
representatives. Thus talk of an 'international agreement' between
state A and state B to limit arms production or to control the selling of
computer technology refers not to an understanding between the
armament manufacturers of A and B or to a pact between their
computer firms but to an arrangement by state A's governmental
representatives with those of state B.

This state and government oriented view of the word 'international' has been increasingly challenged over the past three
decades. The belief has grown that the term should not be used
synonymously with 'intergovernmental' to mean 'interstate' or
relations between the official representatives of sovereign states.
Instead the term has come to include activities between individuals
and groups in one state and individuals and groups in another state as
well as intergovernmental relations. The first types of relationships –
those not involving activities between governments only – are known
as transnational relations. Connections between one branch of
government in one state (say a defence ministry) and a branch of
government in other country (its defence ministry or its secret service,
for example) and which do not go through the normal foreign policy-
making channels are called transgovernmental. All these relationships – intergovernmental, transnational and transgovernmental –
are now usually included under the heading 'international'.

The use of the term 'organizations' is confused by the dual meaning of its singular form and its interchanging in many books with the word 'institutions'. International relations, whether between governments, groups or individuals, are not totally random and chaotic but are, for the main part, organized. One form of the organization of international relations can be seen in institutions – 'the collective forms or basic structures of social organization as established by law or by human tradition' (Duverger, 1972, p. 68) – whether these be trade, commerce, diplomacy, conferences or international organizations. An international organization in this context represents a form of institution which refers to a formal system of rules and objectives, a rationalized administrative instrument (Selznick, 1957, p. 8) and has 'a formal technical and material organization: constitutions, local chapters, physical equipment, machines, emblems, letterhead stationery, a staff, an administrative hierarchy, and so forth' (Duverger, 1972, p. 68). Inis Claude (1964, p. 4) makes the following distinction: 'International *organization* is a process; international *organizations* are representative aspects of the phase of that process which has been reached at a given time'. Some writers confusingly refer to such international organizations as international institutions and also reference is often made to 'the institutions' of an organization, such as its assembly, council and secretariat. This use of 'institutions' to refer to the detailed structure of an international organization or as a synonym for international organizations is more restricted than the sociological meaning of the word. As can be seen from Duverger's definition, it has a wider use that encompasses the notion of a system of relationships that may not manifest themselves in formal organizations of bricks and mortar, headed notepaper, a ready acronym such as NATO or WHO and an international staff. An institutional framework adds 'stability, durability and cohesiveness' to individual relationships which otherwise might be 'sporadic, ephemeral, and unstable' (Duverger, 1972, p. 68). In personal life these institutions that bind people together may be represented by an organization such as the Mothers' Union, the Roman Catholic Church or a trade union organization, but may also take the form of the less formal structures of the family or of a religion or of private property. At an international level, relations may be given a 'stability, durability and cohesiveness' – they may be organized – by the practice of diplomatic method or adherence to the tenets of international law or by regular trading – all institutions in the wider sense – as well as by the activities of such international organizations as the World Movement of Mothers, the World Council of Churches or the International Labour Organization (ILO).

This book is concerned not so much with the broader notions of international organization and international institutions but the more concrete manifestation of regularized international relations as seen in international organizations with their formal and material existence separate from, though for the most part dependent on, states and groups within states.

International Organizations up to the First World War

Accounts of the rise of international organizations rarely begin historically in 1919 at the Versailles Peace Conference – but it is a good time and place to start. Gathered together were the representatives of the victorious powers ready to write a peace treaty, many national interest groups, international non-governmental organizations (INGOS) wanting to advance public health, the lot of the workers, the cause of peace or the laws of war. The states' representatives were also concerned to create a new, permanent world organization that would deal with the problem of peace and security and economic and social questions. They drew on almost a century of experience of peacetime co-operation between European states and some half century of the work of the public international unions. Their activity was underpinned by the existence of private international associations, was foreshadowed in the Hague Conferences of 1899 and 1907 and in plans advanced before and during the war, and was moulded by the wartime experience of co-operation. The organizations they established – the League of Nations and the ILO being the leading ones – had structures determined by this background. This brief history will examine the lead-up to the creation of the League of Nations: the rise of INGOS, the parallel growth of public international unions with their major interest in economic and social questions, and the role of intergovernmental organizations (IGOS) in dealing with peace and security up until 1919. The historical development of international organizations since that date will then be examined to demonstrate the growth of INGOS, economic and social IGOS and IGOS involved with peace and security.

The gathering at Versailles in 1919 was primarily an intergovernmental meeting of heads of state and government, foreign ministers and their advisers. It was mostly concerned with the question of international peace and security while economic and social questions were given only perfunctory consideration. The Conference was faced with the task of writing a peace treaty and organizing relations between states after the most momentous breakdown in interstate relationships in history – the First World War. This war had arrived after a century of comparative peace since the defeat of Napoleon – a hundred years during which a number of forms of international organization had burgeoned. The rise of the phenomena of inter-governmental organizations concerned with international peace and security and with economic and social issues needs some explanation.

An understanding of the reasons why these organizations started to grow in the nineteenth century can be reached by asking the question: why were there no interstate organizations previous to that time? The most obvious reason is that these organizations had to await the creation of a relatively stable system of sovereign states in Europe. The crucial turning point was the Peace of Westphalia, 1648, ending the Thirty Years War which had torn apart late mediaeval Europe. Previous to 1648 the concept of a unified Christian Europe dominated the thinking, if not the practice, of political life in Europe (Bozeman, 1960, p. 514; Hinsley, 1967, chs 1 and 8). The waning temporal power of the Papacy and the Holy Roman Empire demonstrated the difficulties of unifying such a diverse geographical area as the continent of Europe, even when its peoples were threatened by the march of the Ottoman Empire. Despite this, a form of unity was offered by the doctrine, most notably advocated by Thomas Aquinas, of a God-given natural law above mankind, adherence to which provided an opportunity for Christian rulers and their subjects to belong to a greater commonwealth. With the questioning and later rejection of natural law tenets by certain philosophers and the 'civil war' between Christian princes from 1618 to 1648, the prospect of a politically united Europe faded into the past. The Peace of Westphalia and the Treaty of Utrecht in 1713 laid the basis for the sovereign state system in Europe, a system later extended to the rest of the world. This system recognized the right of states, with defined geographical boundaries including more or less settled populations (territoriality), to have their own forms of government (non-intervention) and to conduct relations with each other on an equal legal basis (sovereign equality). Most rulers no longer utilized the natural law to guide relations between states but instead the concept emerged of an international law founded on the practice of states in voluntarily making mutual agreements based either on treaty or on custom. 'The Westphalia conception includes the idea that national governments are the basic source of order in international society.' For international relations it means 'decentralized control by sovereign states' (Falk, 1969, pp. 68–9).

Given the existence of the sovereign state system, why did governments not create a network of international organizations throughout the eighteenth century? Inis Claude (1964, p. 17) sets four preconditions before such action could be taken: the existence of a number of states functioning as independent political units; a substantial measure of contact between these subdivisions; an awareness of problems that arise from states' co-existence; and their recognition of 'the need for creation of institutional devices and systematic methods for regulating their relations with each other'. Only the first of these prerequisites manifestly existed before the nineteenth century. A form of diplomacy existed between the courts of the European powers and trade and travel grew throughout Europe during the eighteenth century. The measure of contact built up between states in the 150 years following Westphalia could scarcely be described as substantial and an all too common form of contact was warfare. It has been calculated that there were sixty-seven significant wars in the period from 1650 to 1800, a time particularly noticeable for the large number of major wars in which Great Powers participated on each side (Wright, 1965, pp. 636–51).

The international systems which existed outside Europe in the period before the area was integrated into the European system in the nineteenth century, also showed little propensity for creating international organizations. The various arrangements of the Chinese Empire ranging from the feudal system of the Western Chou period (starting some 1100 years BC) to the imperial rule of the Manchus (from the latter half of the seventeenth century until the revolution of 1912); the divided warring India of the statesman Kautilya (about 300 BC) to that of the decaying Mogul Empire of the seventeenth century; and the Islamic Ottoman Empire were all familiar with war, trade, alliances, federations and even forms of diplomacy, but none produced the permanent institutions of international organizations. One possible exception is the Amphictyonic Councils of ancient Greece

> which were something between a Church Congress, an Eisteddfod and a meeting of the League of Nations Assembly . . . Although the main purpose of these conferences, as of the permanent secretariat which they maintained, was the safeguarding of shrines and treasures and the regulation of the pilgrim traffic, they also dealt with political matters of common Hellenic interest and, as such, had an important diplomatic function. (Nicolson, 1969, pp. 18–19)

Apart from this, the various polities in the systems mentioned, as in those of pre-nineteenth century Europe, found that contact with other political units was either in a belligerent form or, if peaceful, could be satisfied by the skills of the merchants and the occasional envoy.

The reasons why the nineteenth century provided such fertile ground in Europe for international organizations can be found in Claude's final two points: an awareness of the problems of states' co-existence and the recognition of the need for means different from those already used to regulate relationships. Governments' growing acceptance of new devices with which to conduct their relations arose partly out of the changed political situation post 1815 and partly from economic and social developments.

Peace and Security

First, the Vienna Congress of 1814–15 codified the rules of diplomacy thereby establishing an accepted mode of regular peaceful relationships between most European states. This was an important development in one of the key institutions governing interstate relations, turning diplomacy from a rather discredited activity to one that served the international system as well as the individual state (Nicolson, 1969, ch. 1).

The American Revolution, which led to the independence of the United States of America in 1776, and the French Revolution of 1789 brought into play novel political factors on the international scene. Previously the important European states had been monarchies of one form or another and the interests of the state and those of the ruler were held to be convergent. Cromwell's Commonwealth in England deviated from this pattern and later, when James II was considered unsatisfactory by certain political leaders, a new dynasty was installed. Still it was the king's parliament, the king's army and the king's peace that existed in England. The two revolutions in America and France made a change by popularizing the state. The state no longer, even in legal theory, had to be the property or the trust of a monarch but could be the instrument of popular will: '. . . Governments are instituted among Men, deriving their just Powers from the Consent of the Governed, that whenever any form of Government becomes destructive of these ends, it is the Right of the People to alter or to abolish it.' (The American Declaration of Independence).

There were immediate and noticeable effects on international relations of these two revolutions: the victory of the American settlers weakened Britain, the new revolutionary France was soon at war with the rest of Europe and Napoleon, the son of the Revolution and Madame Guillotine, had marched his armies across Europe from Iberia to Russia, from the Mediterranean to the Baltic. It took the might of Austria, Britain, Prussia and Russia to defeat Napoleon and to restore the pre-revolutionary monarchy to France.

The representatives of the victorious Powers, meeting at Vienna in 1814, had the details of a peace treaty to prepare, but they also had wider problems for consideration. They had had to combine in order to defeat Napoleon and to prevent him from turning Europe into a French empire. Their temporary unity had overcome their foe and given them a chance to return to a system of sovereign states based on the Westphalian concept. The states represented at the Congress of Vienna took the opportunity of standardizing and codifying the rules of diplomatic practice and pronouncing on other problems in the international system such as slavery. Their major contribution, however, was their mutual promise to 'concert together' against any future threat to the system. By Article VI of the Treaty of Chaumont, Austria, Britain, Prussia and Russia

> agreed to renew at fixed intervals, either under the immediate auspices of the Sovereigns themselves or by their respective Ministers, meetings for the examination of the measures which at each of these epochs shall be considered most salutary for the repose and propriety of the Nations and for the maintenance of the peace of Europe. (Hinsley, 1967, p. 195)

Previously states' representatives had met to sign peace treaties at the end of a war, but the agreement that emerged after the Congress of Vienna was to meet in times of peace to prevent war. After 1814 the Great Powers met together to discuss questions such as Greek independence and revolution in the Italian peninsula. Furthermore, the gatherings were regular – 'at fixed intervals' – another novel concept for governments.

These Congress meetings, as they were termed, saw a diplomatic struggle between Britain, represented by Foreign Minister Castlereagh, and the Holy Alliance of the reactionary rulers of Austria, Prussia and Russia over the aims and methods of common action. The Russian Czar's idea of the Great Powers intervening in Europe to uphold the status quo was opposed relentlessly by Castlereagh who was more appreciative of the forces of change in Europe. Eventually what emerged from the Congress system was the looser format of the Concert of Europe with the Great Powers consulting together on problems as they arose rather than trying to pre-empt them at regular meetings. The concept remained of a group of powerful countries discussing questions of mutual interest at a gathering of ambassadors or members of government: this was an innovative improvement on traditional bilateral diplomacy. Despite this innovation, many of the decisions concerning war and peace during the nineteenth century were made in the chanceries of Europe with little prior discussion with other governments, except to arrange alliances.

During the third quarter of the nineteenth century there was a reversion to holding international meetings after conflict rather than using them to prevent a war. The Paris Peace Conference ended the Crimean War in 1856, Vienna in 1864 the Schleswig Holstein War, Prague the Seven Weeks War in 1866 and and Frankfurt brought to a close the Franco-Prussian War in 1871. However, the thirty-five years before the start of the First World War saw the Great Powers of Europe again trying to avoid conflict by mutual agreement: the Berlin Congress, 1878, after the Russo–Turkish War, attempted a more long-term settlement of the Balkan question, the Berlin Congress of 1884–5 agreed on the division of Africa, and the Algeciras Conference in 1906 temporarily relieved pressure over rival claims in North Africa. But these gatherings did little to ease the basic tensions between the Great Powers – their growing empires and wish for expansion, their alliances, their increased military might.

The period from the end of the Congress system in 1822 to the First World War was, however, not one of a straightforward descent into Armageddon. Apart from powers continuing the practice established by the Concert of Europe of meeting together to decide matters of general European concern, there were other landmarks which demonstrated the efforts of governments to take a more organized approach to the problems of peace and security. A factor pressing states in this direction was the internationalization of the European system. Northedge (1976, pp. 73–5) has discerned seven major stages in this process of expansion, starting with the Treaty of Paris in 1783 by which the United States received international recognition. Of these seven steps, five were taken before the start of the twentieth century: the inclusion of the United States; the recognition in 1823 of the new Latin American states by Canning, Britain's Foreign Secretary; the admission of the Ottoman Empire (and Rumania) into the Concert System by the Treaty of Paris, 1856; Japan's joining the system after the opening up of that country by Commodore Perry in 1853; and the imposition in the mid-nineteenth century of diplomatic relations and unequal treaties by Britain on China thereby making it a rather unwilling member of the internationalized European system.

This extension of the system faced the leaders of the major European powers with a dilemma. In seeking to control events within Europe they could continue holding conferences among themselves, admitting to the negotiating chamber any other power with an obvious interest. Such intimate arrangements were less likely to work if the number of powers in attendance doubled or tripled and if these representatives came from lands outside the central stage of Europe. Yet if general rules for the maintenance of the state system were to be successful, either the non-European states had to be forced to follow the wishes of the Great Powers (as happened with China in the mid-nineteenth century) or they would have to be given the chance to subscribe voluntarily to the tenets. The latter option was taken up in the Declaration of Paris at the end of the Crimean War in 1856 which established the principle of free navigation for traders on all international rivers and also dealt with the question of naval warfare, the abolition of privateering, rules for neutral flags in times of war and blockades. As Hinsley (1967, p. 233) comments: 'To be effective these rules required the accession of other states beyond the signatories of the Declaration (the Great Powers, including Turkey, and Sardinia); fourteen other states acceded to them in 1856, Japan in 1886, Spain in 1908, Mexico in 1909'. Furthermore, Protocol 23 of the Treaty stated 'the desire that States . . . should, before appealing to arms, have recourse, so far as circumstances allow, to the good offices of a friendly power. The Plenipotentiaries hope that governments not represented at the Congress will unite in the sentiment which has inspired the desire recorded in the Protocol.' How much easier to bring other governments into general agreements from the beginning and how much more sensible to have meetings about these matters convened separately from a congress primarily aimed at ending a war. Such thoughts were scarcely the main motivating force behind Czar Nicholas's call in 1898 for an international conference to discuss disarmament – he was more concerned with the ability of his own country to stand the financial strain of the arms race. Twenty-seven states attended this conference and, whilst most of them were European countries, China, Japan, Mexico, Siam and the United States also sent representatives. The Second Hague Conference of 1907 drew a response from forty-four states including eighteen Latin American countries (Brown, 1909, p. 528).

Although the Hague meetings did not prevent the catastrophe of August 1914, they did produce some modest achievements and also pointed the way for the institutional development of organized international relations. A panel of arbitrators was established with the intention of making their services available on a regular basis and the First Conference adopted a Convention for the Pacific Settlement of International Disputes. Precedents for such moves can be found in the Alabama Case (1871) when Britain and the USA settled a dispute by arbitration rather than conflict, the Pan-American Conference of 1889, at which seventeen North American and Latin American states tried to establish an arbitration tribunal for disputes but ended up with an agreement on *ad hoc* tribunals, and the Anglo–American Arbitration Treaty negotiated in 1897. The latter two attempts were not very successful – the Pan-American agreement was signed by eleven states and only ratified by one, the Arbitration Treaty was subject to stringent British reservations and failed to obtain the approval of the US senate (Hinsley, 1967, pp. 267–8).

Despite these meagre results, the Hague conferences and the corresponding American efforts still represented an advance in the method of arranging relations between states. Hinsley (1967, p. 266) points out the increase in the number of arbitration treaties post 1870 and the need to regularize international contacts by states new to the 'comity of nations' as being the driving force behind the legalistic approaches of the Hague and inter-American conferences. Claude (1964, p. 26), describing the Hague conferences as meeting in an 'atmosphere heavy with unreality' underlines the diplomatic difficulties in the way of any state wishing to turn down the Czar's invitation. Whatever the motivation for the Hague meetings, once government representatives were there they experienced the innovation of conference diplomacy even with recommendations ('*voeux*') being passed by a majority vote. The legalistic notions behind the Hague concept – that the creation of the correct institutions to make judgements on international disputes would contribute significantly to peace – were later to inspire the Permanent Court of International Justice (PCIJ) and the International Court of Justice (ICJ) and the wide membership of the two conferences was a precursor of the League of Nations' Assembly. The verdict of Inis Claude (1964, p. 28) is that

> the abortive system of the Hague called attention to the emerging reality of a global, rather than a merely European, state system, the demands of small states for participation in the management of that system and the need for institutionalized procedures as well as improvised settlements, in the conduct of international relations.

This is a superficially attractive opinion but it is perhaps far-fetched in typifying Hague as anything resembling a global state system – even an emerging one. It was more a demonstration that the European state system, with European-based law, European diplomacy and other European institutions, had been extended to include outsiders. Whilst the conferences certainly brought out the demands of smaller states and 'the need for institutionalized procedures' – presumably new procedures such as arbitration – the continuation of Great Power diplomacy in Europe, North Africa, the Middle East and China demonstrated that the time was not then ripe for the general adoption of such changes. The Concert System of the early part of the century may have lasted to the end of the nineteenth century but by then it only masked struggles and complex alliances. It was too much to expect the Hague meetings to reverse completely this downward spiral. Whilst the methods used at the Hague and some of the recommendations were useful models for later consideration, the two conferences primarily indicated the limits reached in the institutionalization of international relations by the end of the nineteenth century. A system so imbued by the primacy of the needs of individual governments and which had passed over the idea of collective action implied in the Concert for the more straightforward and ruthless advancement of state interest, was scarcely a good breeding ground for institutional innovation.

Economic and Social Questions

In the area of economic and social matters the nineteenth century was also a period of growth in international co-operation. Another consequence of the French Revolution and the Napoleonic Empire lay in the popularization of the state, already mentioned. It seems far-fetched to claim (Gerbert, 1977, p. 11) that during the post-Napoleonic period 'the advance of democratic ideas, the belief that all human beings were of equal value, fostered the notion of egalitarian participation by all states in international organizations responsible for ensuring peace and progress'. What the French – and indeed the American – Revolution did was to make the state more responsive to the needs of a wider section of the population. The demands of the new middle class, let alone the working class, were not just for a nightwatchman state. By the end of the nineteenth century a number of European governments were increasingly intervening in the economies of their countries and were becoming more involved with the welfare of their citizens, a fact that was to be reflected in their international relationships. J. M. Keynes (1919) wrote of the pre-1914 world economy: 'the internationalization of economic life was almost complete'.

During the nineteenth century the states of Europe were, of necessity, fashioning new means for co-operation over the issues of peace and conflict and were being faced with a growing need to co-ordinate action in the socio-economic areas of life. A further consequence of industrial development was an improvement in communications. The steamship replaced sail, the railway overtook the stagecoach, the telegraph was introduced in 1837, and by 1850 a submarine telegraph cable joined England and France. By increasing common links, these changes underlined the need for co-ordination between states and also made communications between governments easier. Faster travel allowed government delegations to convene together more readily; the telegraph gave them the possibility of consulting with and receiving instructions from home.

Commerce was being increasingly internationalized and many nineteenth-century activities of the public international unions or international agencies reflected this, bringing together the representatives of states to manage an aspect of public life normally associated with travel, communications, commerce or welfare, the good governance of which would otherwise be affected by state boundaries. In 1804 the Convention of Octroi set up a centralized supra-national administration to subject the navigation of the Rhine to international control, but this was done at a time when Europe was dominated by Napoleonic France. The first post-Napoleonic agencies followed the opening up of the international waterways to all traders by the Congress of Vienna (Articles 108–16 of the Final Act of the Treaty of Vienna). An international commission for the Elbe was established in 1821, one for the Rhine in 1831, and Article 15 of the Treaty of Paris, 1856, established a European Danube Commission to supervise the free navigation of that river, independent of national control as the 'system of national administrations had utterly broken down, incompetent to deal with the modern world of shipping and international trade' (Woolf, 1916, p. 373). The idea of having a group of experts and administrators performing particular functions on behalf of states was taken further by the establishment in 1868 of the International Telegraphic Bureau (later named the International Telegraphic Union – ITU) and the General Postal Union (later Universal Postal Union) in 1874. Both organizations were a response to technological advances and the patent need to co-ordinate national developments in these areas. As government involvement in the social and economic sphere of its citizens' lives grew, so did the requirement to ensure that these activities were not unduly confused by the existence of national borders. The International Bureau of Weights and Measures (1875), The International Union for the Publication of Customs Tariffs (1890) and the Metric Union helped to ease international trade, whilst the international health offices established in Havana and Vienna in 1881 and Paris in 1901 demonstrated increased government concern in matters of public health and a recognition that disease knew no frontiers.

A major innovation of these agencies was their secretariats. At the end of the seventeenth century William Penn had included international civil servants modelled on the clerks of the English House of Commons in his proposals for a general European parliament. However, it is more often the bureaux of the public international unions which are seen as the forerunners of the secretariats of later universal organizations such as the League of Nations. The international aspect of the bureaux should not be overestimated – for the most part they were based on the nationals of their host country, though they did provide continuity and a sense of purpose. In many of these unions representatives of a few selected member states formed a governing body which directed policy between the regular policy-making conferences of all the member states. This structure pointed up the tension between the desire of states not to be bound by actions to which they had not agreed and the need for the unions to function efficiently. In the end most of the organizations struck a balance by allowing the governing body to deal with non-controversial technical questions, responsibility for which the national governments were happy to delegate, whilst the conferences agreed on the broad policy lines.

In the latter half of the nineteenth century, the rise of the public international unions was mirrored by that of the private international associations. National humanitarian, religious, economic, educational, scientific and political organizations arranged international meetings. Probably the first such gathering was the World Anti-Slavery Convention of 1840: it was this sort of association that spawned permanent organizations with the machinery of secretariats, boards and assemblies (Woolf, 1916, p. 165). The interest of governments in their citizens' activities, outside those that might endanger the security of the state, was fairly minimal, and there were few official restrictions on those who wished to travel and indulge in meetings of the International Institute of Agriculture, the International Law Association or the Universal Peace Congress, although the representatives of anarchist, socialist and working men's associations normally received police attention when they crossed frontiers. According to the Union of International Associations, whilst the number of intergovernmental organizations rose from seven in the 1870–4 period to thirty-seven in 1909, the number of international non-governmental organizations had already reached 176 by the latter date (*Yearbook of International Organizations*, 1974, vol. 15, tabs 1 and 2).

The relationship between the international public and private associations has usually been symbiotic. Whilst many of the private associations clearly reflected individual interests of little concern to the state, some of them demonstrated the necessity for governmental activity and co-operation across frontiers. The International Committee of the Red Cross, a private international union, promoted the intergovernmental Geneva Conventions of 1864, 1906, 1929 and 1949. In some cases a private union was a forerunner of a public international union: for example, the International Association of the

Legal Protection of Labour led to the establishment of the International Labour Organization (ILO) in 1919. The Union of International Associations, established in 1910 because of the growth of private unions, laid down as conditions of membership that the association should possess a permanent organ; that its object should be of interest to all or some nations and not be one of profit; and that membership should be open to individuals and groups from different countries. Despite this distinction between private and public associations, a number of the organizations had mixed memberships with representatives of government bodies sitting together with individual members. Present-day examples are the International Statistical Institute and the International Council of Scientific Unions (Bowett, 1970, pp. 4–5).

This rise of international public and private associations during the nineteenth century was a response to scientific, and technological changes. An American writer (Chamberlain, 1955, p. 87) observed that

Events in the international society have been following those in the national societies of which it is composed. The same new inventions, the same intensification and complication of social life have led to a great increase in international regulations which have to do with the relations of states in the economic and social fields and which affect the daily lives of individuals.

The functional approach taken by both the private and public associations – that it made sense to co-operate across frontiers on specific matters of a technical or administrative nature – came into its own during the First World War. The pressures of the war economy forced the Allies to consider afresh the organization of important areas of economic life. On the political side it was found necessary in 1916 to co-ordinate the war effort through the Inter-Allied Committee, consisting of prime ministers, relevant ministers and the necessary experts and which was advisory in character with its proposals subject to the approval of the governments involved. As the war continued, the Allies established a Supreme War Council, served by a permanent secretariat, which had authority over the range of inter-Allied councils covering the economic, military and political aspects of the war. On the economic side the aim was to make the maximum use of limited resources by pooling them and distributing them where most needed. The executive committees of these councils consisted of government officials such as Britain's Arthur Salter and France's Jean Monnet who had a wide remit to organize provision of food and transport in a way that functioned best rather than to suit national sensitivities.

The Foundations of the League of Nations

The participants at the Paris Peace Conference of 1919 had the dual task of making a settlement of victor over vanquished and of establishing a functioning international system after the disturbances created by a world war.

During the course of the war individuals, groups and governments had started work on plans for organizing post-war international relations so that 'the Great War' would be 'the war to end all wars'. President Wilson of the United States was committed to 'a general association of nations' and his adviser, Colonel House, drew up plans to this end. An official British commission under Lord Phillimore had examined a number of schemes, including those of the sixteenth- and seventeenth-century philosophers, and had decided that whilst international relations could not be radically changed, a more organized form of interstate diplomacy was desirable with states submitting disputes to a Conference of the Allied States. The French proposal, advanced by Leon Bourgeois, was more robust. It imagined an international tribunal to pronounce on issues open to legal decisions, an international body of delegates of the League member states which would take decisions on disputes, and an international force with a permanent staff which would ensure the execution of the tribunal's decisions and overcome any armed opposition to the League. In his scheme, the South African statesman, Jan Smuts, stressed the need for a small Council of League members to discuss international affairs and he placed store on deliberation and delay during disputes so that public opinion could be organized to cool down war passions.

At the Versailles Peace Conference, President Wilson himself chaired a special Commission on the League of Nations at which the British–American–South African ideas, as expressed in the Hurst–Miller draft, were dominant. The statesmen moulding the new League found that the plans before them relied heavily on the experience of the previous hundred years – the Congress and Concert systems, the public international unions and their private counterparts, and the Hague meetings. They also had something else on their minds – the wartime experience. One side of the coin was the determination to prevent the collapse of international relations into general war: the other side was the experience of Allied co-operation during the war which helped the leaders to decide at Versailles on particular schemes for their post-war relationships.

The Covenant of the League of Nations reflected the somewhat jumbled hopes and fears of the Allied and Associate powers' leadership. The new organization had as its aim the promotion of international co-operation and peace and security. To achieve this, they desired the form of relations between states to be open, lawful, just and peaceable.

In line with what had been sought at the Hague meetings of 1899 and 1907, the Covenant stressed the need to control the sinews of war. Whereas agreements of the nineteenth century had dealt with the laws of war and the Hague conferences had not come forth with any radical suggestions on the topic, the arms race preceding the war and the carnage of 1914–18 led to the inclusion of Article 8 in the Covenant, recommending the reduction of armaments and the limitation of the private manufacture of armaments.

Article 10 by which the Members of the League undertook

> to respect and preserve as against external aggression the territorial integrity and existing political independence of all Members of the League

was the work of President Wilson who based this idea on the experience of the Pan-American Union formed some twenty years previously. The British watered this down by a more Concert-like addition that, when the need arose, the members of the League Council would 'advise upon the means by which this obligation shall be fulfilled'. However, the British delegation were willing to see a 'musketeers' oath' placed in Article 11 by which

> Any threat of war . . . is hereby declared a matter of concern to the whole League and the League shall take any action that may be deemed wise and effectual to safeguard the peace of nations.

The British were also enthusiastic about the inclusion of Article 19 which allowed another element of the old European Concert into the League system – the prevention of conflict by the prior consideration of situations that might threaten peace.

The core of the League system was Articles 12–16 which outlined how states in dispute should conduct their relations. The promise of the Hague conferences was to be fulfilled in the establishment of a Permanent Court of International Justice (Article 14) and a stress on arbitration, conciliation and mediation (Articles 12, 13 and 15). Articles 12–15 took up Smut's idea of a breathing space during which war would be precluded whilst countries attempted to settle their disputes peacefully and public opinion would thereby be allowed to restrain any rush to war. States resorting to war in disregard of the processes established under Articles 12, 13 or 15 were deemed

> to have committed an act of war against all other Members of the League, which hereby undertake immediately to subject it to severance of all trade or financial relations.

This section reflects closely the wording of Jan Smuts in his 'The League of Nations: a practical suggestion' (Henig, 1973, p. 34). There was a notion expressed by Lord Cecil, the British minister, that the war had shown such action, including blockades, to be a potentially powerful instrument for peace.

President Wilson's wish for 'open convenants, openly arrived at' as opposed to the secret agreements which he felt had contributed to the outbreak of the First World War, ended up in Article 18 whereby new treaties were to be registered with and published by the League's secretariat.

To be truly global the League system would have had to cover the colonized world as well as just the sovereign states. There was pressure from the Americans for an extension of the international system, yet in the end the colonial powers' refusal to consider such a trespass on their territory blocked these plans. All that remained was the compromise over the treatment of the ex-colonies of the defeated powers – the mandates system of Article 22 and a paragraph in Article 23 whereby League members would

> undertake to secure just treatment of the native inhabitants of territories under their control.

Article 22 also contained other clauses concerning economic and social questions which reflected the growth in their international aspect as seen in the public and private international unions of the previous fifty years and in the effects of the war. An organization to secure fair and humane conditions of labour was to be established; traffic in women, children and drugs controlled; the trade in arms supervised; freedom of commerce and communications ensured, particularly in the war-ravished areas; and steps taken internationally to control disease.

Such aims presumed a re-shaping of international politics with new institutions to serve the purpose of peace. Whilst schemes abounded for such innovations, the statesmen present at the Paris Conference drew heavily on their own experience of co-operation during the war and of previous institutional developments. The Inter-Allied Supreme Council established during the war formed the basis of the Council of Ten, the inner negotiating group of the Paris Peace Conference, and its continuation can be seen in the Council of the League of Nations which was created as a forum for the Great Powers (Hankey, 1946, p. 26). Whilst nostalgia for the Concert may have affected the thinking of those who advanced plans for a post-war organization, it seems more likely that the Great Powers determining the actual settlement just decided to carry on as they had done – relatively successfully – for the previous four years. The same can be said about the social and economic institutions associated with the League. Whilst the ILO had the work of the International Labour Office at Basel (established in 1901) to build on, and the Red Cross organizations mentioned in Article 25 of the League Covenant had been functioning for some fifty years, the real stimulus to the inclusion of social and economic co-operation in the League's work was the wartime effort mentioned above (pp. 14–15). Indeed people such as Salter and Monnet remained prominent in League efforts in this area.

The Hague conferences are often seen as the model for the Assembly of the League with each state, regardless of size, having one vote and being able to make its contribution to the debates on the great questions of war and peace. This does not answer the question of how the smaller states (or, in truth, non-Great Powers) were willing and were able to press their demand for such an Assembly and why the Great Powers agreed to this request. Again the answer can be found in the wartime experience. Apart from the fact that two small states – Serbia and Belgium – had figured in the immediate causation of war, by the time the war had ended British Empire and Dominion states had made a noticeable contribution to the war effort and a number of other smaller states had come in on the Allied side. Furthermore the entry of the USA into the war, the dominance of President Wilson at the Paris Conference and the insistence of American politicians on his writing into the Covenant a reference to 'regional understandings like the Monroe Doctrine' (Article 21) meant that there would most likely also be a strong Latin American presence in any post-war peace organization. The First World War started in Europe but ended as a global war: it was fought over four continents by troops from all continents. This made it impossible for any post-war institution such as the League Assembly not to be open to universal membership, albeit determined by the restrictions of Article 1 of the Covenant. However, the Assembly was by no means seen as the central institution of the League by framers of the Covenant: the powers given to the Council compared favourably with those of the Assembly and the intention of a number of the Paris peacemakers that the Assembly should only meet every four years whereas the Council would meet more frequently, demonstrated the original favour shown to the Council.

The secretariat of the League is often seen as being based on the model of the bureaux of the public international unions of the nineteenth century. Whilst these may have provided examples of how an international secretariat may work, this by no means explains why the model was adopted rather than the idea of a secretariat with a political role or the stronger executive allowed for by the ILO. Once more the answer lies in the wartime experience, specifically that of the international secretariat of the Supreme War Council headed by Sir Maurice Hankey. The genesis of the Supreme War Council can be found in the Committee of Imperial Defence, established in 1902, which had Hankey as its secretary and which also had a number of deputy secretaries with specialized knowledge. Its task was to make war plans and to co-ordinate with the Dominion governments and its lineal successor was the wartime Imperial War Cabinet of which Hankey was again secretary. It is perhaps not surprising that Hankey was the choice for the job of secretary of the Supreme War Council which by the end of the war brought together the representatives of the British Empire, France, Italy and the United States. The next step seemed logicial: 'The machinery that had stood the terrible test of war inevitably became the nucleus of the Peace Conference . . . The International Secretariat of the Supreme War Council was brought up from Versailles and attached to the Secretariat-General of the Peace Conference' (Hankey, 1946, pp. 26–7). When consideration was given to a secretariat for a newly-emerging League of Nations, there was some support for 'a permanent organization presided over by a man of the greatest ability' as Lord Cecil wrote in his memorandum to the Imperial War Cabinet, 24 December 1918. He suggested a 'Chancellor' who as well as heading the League secretariat would be the 'international representative of the League . . . the suggester, if not the director, of its policy'. He was in fact proposing a secretariat with a political role and it was fitting that he chose a politician for the job – the Greek premier, Venizelos. However, Venizelos thought his own country needed him more than the League, as did Masaryk of Czechoslovakia and President Wilson, both of whom were apparently considered. This inability to persuade any active politician to take on such a thankless task, and French opposition to the plan, meant a return to the established model: the word 'Chancellor' was replaced by that of 'Secretary-General' in the draft Covenant and the faithful Hankey was offered the job. As Colonel House, President Wilson's adviser, explained: 'Hankey had during the war done the type of work contemplated for the Secretary-General'. When Hankey declined the position another British civil servant, Sir Eric Drummond, was appointed in his stead (Barros, 1979, pp. 1–9). It seems that the drafters of the Covenant intended that the new secretariat of the League, whilst remaining administrative rather than political, would also carry on the co-ordination role of Hankey's wartime office:

> There shall be placed under the direction of the League all international bureaux already established by general treaties if the parties to such treaties consent. All such international bureaux and all commissions for the regulation of matters of international interest hereafter constituted shall be placed under the direction of the League. (Article 24)

This somewhat underestimated the bureaucratic urge for self protection of the existing agencies once the immediate pressures of war had ceased. These plans were finally undermined when the USA did not join the League. Existing international organizations of which the USA was a member were unwilling to risk her membership by too close a connection with the League.

The League's Activities

If the institutions of the League were fashioned by the immediate experience of wartime co-operation rather than by seventeenth-century writers, the activities pressed by the members through these institutions were also more determined by memories of 1914–18 than by abstract concepts.

During the 1920s the League provided a useful but modest addition to international diplomacy. Regular annual meetings between states' representatives allowed the discussion of threats to peace and security and a more long-term consideration of questions of disarmament, guarantees of frontiers and the evolution of the League system. The Council – voicing the concern of the French and British governments – was able to dampen conflict between Greece and Bulgaria in 1925 and also solved the Turkish–Iraq dispute over Mosul. The League was by no means the only method used by states to place their relations with each other on a more peaceful and organized basis: Sweden and Finland used mediation to solve their dispute over the Aaland islands in 1920; the Locarno Treaty guaranteed French–Belgium–German frontiers thus allowing Germany to become a League member in 1926; the Kellogg–Briand

Pact allowed both League and non-League members to renounce war as an instrument of national policy; and by the end of the decade the Preparatory Commission for Disarmament which included US and Soviet delegates had started work.

On the economic and social side the League provided valuable co-ordination for efforts that had previously been disparate and also provided machinery through which problems could be studied and eventually tackled on a cross-national basis. Refugees from Russia and Turkey were aided; protection of minorities was placed on a regular international footing. The importance of co-operation on economic questions had become accepted after the experience of the Depression and by 1939 the Bruce Report recommended that the League Assembly strengthen its economic programme and establish a Central Committee for Economic and Social Questions to this end.

However, in the end the system created in 1919 was not allowed to prevent the Second World War in 1939. Rather than an organization helping to achieve collective security, disarmament, the peaceful settlement of disputes and respect for international law, the League eventually became an empty shell abandoned by countries unwilling to involve themselves outside their domain or give teeth to the League's Covenant. The United States' failure to join the League undermined its claim to universality and its hopes of taking effective action in areas outside Europe – in Manchuria, Ethiopia and Latin America. French policy was aimed at securing their country against future German attack, by a system of alliances if need be, and France attempted to make the League more of a collective security organization which would serve its own interests in Europe. British leaders in the interwar period showed themselves unwilling either within the League or outside it to commit themselves to the auto-matic defence of other countries: the logic of the alliance and of collective security.

A more serious threat came from those governments who were unsatisfied with the Versailles settlement: originally the Soviet Union, then Mussolini's Italy and finally Nazi Germany and Imperial Japan in the 1930s. These revisionist powers all had a deep-seated dislike of the post-1919 status quo which, in the cases of Germany, Italy and Japan led them to reject the institutions of the existing international system – treaties, diplomacy, international law, the international economic order and international organizations such as the League. In the case of the Soviet Union, the distaste for the European bourgeois democracies and their associated forms of international relations became attenuated over time by the need to secure the Soviet motherland from outside attack even if this meant membership of the League or alliances with non-socialist states.

Of the major Allied and Associated states that had fought the First World War, Russia had undergone a revolution and had retracted into a protective shell, both the USA and the United Kingdom had withdrawn their troops from the European continent after the immediate post-war hiatus and the French Third Republic became crippled by internal political divisions. During the 1930s the European political system which had helped to create the League of Nations came under attack from the revisionist states. Japanese attacks on China and her occupation of Manchuria from 1931 onwards underlined the unwillingness of League members to act in the Asian and Pacific areas without United States' support; full-scale military aggression by Italy against Ethiopia (Abyssinia) in 1935 brought only desultory League economic sanctions which were undermined by British and French concern not to push Italy into the arms of Germany, and Hitler's withdrawal of Germany from both the League and the Disarmament Conference in 1933 presaged a whole series of aggressive measures that went unchecked by the League's remaining members. It has been argued by J. Brierly (1946, pp. 84–92) that is was not the League system that failed. Indeed it can be seen as having a good deal of success, especially given the unfavourable conditions: it is scarcely surprising that in this period of uncertainty, isolationism and economic protectionism international institutions created to further international co-operation were so severely tested.

The whole League system can be seen as a crucial link which brought together the strands of pre-1914 international organizations and wartime co-operation into a more centralized and systematic form on a global scale, thus providing a stepping stone towards the more enduring United Nations.

Post-Second World War Organizations

The Second World War is often seen in negative terms as far as international organizations are concerned: the League of Nations and the ILO had just a residual presence in Geneva; a few other technical or humanitarian agencies – in particular the Red Cross – were kept going by the hard work of the neutral states and their citizens. Yet the war years provided the furnace within which some of the most important post-war organizations were fashioned. The experience of wartime co-operation was crucial in determining the institutions and aims of the United Nations Organization and the various economic organizations that resulted from the Bretton Woods negotiations of 1944–6. The wartime summit conferences and the intense diplomatic activity between Britain, the United States and the Soviet Union culminated in these three states, together with China, deciding on the basic structure of the UNO at the Dumbarton Oaks meeting of 1944 and the Yalta Summit of February 1945.

The Formation of the UN

Whilst the institutions of the UNO superficially resemble those of the League – Council, Assembly, Court, Secretariat – there are important differences, not just ones of detail. The UNO was negotiated whilst the war was still being fought, with the failures of the 1930s and the burdensome task of defeating the Axis Powers on the minds of Allied politicians. Emphasis was placed on carrying over wartime Great Power co-operation into peacetime with a council that would be dominated by the Big Three plus France and China and which would have prime responsibility for the maintenance of peace and security. This political solution contrasted to the legalism of the League Covenant but was also a reflection of reality: it had been the joint Anglo–American–Soviet forces that had saved the world from Axis domination. The role of the other states was not forgotten – after all, many small states and Commonwealth countries had again played an honourable and important role in the war effort and a number of the European governments-in-exile in London had contributed to the debate about post-war institutions. There was no going back from the League Assembly in making plans for the UNO but at least it could be made clear that the council body was to bear the prime responsibility for peace and security matters. It was recognized that the new organization would need a secretariat, if only to carry out the administrative duties. However, the introduction of an executive and political role (Articles 98 and 99) needs some explaining. The forerunner of the executive role can be seen in the secretariat of the ILO, especially when Albert Thomas was Secretary-General (Pheelan, 1949), whilst Cecil's idea of a chancellor and President Roosevelt's notion of a world moderator may have been a model for the political role of the UN's secretary-general. Furthermore the powers meeting at Dumbarton Oaks had the practical example of the United Nations Relief and Rehabilitation Agency's director general available – in this case the director general had a non-voting seat on the Central Committee of the USA, USSR, United Kingdom and China and had wide executive powers (Royal Institute of International Affairs, 1946, pp. 18–21).

Preparation for the formulation of the United Nations Organization was extensive, particularly in the USA where numerous private organizations produced proposals which were fed into the official planning process (Russell and Muther, 1958, pp. 215–24). All the major powers at Dumbarton Oaks and at the later San Francisco Conference which drafted the UN Charter were aware of the need to avoid the 'mistakes' of the League of Nations – the confusion of responsibility for peace and security between Council and Assembly, a legalistic approach to international peace and security, the restrictions of all members having a veto. But the nature of what was decided was determined by the reality of wartime co-operation: the UN was to be primarily a peace and security organization based on the concept of the Four Policemen, that is, the USA, USSR, the United Kingdom and China as protectors of the world against a recurrence of Axis aggression. The San Francisco Conference of all the founding members added important elements to this core: the economic and social aspects of the organization were filled out (the League's Bruce Report providing the groundwork), and trusteeship was added to the Charter as was the Declaration Regarding Non-Self-Governing Territories (Chapter XI).

The creation of the UNO contrasts to that of the League of Nations. The League's creators – Clemenceau, Lloyd George, Wilson and their advisers – had a number of draft proposals before them, based on work during the war. However the political decisions were made after the end of hostilities and were tied to the peace settlement. As suggested above, the League established by the leaders of the major victor powers scarecely looked brand new, more a continuation of nineteenth-century wartime and peace conference practice institutionalized and given some purpose. By comparison, the birth of the United Nations Organization seemed the result of the more deliberative consideration of future needs. It was based less on existing practice than had been the case with the League. After all, the experience of the major powers with the League had not been happy: the USA had not joined, the USSR had been expelled in 1939 for invading Finland, China had seen the League powerless to act against Japanese invasion of its territory and Britain had chosen appeasement and then rearmament rather than action through the League to combat the advance of Hitler in the late 1930s. Despite this, these four countries recognized at the Moscow Conference of October 1943 'the necessity of establishing at the earliest practicable date a general international organization, based on the principle of the sovereign equality of all peace-loving States and open to membership by all such States, large or small, for the maintenance of international peace and security' (Royal Institute of International Affairs, 1946, p. 13). There was even a lively debate between the British and American governments as to the basis of such an organization – whether it should have a strong regional element, as advocated by Churchill, or whether the emphasis should be universalist as Roosevelt came to believe. Unlike the case of the League, there was not the range of inter-allied institutions on which to base the organization of the UNO. The major exception is that of the Security Council which grew naturally from four-power wartime co-operation, though even here it was recognized that non-permanent members chosen from the lesser powers should be included. In contrast to the League, the work of the drafting of the United Nations Charter was undertaken whilst the war was being fought and the document was signed at San Francisco on 26 June 1945, some six weeks before the end of the war in the Far East. The proposals germinated in Allied chancellories, particularly in the various US government departments, the blueprint worked out by the Big Four at the tough negotiations at Dumbarton Oaks and the confrontation of this draft with the demands of the other allied countries meeting at San Francisco was bound to produce a hybrid. The US Senate Committee of Foreign Relations provided an appropriate epitaph for these efforts when referring to the Charter:

> While it may be that this is not a perfect instrument, the important thing is that agreement has been reached on this particular Charter, after months and even years of careful study and negotiation, between the representatives of 50 nations. (Russell and Muther, 1958, p. 939)

Like the League Covenant, the UN Charter reflected the circumstances of the time in its vision of how to obtain peace and security – by the mechanisms of peaceful change and settlement and by Great Power enforcement of the peace. With the experience of the League behind them, the Allies knew not to provide for just a particular peace (as seemed to be the case in 1919) but also to fashion instruments able to deal with the unforeseeable future. The Charter was far more successful in doing this than the League Covenant. Of course, the Charter was blessed with the signatures and ratification of the major victor powers, something the Covenant never achieved, but there were more basic differences. The Covenant contained a particular formula for maintaining peace – a rather legalistic machinery which became dated even before the end of the 1920s. The Charter also established machinery that soon became outmoded – the Military Staff Committee of Articles 46 and 47 being the prime example – but on the whole it left the task of obtaining and maintaining peace and security to the political decisions of the UN membership made at the appropriate time. Rather than re-establish the tripwires of Articles 11–16 of the Covenant, which were avoided by some states and trampled on by others, the Charter provided a set of tools (Chapter VI – Pacific Settlements of Disputes, Chapter VII – Action with Respect to Threats to the Peace, Breaches of the Peace and Acts of Aggression, Chapter VIII – Regional Arrangements) which members could take up in order to help fashion a settlement of their problems.

Post-war Developments

The way that the UNO has worked in the post-war world and the mode of development of other international organizations has been affected by the international environment since 1945. S. J. Michalek (1971, p. 387) has written that 'the successes or failures of international organizations stem not so much from their formal–legal covenants as from changing configurations and distributions of power, systemic issues and forces, and the attitudes and resources of member states'. A brief examination of these developments post-war will help to set the historical context for the behaviour of international organizations during that period.

The international system that emerged in 1945 was still one based on the sovereignty of states and it seemed that the European system had emerged victorious despite being challenged by the Axis powers. The work of the San Francisco Conference and the statements of the Great Powers at conferences from Moscow, November 1943, to Potsdam, August 1945, pointed to a belief in the tried and tested system of diplomacy, international law and international institutions. Developments in the international system since 1945 have severely tested the efficacy of the old European mode of adjusting relations between states and have to a certain extent amended it to suit new demands.

A former British diplomat who had much to do with the organization wrote: 'The United Nations is a mirror of the world around it, if the reflection is ugly, the organization should not be blamed' (Gladwyn, 1953, p. 390) and a Rumanian ex-ambassador made the point more generally: '. . . international organizations have always mirrored the world power structure of the given period' (Brucan, 1977, p. 95). What sort of post-war world has the UNO – and other international organizations – reflected?

First, it has been a world which has seen a substantial increase in the number of states and in the range of state types, measured by a variety of indicators. During the life of the League, sixty-three states had been members and in 1945 fifty-one governments signed the UN Charter. Another twenty-five states joined during the following ten years and by the end of 1960 there were 100 members. In 1982 membership reached 157, covered all the inhabited continents and included mini-states such as the Seychelles and Grenada as well as giants such as China and the Soviet Union. The political spectrum ranges from right-wing military dictatorships, the apartheid state of South Africa, through the parliamentary democracies to states with Marxist governments of the most totalitarian kind. The economic development of the membership is as varied as the consumerist USA and poverty-stricken Upper Volta, welfare state Sweden and broken-backed Lebanon. Powers such as the Soviet Union, United States, France and the United Kingdom have world-wide connections; some members, Saudi Arabia for example, can be regarded as regional powers, whilst most countries have significant relationships only with their immediate neighbours, their former colonial power and maybe one of the superpowers. A growing number of states provides the possibility of a larger number of international organizations and a wide variety in the nature of states suggests that this will be mirrored in those organizations.

This growth in the number of states in the system has resulted in the universalist institutions of the UN and its associated agencies being underpinned by a variety of international organizations with more limited membership. Some of these are confined to particular geographic areas – the Organization of American States, the Arab League, the Organization of African Unity – whilst others are geographically and ideologically defined: NATO, the Warsaw Treaty Organization, the OECD, the Association of South East Asian Nations (ASEAN). The functional areas covered are varied, ranging from the economic interests of the European Free Trade Association to the cultural, social and juridical remit of the Nordic Council and the obvious concern of the International Whaling Commission and the International Commission for Southeast Atlantic Fisheries. The universalist UN deals with issues that motivated the League – international peace and security – and has developed a prominence in areas that the League at first neglected: economic and social issues, the position of colonial peoples. The wide range of other IGOs have reflected these concerns. The Bretton Woods institutions – the IMF, IBRD, GATT, IDA, IFC – have provided the organized basis of the post-war non-communist economic system. The OAU, OAS and Arab League have helped in peacefully settling disputes and have provided much of the inspiration for the UN's later work on decolonization. However, some organizations have demonstrated the different interests of the growing number of sovereign states that cannot be satisfactorily accommodated at the UN whether they be the security concerns of NATO and the Warsaw Treaty Organization or the desire for a better price for their exports expressed in OPEC or the wish to develop a regional identity as demonstrated in the Nordic Council, the Caribbean Community and the European Community.

Scientific progress has allowed greater ease in communications since 1945. Also there has been more to communicate between countries: there are more people, more industrial and agricultural production, more money, more writings and so on. Governments have continued to intervene in economic and social affairs and also in educational, scientific and cultural matters. Faster travel and transport and the advent of telecommunications have meant that contacts between peoples, groups and governments are more numerous, regular and widespread. Keohane and Nye (1971, p. xii) identify four major types of global interaction:

1) communication, the movement of information, including the transmission of beliefs; 2) transportation, the movement of physical objects, including war material and personal property as well as merchandise; 3) finance, the movement of money and instruments of credit; 4) travel, the movement of persons.

These interactions have resulted in a growth in the number of inter-governmental technical, economic and social organizations and the spread of organizations between individuals and non-governmental groups.

The rise of international non-governmental organizations (INGOS) allowed for by the increase in global interactions has been one of the noticeable developments in international relations since the Second World War. Article 71 of the UN Charter authorized the Economic and Social Council to 'make suitable arrangements for consultation with non-governmental organizations which are concerned with matters within its competence' and there are now 640 INGOS on ECOSOC's books. As well as these INGOS, which by nature are concerned with economic, social, educational, cultural and scientific questions, a whole range has grown up in other spheres and they now have similar symbiotic relations with the UN specialized agencies. The trade union and employee organizations have an established relationship with the ILO and scientific and specialist associations have consultative status with the FAO and UNESCO. The 1972 Stockholm UN Conference on the Human Environment was a gathering place for many non-governmental ecology groups and such organizations as Friends of the Earth, the International Union for Conservation of Nature and Natural Resources and the World Wildlife Fund have since acted as shadows to UNESCO and the United Nations Environment Programme (Boardman, 1981, pp. 118–23; Willets, 1982, *passim*.). On a more regional scale, the European

Community structure encourages INGO activity both through its Economic and Social Committee and by its general decision-making procedure. This has led to Community-wide interest groups being formed to represent producer, consumer and worker interests at a European Community level (Archer and Main, 1980, ch. 1).

Even excluding the INGOs associated with the European Community and EFTA, the total number of these organizations has mushroomed from 176 in 1909 to 1,253 in 1960, 1,993 in 1970 and now stands at well over 2,000 (*Yearbook of International Organizations*, 1981, tab. 2). Many of these have little direct influence on IGOs, let alone governments. They are either weak in membership and organization or are concerned with activities of seemingly little interest to the authorities: chess, stamp collecting, esperanto, nudism. Yet their very number can be seen as presenting a potential power in the mobilization of social forces separate from the agents of government. Because of this the spread of INGOs is an important political as well as social factor in international life.

The creation of a near-global economy in the post-war years has gone hand-in-hand with the extension of another form of non-governmental activity across frontiers – the multinational or trans-national corporation. Such firms have been partly responsible for scientific and technical achievements and the internationalization of economic factors but they have also been encouraged by the more general trend in this direction.

One of the major post-war developments in the political world that the United Nations very quickly mirrored was the division between the Soviet-led bloc and the United States-led bloc – the East–West Cold War. Such a divide between the major powers has been seen in the restrictions placed on the functioning of the UN and some of its agencies, in the type of peace and security questions that the Organization has handled and in the creation of bloc-oriented organizations such as the North Atlantic Treaty Organization (NATO) in 1949 and the Warsaw Treaty Organization in 1955.

With the increase in the number of states brought about mainly by the process of decolonization, international organizations have started to reflect another factor – the growing importance of the Afro–Asian–Latin American states, often called the Third World. The creation of a group of states standing outside both the East–West military and political divisions is often dated from the Bandung Conference of non-aligned states held in April 1955. In 1960 sixteen African states became independent and joined the United Nations and since then the Third World has appeared to function in inter-national forums not just as a non-aligned grouping but also as an economic force with its own demands concerning the ending of the

Western-oriented, market-based global economy and the adoption of a New International Economic Order. In this context the Third World often appears under the nomenclature of the Group of Seventy-Seven (or G77) originally adopted by the Third World states attending the first United Nations Conference on Trade and Development (UNCTAD). (Words do not always mean what they appear to say – the membership of G77 is now well over 100). The demands of these states have been felt both within previously existing organizations and by the creation of new organizations supporting the needs of G77 states such as the Association of South East Asian Nations or the Organization of African Unity (OAU).

Whilst the East–West and North–South divisions can be seen as major developments in the post-war world, interstate relations in a thirty-five-year period cannot be reduced to such slogans. The history of relationships between the Western countries and the Soviet Bloc contains an important strand of co-operation which has waxed and waned over this period: in the immediate months following the end of the Second World War, both the Soviet and the US governments were anxious not to be the first to break up the wartime alliance, but the period from 1947 to 1954 was one of the deepest confrontation between the two sides. Whilst the demise of Stalin saw a lifting of Cold War feeling in the mid-1950s, crises in the Middle East, Berlin and, in 1962, Cuba stressed the adversary side of East–West relations. The conscious attempt to decrease tension between the two sides made in the late 1960s and the 1970s – detente – demonstrated that even when the systems were in competition and were rivals, agreement could be reached over important areas of international relations. Even when the Cold War looked frozen solid – at the time of the Korean War – the major powers kept contact with each other both bilaterally and through international organizations such as the UNO.

Likewise the North–South divide is by no means a story of two contending monolithic blocs. Both sides have serious internal divisions: the 'North' includes the Soviet-group countries which claim a special position in relation to the Third World by virtue of their non-colonialist past; even Western Europe contains former colonialist states with strong connections with the South, such as France, and countries such as Sweden which are just developing trade links; the OPEC states are members of G77 but many have considerable wealth and have obtained some of this at the expense of the world's poorest states which have to import oil; some Third World states' economies are integrated into the semi-global economy led by the West whilst others, such as Vietnam and Cuba, are part of the socialist bloc economy. Contacts across the North–South divide are often expressed in institutional form – the Lomé Convention between the European Community and a number of African,Caribbean and Pacific (ACP) states; the Commonwealth; the Council for Mutual Economic Assistance (Comecon) of which Vietnam, Mongolia and Cuba are members as well as the European Soviet Bloc states.

International organizations do not exist in a political vacuum. They are part of the modern state system and their institutional forms and activities reflect the hopes and fears of the governments of states within that system. The brief history above of the rise of international organizations demonstrates how closely they have been tied to the life of modern industrial society and the expansion of the European international system to the rest of the world. With the growth in the number of states, the activities of government and groups within the state and the number of potential areas of conflict – and prospects for co-operation – between East and West, North and South, the climate for international organizations has been favourable in the post-Second World War period. This is not to say that with a future different configuration of states, the role of these organizations may not decline. A world empire would have little use for them, preferring the use of force or bilateral diplomacy – it was noticeable that Nazi Germany had little time for international organizations. A world in which war becomes more endemic than at present may have need for international organizations but may find that they are physically unable to function. A world of continental federations may have use for organizations to ease relations between the continents but within each federation 'international' organizations may have turned into new political federal institutions. A world in which mankind decides to confront universal problems such as overpopulation, pollution and destruction of the environment and starvation by the use of effective international organizations will see a shift in the balance of political activity from the sovereign state to a number of strengthened global functional (but also highly political) institutions.

A Working Definition

This chapter started with an examination of the words 'international' and 'organization' and continued with an account of the historical rise of those institutions known as 'international organizations'. It is now possible to define 'international organizations' within the context of that account. This can be done by examining the essential characteristics of international organizations and adding some of the more noticeable elements which, whilst not necessary preconditions in the identification of international organizations, are often important contributory factors that distinguish them. After under-taking this all-embracing definition, the next chapter will disaggre-gate international organizations, looking at the ways various *kinds* of organization may be typified.

The *Yearbook of International Organizations* lists eight criteria for inclusion under the rubric of international organization. They can be summarized thus:

1 The aims must be genuinely international with the intention to cover at least three states.
2 Membership must be individual or collective participation, with full voting rights, from at least three states and must be open to any individual or entity appropriately qualified in the organization's area of operations. Voting must be so that no one national group can control the organization.
3 The constitution must provide for a formal structure giving members the right periodically to elect governing bodies and officers. Provision should be made for continuity of operation with a permanent headquarters.
4 Officers should not all be of the same nationality for more than a given period.
5 There should be a substantial contribution to the budget from at least three states and there should be no attempt to make profits for distribution to members.
6 Those with an organic relationship with other organizations must show it can exist independently and elect its own officials.
7 Evidence of current activities must be available.
8 There are some negative criteria: size, politics, ideology, fields of activity, geographical location of headquarters, nomenclature are irrelevant in deciding whether a set-up is an 'international organization' or not (*Yearbook of International Organizations*, 1976/7).

Wallace and Singer (1970, pp. 245–7) distinguish intergovernmental organizations by three criteria:

1 The Organization 'must consist of at least two qualified members of the international system . . .' and should have been 'created by a formal instrument of agreement between the governments of national states'. Bilateral international organizations are included on the grounds that they are still international organizations and because otherwise certain multilateral organi-zations (for example, the Rhine River Commission) would have

to be excluded for the periods when their membership was reduced to two.

2 '[T]he organization must hold more or less regular plenary sessions at intervals not greater than once a decade.'

3 The organization should have a permanent secretariat with a permanent headquarters arrangement and which performs ongoing tasks.

Plano and Riggs (1967, pp. 12–13) list eleven essential features of nineteenth-century intergovernmental institutions. These are the 'basic characteristics and the procedures' of early international organizations which 'have become commonplace features of modern international institutions'. Other writers have produced less exhaustive though more precise criteria for international organizations. Bennett (1977, p. 3) lists their common characteristics as being

(1) a permanent organization to carry on a continuing set of functions; (2) voluntary membership of eligible parties; (3) a basic instrument stating goals, structure, and methods of operation; (4) a broadly representative consultative organ; and (5) a permanent secretariat to carry on continuous administration, research and information functions.

The eminent Soviet international lawyer, Professor G. I. Tunkin, refers to international organizations as 'permanent bodies' that states create 'to handle matters entrusted to them' and which result from international agreements: 'Any contemporary international organization (intergovernmental) is created by states by means of concluding an international treaty for the purpose' and 'A constituent instrument of an international organization provides for certain rights and capabilities of the organization which lead to the conclusion that the organization possesses a certain degree of international legal personality' (Osakwe, 1972, pp. 24–30).

Another Soviet author, Professor Grigorii Morozov (1977, p. 30), defines an international organization 'in the light of the basic tenets of the socialist conception':

In its most general form as a stable, clearly structured instrument of international co-operation, freely established by its members for the joint solution of common problems and the pooling of efforts within the limits laid down by its statutes.

[Such organizations] have, as a rule, at least three member countries. These may be governments, official organizations or non-governmental organizations. International organizations have agreed aims, organs with appropriate terms of reference and also specific institutional features such as statutes, rules of procedure, membership etc. The aims and activity of an international organization must be in keeping with the universally accepted principles of international law embodied in the Charter of the United Nations and must not have a commercial character or pursue profit-making aims.

Paul Reuter (1958, p. 214) considers an international organization as a group normally, but not exclusively, of states 'which can permanently express a juristic will distinct from that of its individual members'. Charles Pentland (1976, p. 626) describes international organizations as institutions with 'formalized sets of relationships expected to persist for a considerable time' whose institutional quality 'is found in their legal, institutional fabric, their political organs and bureaucratic structures, and their physical and symbolic presence'. Pierre Gerbet's definition is succinct:

> The idea of an international organization is the outcome of an attempt to bring order into international relations by establishing lasting bonds across frontiers between governments or social groups wishing to defend their common interests, within the context of permanent bodies, distinct from national institutions, having their own individual characteristics, capable of expressing their own will and whose role it is to perform certain functions of international importance (Gerbet, 1977, p. 7)

Virally (1977, p. 59), the French writer on public international law, after examining other definitions, issues his own to the effect that international organizations 'can be defined as an association of States, established by agreement among its members and possessing a permanent system or set of organs, whose task it is to pursue objectives of common interest by means of co-operation among its members'.

What then are the irreducible essential characteristics of international organizations and what are the other elements which often typify such organizations? The outstanding features come under three headings:

1 *Membership*: an international organization should draw its membership from two or more sovereign states, though membership need not be limited to states or official state representatives such as government ministers. (Further distinctions between interstate,

intergovernmental and international non-governmental organizations will be made in Chapter 2.) Wallace and Singer's case for choosing two as the minimum membership is accepted here in preference to the *Yearbook of International Organizations* and Morozov's choice of three.

2   *Aim*: the organization is established with the aim of pursuing the common interests of the members. It may end up not undertaking this task or favouring the interests of one member over that of another but it should not have the express aim of the pursuit of the interests of only one member, regardless of the desires of others.

3   *Structure*: the organization should have its own formal structure of a continuous nature established by an agreement such as a treaty or constituent document. The nature of the formal structure may vary from organization to organization but it should be separate from the continued control of one member. It is this autonomous structure that differentiates a number of international organizations from a series of conferences or congresses.

So an international organization can be defined as *a formal, continuous structure established by agreement between members (governmental and/or non-governmental) from two or more sovereign states with the aim of pursuing the common interest of the membership.*

Other factors are often associated with most international organizations: their institutions usually consist of a plenary gathering of all the membership (often called an assembly or conference), a more regular meeting of a limited number of members, quite often with executive powers, and a permanent secretariat of an international nature. 'International' in this context can mean either being drawn from several countries or being chosen to serve the organization regardless of nationality or being financed by the organization's other institutions. Some organizations also have institutions with judicial or quasi-judicial powers. This book will adopt the *Yearbook of International Organizations* and the Morozov proviso that the international organizations dealt with are to exclude those established with the purpose of making a profit for the members. This rules out international business corporations, cartels and transnational or multinational enterprises. However, these will make an appearance in the next chapter before being removed from the remit of the book. The following chapter will consider the various types of international organizations as determined by aims, activities and functions, membership and structure.

2

Classification of International Organizations

The definition of an international organization as a formal, continuous structure established by agreement between members, whether governmental representatives or not, from at least two sovereign states with the aim of pursuing the common interest of the membership, covers a wide range of institutions even if profit-making associations are excluded. Although useful observations can be made even about the total genus of international organizations, a more useful and informative study is possible if various types of international organizations, with common features separating them from other international organizations, can be identified.

In this chapter international organizations will be examined from three perspectives which tend to break down the totality into subgroups. The three headings provide a description of types defined by membership, by aims and activities and by structure.

Membership: 1. What are the Building Blocks?

From the discussion in Chapter 1 about membership and the description of the history of international organizations, it should be clear that their existence is closely associated with that of the sovereign state but that membership of some international organizations is not necessarily drawn from sovereign states or their governmental representatives. The first distinction between the kinds of international organizations is those which are interstate or intergovernmental and those whose membership is non-governmental. A further category could be made of international organizations with mixed membership.

IGOs

According to the UN Economic and Social Council 'Every international organization which is not created by means of intergovernmental agreements shall be considered as a non-governmental international organization' (Economic and Social Council, Resolution 288 (x) of 27 February 1950). This suggests a distinction between intergovernmental organizations (IGOs) and international non-governmental organizations (INGOs – sometimes shortened to NGOs). There is still some discussion as to whether intergovernmental organizations are the same as interstate organizations. Three points can be made about this latter distinction:

1   Some organizations allow membership by countries which are not sovereign states but which have governments and which are usually non-self-governing territories. Examples of international organizations that have accepted such members are the International Telecommunications Union (ITU), the Universal Postal Union (UPU) and the World Meteorological Organization (WMO) (Klepacki, 1973, p. 5). Can such organizations be called 'interstate'?

2   Klepacki also divides international organizations into those having interstate organs, made up exclusively of heads of state, and those having intergovernmental organs with governmental representatives.

3   The international lawyer Jenks (1945a, pp. 18–20) claims a fundamental distinction between organizations based on a treaty between states and one between governments. An interstate treaty includes all the institutions of the state – administrative, executive, legislative and judicial – whereas an intergovernmental organization is established purely by the administrative branch of government.

D. W. Bowett comments on Jenks's distinction that 'in practice [it] is not regarded as having this significant difference in effect' (1970, p. 11), and the political scientist should perhaps extend Bowett's words to refer to all the distinctions between interstate and intergovernmental. Any interstate agreement has to be made by an agent for those states and it matters little whether his or her nomenclature is that of head of state or head of government. Indeed in many countries, including the USA and the USSR, this distinction is longer made, whereas in some states where it is made, the head of state no longer has treaty-making powers, for example in Sweden. It will be the practice of this book, unless otherwise stated, to use the terms 'intergovernmental organization' and 'interstate organizations' interchangeably.

TNOs: from INGOs to BINGOs

The traditional notion of international organizations being established between governments is based on the sovereign state view of international relations which contains three important elements: that, with few exceptions, only sovereign states are the subjects of international law; that sovereign states are equal in their standing in international law; that sovereign states are constitutionally self-contained and international law cannot interfere with the domestic jurisdiction of their governments. This doctrine has important consequences for international organizations.

In theory, such organizations, if they were to be recognized as having any standing in international law, should only consist of sovereign states in their membership. However, as has been seen, the UPU, ITU and WMO all allow non-self-governing territories to become members and even the League of Nations opened its membership to 'Any fully self-governing State, Dominion or Colony' (Article 1.2), a position that fell short of admitting only sovereign states.

Secondly, the notion of the sovereign equality of states would allow states to have equal voting power in any international institution such as an assembly or a council of an organization. The creation of executive councils in the early public international unions placed some states in a constitutionally favourable position in those organizations and that situation was entrenched in the League Covenant with the Council having permanent members.

Finally, the inviolability of sovereignty can be protected within international organizations by the doctrine that states cannot be bound by agreements to which they are not party. This would effectively rule out decisions by anything short of unanimity (with abstaining states not being bound) and by executive secretariats or councils which could act without the express consent of all the membership. Certainly any interference with questions of domestic jurisdiction by international organizations would not be allowed. Even Articles 15 and 16 in the League Covenant produced a fear amongst some sections in the USA that member countries might be obliged to carry out actions against their will but in support of the League. Clearly the UN Charter, allowing majority decisions, breaks with the unanimity principle. Furthermore, although Article 2.7 of the Charter states that

Nothing contained in the present Charter shall authorize the United Nations to intervene in matters which are essentially within the domestic jurisdiction of any state or shall require the Members to submit such matters to settlement under the present Charter

it continues with the important exception that

this principle shall not prejudice the application of enforcement measures under Chapter VII.

Against these seeming shortfalls from the 'sovereign state' model of international relations, it could be argued that states were exercising their sovereign rights in allowing non-sovereign states to become members of international organizations, in agreeing to restricted membership institutions or executive secretariats and in allowing majority voting or exceptions to the domestic jurisdiction clause. The state-centric model of international relations would allow inter-actions between the government of one state and the domestic society of another state but would insist that international politics is about relations between the governments of two or more states and not between the members of those states' societies (Figure 2.1). Thus international organizations are interstate, intergovernmental organi-zations by this reckoning.

State A   State B

Government	← IGO →	Government
Departments Military, etc.		Departments Military, etc.
Non-governmental Organizations:		Non-governmental Organizations:
Economic Social Religious Political, etc. Business Organizations		Economic Social Religious Political, etc. Business Organizations
Individuals		Individuals

Figure 2.1   *Intergovernmental Relations and Organizations*

This is clearly not the case. What are commonly and reasonably called 'international organizations' often contain members that are not states or governmental representatives but are drawn from groups, associations, organizations or individuals from within the state. These are *non-governmental* actors on the international stage and their activities give rise to *transnational interactions*. Figure 2.2 typifies international relations seen from a viewpoint that admits the importance of transnational relations.

State A   State B

Government	← IGO →	Government
Departments Military, etc.	← TGO →	Departments Military, etc.
	Hybrid INGO	
Non-governmental Organizations:	← INGO →	Non-governmental Organizations:
Economic Social Religious Political, etc.	← INGO →	Economic Social Religious Political, etc.
Business Organizations	← BINGO →	Business Organizations
Individuals	← INGO →	Individuals

Figure 2.2   *Transnational Relations and Organizations*

Keohane and Nye (1971, p. xii) have defined transnational interactions as covering 'the movement of tangible or intangible items across state boundaries when at least one actor is not an agent of a government or an international organization'. They list four major types of global interaction–communications, transportation, finance, travel – and note that many activities contain several of the types simultaneously.

When such relationships between more than two participants become institutionalized by agreement into a formal, continuous structure in order to pursue the common interests of the participants, one of which is not an agent of government or an international organization, then a *transnational organization* (TNO) has been established. In contrast to an intergovernmental organization, a TNO must have a non-state actor for at least one of its members.

Three sorts of TNOs are commonly identified in the literature:

1   *The genuine INGO* which is an organization with only non-governmental members. Such organizations bring together the representatives of like-minded groups from more than two countries and examples are the International Olympic Committee, the World Council of Churches, the Salvation Army and the Universal Esperanto Association.

2   *The hybrid INGO* which has some governmental and some non-governmental representation. If such a hybrid organization has been established by a treaty or convention between governments, it should be counted as an IGO, an example being the ILO which has trade union and management (i.e. non-governmental) membership as well as governmental representatives. However, some INGOs have a mixed membership and are not the result of a purely intergovernmental agreement. An example is the International Council of Scientific Unions which draws its membership from international scientific unions, scientific academies, national research councils, associations of institutions and governments (Judge, 1978, p. 57).

3   *The transgovernmental organization* (TGO) which results from 'relations between governmental actors that are not controlled by the central foreign policy organs of their governments' (Keohane and Nye, 1971, p. xv). Such relationships are fairly common if the term 'governmental actors' is widely defined to include anyone engaged in the governmental process of a country – in the legislature, judiciary or executive, at local government level or as part of a regional government. Much of these contacts tend to be informal or non-institutionalized but organizations do exist such as the International Union of Local Authorities (IULA) which brings together the local government authorities of the European Community, the International Council for the Exploration of the Sea (ICES) which has established a network of co-operation between government marine research laboratories, Interpol, the International Criminal Police Organization, and the Inter-Parliamentary Union.

A fourth category of TNOs is sometimes made: that of the Business International Non-governmental Organizations (BINGOs), alternatively called multinational enterprises or corporations: MNES, MNCS.

Before deciding whether to include this group, the nomenclature should be sorted out. All the descriptions used above have their critics. The use of 'BINGO' though no doubt having its attractions, would exclude those international business organizations that are definitely governmental, such as the Soviet airline 'Aeroflot', or which have a strong governmental stake, such as British Petroleum pre-1977. The use of the word 'multinational' – or 'international' – to describe large corporations functioning in several countries has been challenged on the grounds that it makes them sound as if their management is recruited internationally and their decision-making is not centred in any one country. This does not seem to be true of the leading US companies with overseas interests: a survey of these in 1970 revealed that only 1.6 per cent of their top level executives were non-Americans (Barnet and Muller, 1975, p. 17). The United Nations Group of Eminent Persons reported the 'strong feeling that [the word] transnational would better convey the notion that these firms operate from their home bases across national borders' without any form of state control. Another UN discussion produced the distinction between

'transnational corporations' for enterprises operating from their home bases across national borders ... [and] the term 'multi-national corporations' for those established by agreement between a number of countries and operating in accordance with prescribed agreements. (Judge, 1978, pp. 35–6)

Multi- or transnational business enterprises have been excluded from the rest of this study on the following grounds:

1   Both the ECOSOC Resolution 288(x) of 27 February 1950 and the definition used by the *Yearbook of International Organizations* exclude them from the term 'international organization'.
2   Using the definition of an international organization established at the end of Chapter 1, multinational corporations (MNCs) cannot really be described as 'formal, continuous structures established by agreement between members (governmental and/or non-governmental) from two or more sovereign states'. In reality the transnational corporation (TNC), as defined by the UN document quoted above, is an extension across frontiers of a business domiciled in one country.
3   If a MNC is tightly defined as a corporation 'established between a number of countries and operating in accordance with prescribed agreements' then it would certainly come much closer to being defined as an international organization. An example is the Scandinavian Airline System. However, it has been decided to keep

in line with the *Yearbook of International Organizations* and exclude profit-making organizations from the description.

The exclusion of MNCs is not to deny that they have much in common with international organizations, especially organizationally (Wells, 1971, p. 113). Also a number of MNCs may join together to form an international non-governmental organization – for example a users' group designed with a representational, promotional or educational purpose (e.g. International Chamber of Shipping, Oil Companies International Marine Forum). A more borderline case is that of international cartels and the various freight and shipping conferences which do not themselves make a profit but whose clear aim is to advance the profit-making capacities of their members. Shipping conferences, for example, are varied in their structure and permanence but their general aim is to include a number of shipping lines plying a defined ocean route and to come to an agreement about the conditions used for that route – uniform charges, freight tariffs, working conditions, and so forth.

In summary, it should be remembered that MNCs, whilst not defined here as international organizations, are nevertheless 'clearly important international actors' (Wells, 1971, p. 113) as will be seen in the later review of the literature on international organizations (Chapter 3).

Meanwhile two different sorts of 'building blocks' making up international organizations have been identified – the governmental members and the non-governmental members. The mix of these produces different types of international organizations.

Membership: 2. Regionalism Versus Universalism

Another important aspect of the membership of international organizations is the catchment area from which it is drawn. The two extremes of spread of membership are, first, those of the most limited kind with two members drawn from a geographically contiguous area which has many other factors – economic, social and political – in common. The Benelux Customs Union with its associated institutions is perhaps the best example of this limited end of the membership spectrum: the three members of Belgium, the Netherlands and Luxembourg fulfil the criteria of having relatively similar socio-political and economic backgrounds and are certainly geographically contiguous. At the other extreme are the universal organizations which have membership drawn from practically all the sovereign states in the world: the United Nations Organization and many of its specialized agencies fall into this category.

The distinction made in types of international organization based on membership is often that between regional organizations and global or universal organizations. This is a distinction that informs us not just about the extent of membership but also about the aspirations of the organization. Most academic writings on this question have discerned a tension between the trend towards regional organizations and that towards universal aspirations.

In discussing this subject, attention will be predominantly given to IGOS as their membership is more easily defined. However, the general points made can be mirrored in the INGOS.

The major problems arising here are the definition of a region, and thus of a regional organization, and the delineation of one region from another. Matters would be simplified if the world resembled a peeled grapefruit which divided neatly into segments. This would at least make a geographical typology of international organizations easier: those covering a particular segment would be defined as regionalist and those covering the whole, universalist.

However, there seems to be no one satisfactory definition of a region. Bruce Russett (1967, p. 2) cites two American social scientists: Rupert Vance who called a region 'any portion of the earth's surface whose physical characteristics are similar' and Howard Odum whose 1938 study claimed that a region should have 'a relatively large degree of homogeneity measured by a relatively large number of purposes or classifications'. In the social sciences, regions have not just been defined by geographical characteristics but have also been tested on economic, social, cultural and political grounds. Cantori and Spiegel (1970, p. 1) consider regions

to be areas of the world which contain geographically proximate states forming, in foreign affairs, mutually inter-related units. For each participant, the activities of other members of the region (be they antagonistic or cooperative) are significant determinants of its foreign policy; while particular members of certain regions may have extraregional concerns, their primary involvement in foreign affairs ordinarily lies in the region in which they find themselves.

Karl Kaiser (1968, p. 86) introduces a similar element of foreign relationships when writing about regional subsystems. He defines a subsystem as 'a pattern of relations among basic units in world politics which exhibits a particular degree of regularity and intensity of relations as well as awareness of inter-dependence among the participating units', and thus a regional subsystem is a partial international system 'whose members exist in geographical propinquity'. Norman Padelford (1955, p. 25) also allows for the intermix of geographic and political elements in his definition of regions as 'spatial areas which come to be spoken of as "regions" as a result of usage stemming from the practices of groups of states, utterances of statesmen, or the terms of treaties or agreements between groups of states'. In this description, the stress is placed on the *behaviour* of state representatives and whether an area becomes defined as a region is a result of states' activities. Such activities may give rise to an international organization which institutionalizes the relations of the member states in a regional context.

Another problem in dealing with international regions is that of delineation: where does one region end and another begin? If the world divided easily into segments, then the answer would be self-evident, but not even the continents provide such neat packages in international relations. There seems to be no international organization whose membership completely covers one continent and is only drawn from one continent: the OAU is perhaps the nearest but it excludes South Africa; the OAS contains some, but not all, Caribbean states, and includes the USA but not Canada. It seems difficult to decide what *size* a region should be. This can often lead to the term being used very loosely with boundaries 'zones rather than lines', ending in 'transition seldom in definite boundaries' (Russett, 1967, p. 5). Otherwise non-geographic factors (political, cultural) can be used to delineate members of a region. An example of the latter case is the Nordic region where membership is not only drawn from the Scandinavian peninsula but includes Denmark (though not Germany to which Denmark is physically joined) and Iceland, far out in the North Atlantic, because of their cultural and historic links with the peoples of the Scandinavian peninsula. Quite often the problem of delineation is sidestepped by identifying a region's 'core area' and its 'periphery' with sometimes 'intrusive' outsiders (Cantori and Spiegel, 1970, ch. 1). Even here the definition is by no means clear. To take the Nordic case again, a geographical core area would include Norway, Sweden and Finland whilst the cultural–political core area is readily recognized as being made up by Denmark, Norway and Sweden.

Bruce Russett (1967, p. 11) has tackled the problem of regionalism in a comprehensive fashion, focusing on five aspects: regions of social and cultural homogeneity; regions sharing similar attitudes or external behaviour; regions of political interdependence; regions of economic interdependence; regions of geographic proximity. If these five factors are utilized for regional international organizations, it can be said that some organizations are 'more regional' than others. An organization the members of which have strong similarities in each of the five categories could be classified as strongly regional whilst an organization 'scoring' in only one category would be one with a weak regional profile (see Table 2.1 for examples). This helps to move away from the sterile argument in the classification of international organizations: 'are they regional or universal?'

Table 2.1   *Degrees of Homogeneity amongst Five IGOs*

Russett's Factors:	A	B	C	D	E	Total
Organization						
Benelux	3	3	3	3	3	15
European Community	2	2	3	3	2	12
Arab League	2	2	1	1	2	8
Commonwealth of Nations	1	0	1	1	0	3
UNO	0	0	0	1	0	1

Key:

Russett's Factors –
A   Social–cultural homogeneity
B   Attitudes and behaviour
C   Political interdependence
D   Economic interdependence
E   Geographic proximity

Scores
0   No or negligible homogeneity
1   Weak homogeneity
2   Medium homogeneity
3   Strong homogeneity
Totals –
15   Strongest 'regional' identity
0   Weakest 'regional' identity

The entrenchment of this regional/universal dichotomy in writings on international relations seems to be a result of the values attached to the ideal organization of each type: the perfect regional organization brings together states of similar backgrounds to solve problems they could not otherwise deal with at a national level and which would be ineffectively tackled by a wider institution; it can produce a security community between members who will no longer expect to resort to force in their mutual relations and can provide a form of selective security against outside threats; it can perhaps produce political entities which will act as components for a future world government (Carr, 1945, p. 45; Etzioni, 1964; Gladwyn, 1966). The perfect universal organization would, in contrast, stress the indivisibility of world peace and prosperity; it would help link the rich and the poor areas of the world; it would be the basis of a collective security system whereby all countries would unite to protect any one that was threatened (The Independent Commission on International Development Issues, 1980, Introduction; Yalem, 1965, ch. 1). Depending on the stance taken, regional organizations are seen as better or worse in attaining desired ends such as international peace and security, economic growth and prosperity.

Inis Claude (1964, ch. 6) remarks that 'the constitutional problem of achieving a balance between regional and universal approaches to international organization is far from solved' but points to the complementary elements of the two. Indeed, the UN Charter has a good number of references to the regional element in Articles 23(1), 33(1), 47(4), 52–4, 101(3), with Article 52(1) being the most specific:

Nothing in the present Charter precludes the existence of regional arrangements or agencies for dealing with such matters relating to the maintenance of international peace and security as are appropriate for regional action, provided that such arrangements and agencies and their activities are consistent with the Purposes and Principles of the United Nations.

Clearly the superiority of the UN in matters of peace and security is maintained especially as Articles 52(3) and 53(1) underline that regional arrangements should not impair the peaceful settlement of disputes and peace enforcement activities of the Security Council.

Bruce Russett's study (1967, p. 11) demonstrates that when states' institutional, attitudinal, economic, socio–cultural and communications links are examined, a number of groups emerge with the aggregates showing essentially the same boundaries for the different criteria. However, no region or aggregate of states could be discerned as a subsystem of the international system and there was no area within which the inclusions and exclusions were the same for all criteria tested. What emerged were four major areas whose members shared much in common, although there normally was a core group of states with a more intense relationship surrounded by a periphery of 'hangers on':

1 Eastern Europe with the USSR, Poland, Czechoslovakia, Rumania, Bulgaria and Hungary forming the core. Common membership of international organizations for the East European states doubled from 1951 to 1962 – from fourteen to twenty-eight.
2 Latin America – this was becoming less of a group in the 1960s, partly due to Cuba's move to fit in with the East European system.
3 The Western Community – even in the mid-1960s the core group here was that of the original six European Community states (Belgium, Netherlands, Luxembourg, France, Italy and West

Germany) together with the United Kingdom, Denmark, Austria and Switzerland. The outer members included other Western European states such as Spain and Portugal and extra-European countries like the USA, Canada, Australia and Japan.
4   Asia, including some Arab and African states, though with Japan and Taiwan being closer to the Western Community.

There were also three other clusters of less homogenous states which nevertheless adhered together on two or three criteria:

1   The Middle Eastern states
2   Black Africa, especially the ex-French colonies
3   The British Commonwealth which split into a number of overlapping subgroups – the White Dominions, the Asian states, the Caribbean.

Russett remarks that the true description of all these regions contains more than just geographic tags.

Any international organization with a limited number of members most of which are seen to be geographically proximate and/or culturally, economically and politically similar, has traditionally attracted the epithet 'regional'. The Nordic Council, the Organization of Economic Co-operation and Development (OECD), NATO, the Council of Mutual Economic Assistance (CMEA – Comecon) and the Commonwealth Nations have all been labelled such. However, the Russett study brings out four important factors:

1   Regions are difficult to define: using one criterion produces a division of little help; using several criteria may produce, if not conflicting, at least rather uncertain results.
2   Regions are even more difficult to delineate: core areas are fairly easy to identify but one periphery blends into another.
3   Even if the state membership of a region could be defined and delineated, changes take place over time which may loosen the membership or add to it.
4   If the idea of a region is an uncertain and changing one, so is the notion of a regional organization. It is far better to refer to organizations with limited membership (and one of the limits may be that of geography) as opposed to organizations with more open or extensive membership.

This change of nomenclature will help to clarify how an organization is being typified – more limited or more extensive membership – rather than the present classification of 'regional' which can cover anything from a three-member tightly-knit group to a fifty-member multicontinent organization. It should also help in drawing some of the normative sting associated with the term 'regionalism' – whether positive or negative. Regional organizations are often judged by their ability to fulfil certain norms set by academic commentators – for example maintaining peace and security – and are compared to 'universalist' organizations in the performance of these tasks. Studies such as those by Haas and Rowe (1973) which demonstrate the relationship between the UN and various 'regional' agencies in problems of peace and security provide useful information about both state behaviour and the role of international organizations. However, the conclusion should not be drawn that 'regional' organizations can be seen as potential pillars of a world community (de Rusett, 1950, p. 159) or as 'a manifestation of a world in disorder' (Yalem, 1965, p. 141). This makes the heady assumption that the aims of such organizations should concern the creation of world order (or *a* world order) and either they have succeeded or they have failed. Harsh realities about the composition of such organizations can be forgotten: the aspiration of member states may be more modest than that of building world order, a world order, any world order. A division of international organizations into categories denoting the geographical spread of membership or other limits on membership should just indicate what is required and not, either explicitly or implicitly, judge the aims and activities of the organization and its membership.

Aims and Activities

Perhaps the most common way of classifying international organizations is to look at what they are supposed to do and what they actually do. These two interrelated aspects of the behaviour of the organizations get to the heart of their existence and it is by these that they are best classified.

Most international organizations, be they IGOs or INGOs, have their aims stated usually in the basic document by which they have been established. This is not to say that an organization has no other aim except the stated ones. Neither does it hide the fact that each member of the organization may harbour slightly different aims in creating the organization or in joining it. The proclaimed aim is the most apparent statement of the intentions behind the existence of an organization.

The activities that an organization is intended to undertake are also often laid down in its basic documents and they are normally seen to be the fulfilment of the stated aims. This is an area that can be judged by the record of the organization, enumerating the sort of activities it has undertaken. These may vary from the study of 'the scientific, technical, social and economic aspects of poplar and willow cultivation' of the International Poplar Commission of the FAO, the 'administering of the Fourth International Tin Agreement' of the International Tin Council, the development of 'training programs for the training of appropriate personnel to meet the varying needs of the coconut industry' of the Asian Coconut Community to the Program of Trade Liberalization of the Latin American Free Trade Association, the transactions of the International Monetary Fund and the services of the Permanent Court of Arbitration set down in its 1907 Convention (Peaslee, 1974, pp. 1,019, 1,091, 1, 236–8; Peaslee, 1975, pp. 13, 345, 531).

The preamble of the Charter of the United Nations in a lyrical passage that caused much heart searching and dictionary-thumbing at the San Francisco Conference declares:

We the people of the United Nations determined

to save succeeding generations from the scourge of war, which twice in our lifetime has brought untold sorrow to mankind, and

to reaffirm faith in fundamental human rights, in the dignity and worth of the human person, in the equal rights of men and women and of nations large and small and

to establish conditions under which justice and respect for the obligations arising from treaties and other sources of international law can be maintained, and

to promote social progress and better standards of life in larger freedom,

and for those ends

to practice tolerance and live together in peace with one another as good neighbours, and

to unite our strength to maintain international peace and security and to ensure by the acceptance of principles and the institution of methods, that armed force shall not be used, save in the common interest, and

to employ international machinery for the promotion of the economic and social advancement of all peoples

have resolved to combine our efforts to accomplish these aims.

Whilst this passage may not prepare the reader for the present operations of the UNO, it does give an insight into the breadth and depth of activity intended for the Organization by its founders. In contrast, some statements of aims are succinct and limited: for example, Article 1(i) of the agreement establishing the International Institute of Refrigeration states:

> The Contracting Parties resolve to collaborate closely in the study of scientific and technical problems relating to refrigeration and in the development of the uses of refrigeration which improve the living conditions of mankind. (Peaslee, 1975, p. 278)

As can be seen from the two examples of the UNO and theInternational Institute of Refrigeration, the aims of international organizations range from the general and extensive to the specific and particular. The same can be said about an organization's activities which may range from the establishment of a free trade area down to the study of poplars and willows. Peaslee's massive work of documentation gives a good indication of the extent of difference in the aims and activities of organizations: the titles of the study's five volumes demonstrates the point – Part I: general and regional, political, economic, social, legal, defence; Part II: agriculture, commodities, fisheries, food, plants; Part III: education, culture, copyright; Part IV: science, health; Part V: communications, transport, travel.

Other writers tend to define organizations by their activities but in fewer categories. Virally (1977, p. 65) notes both the distinction between general and specialized organizations and that between political and technical ones. Nye (1972, p. 430) uses a threefold division: military security, political organizations, economic organizations. Norman Padelford (1954, p. 205) again has three types: '1. economic and technical arrangements; 2. arrangements for defense purposes; and 3. arrangements providing an organization framework for the consideration of broad political issues'. Haas and Rowe (1973, p. 15) divided 'regional organizations' by their substantive mandate distinguishing between those devoted to economic objectives, those with military and diplomatic activities and 'multipurpose organizations covering all or some of these aims in addition to mandates concerning cultural co-operation, human rights, and social or technological questions'. Charles Pentland (1976, pp. 628–9) cautions against relying too much on formally stated objectives when classifying international organizations according to their activities. He notes that many organizations are 'flexible and multifunctional' and that it is best to group them according to the issues 'in which they are most actively and consistently involved'. He goes on to use the distinction between 'high' and 'low' politics. High politics concerns 'diplomatic and military problems relating directly to the security and sovereignty of states and to the fundamental order of the international system'. Low politics refers to 'the great volume of daily business conducted between states within that political order – concerning economics, social, cultural and technical issues'. Pentland then distinguishes between 'high political organizations . . . most directly concerned with the sovereignty and security of their members' and low political organizations, subdivided into those dealing with economic management or development, those within the narrow technical or functional sectors of international relations and those concerned with social and cultural questions.

This distinction between high and low political issues, although a traditional one, is far less useful now than twenty or thirty years ago. In times of perceived increasing scarcity of resources – even in the richer parts of the world – the security of a country may depend more on economic factors than on the immediate diplomatic and military ones. It is interesting to note that Western summits of heads of state and government drawn from the most powerful West European and North American states plus Japan were throughout the 1970s primarily concerned with economic issues. An argument could be made that during this period the Organization of the Petroleum Exporting Countries (OPEC), the International Energy Agency (IEA) and the International Monetary Fund (IMF) have been involved in 'problems relating directly to the security and sovereignty of states and to the fundamental order of the international system'.

There are certainly two ways in which international organizations may be usefully classified by aims and activities. The first is to take the discrete areas of activity within which the organization acts and to evaluate it on a 'general–specific' scale. The results of such a classification can be seen in Tables 2.2 and 2.3 in which a number of headings are drawn from those used by writers already mentioned. The aims and activities of ten selected IGOs and five INGOs are listed under these heads, giving a clear idea of the range of the organizations. Table 2.4 provides a more general picture of the field of activities covered by both IGOs and INGOs founded between 1693 and 1954. Perhaps the most noticeable trends are those of the steady growth of economic, food, agricultural, trade, commodities, industrial and education organizations, and the decline in new legal, juridical, administrative, cultural, religious, philosophical, ethical, peace and, more surprising, scientific and technological organizations.

These Tables, especially 2.2 and 2.3, disguise the gap between the aspirations and the achievements of each organization: for example the aims of the Arab League are wide-ranging but its activities to date

Table 2.2   Aims and Activities of Ten IGOs by Functional Area

Organization	Broad political	Economic	Social	Labour	Legal and juridical	Defence and military	Food and agriculture	Trade and commodities	Fisheries	Industry	Education	Culture	Human rights	Science and technology	Health	Transport	Other communications
UNO (Charter 1945, 1963 1965)	X	X	X	X	X						X	X	X		X		
Arab League (Pact 1945, JDEC Treaty 1950)	X	X	X	X	X	X				X		X			X	X	X
NATO (North Atlantic Treaty 1949)*	X	X	X		X	X					X	X		X	X	X	X
IMF (Arts of Agreement 1945, 1969)		X						X									
EFTA (Stockholm Convention 1960)		X					X	X		X							
OPEC (Statute 1961, 1965, 1966, 1970, 1971)		X	X	X			X	X	X	X							
Nordic Council (Treaty 1962, 1971)	X	X	X	X	X			X			X	X		X	X	X	X
Permanent Court of Arbitration 1907					X												
International North Pacific Fisheries Commission 1952									X								
International Tin Council 1970				X				X									

* plus council additions

Table 2.3   Aims and Activities of Five INGOs by Functional Area

	Broad political	Economic	Social	Labour	Legal and juridical	Defence and military	Food and agriculture	Trade and commodities	Fisheries	Industry	Educational	Cultural	Human rights	Science and technology	Health	Transport	Other communications
International Olympic Committee											X	X			X		
World Federation of United Nations Associations	X	X	X								X	X					
International Federation of World Trade Unions	X	X	X	X							X		X				
Liberal International	X										X		X				
International Chamber of Shipping		X						X		X	X			X	X	X	X

have not fulfilled the expectations that may arise from reading the Pact. On the other hand the major specific aim of the European Free Trade Association (EFTA) – that of industrial free trade between its members – was achieved well before the date set down in the Stockholm Convention. OPEC seems to have helped achieve 'a steady income to the [petroleum] producing countries' and 'a fair return on their capital to those investing in the petroleum industry' (Article 2c) though it is more arguable whether it has succeeded in bringing about 'the coordination and unification of the petroleum policies of Member Countries' (Article 2a), 'the stabilization of prices in international oil markets' (2b) or 'an efficient, economic and regular supply of petroleum to consuming nations'.

Table 2.4 *Field of Activity of International Organizations Founded 1693–1954*

	1693–1914	1915–44	1945–54
		% by year	
General	6·3	3·5	5·6
Economic	3·3	9·5	12·5
Social science	1·8	1·2	2·1
Labour	8·6	3·0	5·2
Legal/juridical/administrative	10·0	9·2	8·6
Food and agricultural	4·9	5·1	6·0
Trade and commodities, industry	5·7	8·3	9·2
Educational	8·6	11·6	12·1
Cultural and religious	17·9	17·6	10·4
Philosophy, ethics and peace	7·1	5·0	4·0
Science and technology	13·5	10·6	9·5
Health	9·4	10·5	9·6
Transport	2·0	4·5	4·5
Others	0·9	0·4	0·7
Number	509	666	803

Source: Adapted from G. P. Speeckaert, 1957, p. xiii.

However great the shortfall between the aims and activities of an organization, both can help in the classification of international organizations by the extent of their intended and actual activity.

International organizations may also be typified by their aims and activities in another way: by consideration of the orientation of activities involved. Cantori and Spiegel (1970, p. 362), when dealing with 'regional' organizations, identify three kinds of orientation: organizations aimed at settling disputes between members 'either through the diplomatic process or through more elaborate peacekeeping machinery'; organizations designed 'to present a common military and, perhaps, diplomatic front against an outside actor or actors'; and those intended to deal with economic relations and other technical problems.

This division can be adapted and broadened to cover international organizations generally. When examining the aims and activities of organizations, the sort of relationships they are intended to create among their members should be considered. Three major divisions are identifiable:

1 Organizations that aim at encouraging *co-operative* relations between members which are not in a state of conflict. The organizations would be intended to increase already existing co-operation or to turn a relationship of indifference into one of co-operation (Figure 2.3).

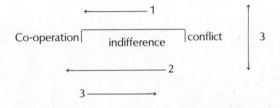

Figure 2.3 *International Organizations' Orientation in Relations Between States*

2 Organizations intending to decrease the level of *conflict* between members by means of conflict management or conflict prevention. Such an organization would help to move an existing relationship from that of conflict (or potential conflict) to that of less conflict, indifference or even co-operation.
3 Organizations with the aim of producing a *confrontation* between members of differing opinions or between members of the organization and specific non-members. This can either harden already existing attitudes or can move them from the co-operative or indifferent points on the scale to that of conflict.

Many organizations incorporate an element of divisions 1 and 2 in their aims and activities and others include 3 with some elements of either 1 or 2 or 1 and 2 (Figure 2.3). This admixture is shown for ten IGOs in Table 2.5. By far the greatest orientation in the stated aims and activities of these ten organizations as portrayed in their basic documents is that of co-operation, an understandable finding. It should, however, be noted that the stated aims and activities of organizations are not always reflected in their actual behaviour. The good intentions of co-operation are sometimes laid aside and the instruments of conflict management do not work every time. The actual behaviour of organizations is considered in Chapter 4.

Table 2.5   *Aims and Activities of International Organizations*

	Co-operation	Conflict management	Confrontation
UNO	Arts 1.2–1.4, 10, Ch. IX	1.1, 2.3, 2.4, Ch. VI, 52	Ch. VII, 53
Arab League	Arts 2–4, JDEC 7 and 8	Arts 3, 5–6 JDEC 1–7	Annex re Palestine
NATO	Arts 2–5	1, 2	
IMF	Arts I–VI, VIII 4–6, XXI–XXXII	Art VIII, 2–3	
EFTA	Arts 2–30	31–33	
OPEC	Arts 2, 4, 7d		
Nordic Council	All provisions		
Permanent Court of Arbitration		All provisions	
International North Pacific Fisheries Commission	Arts III, IV, VIII–X		
International Tin Council	Arts 1, 8, Ch. VII, VIII	Ch. XIII	

Structure

One of the easiest ways used to classify international organizations is by the structure of their institutions and the comparative power of these institutions. Since the rise of international organizations in the mid-nineteenth century, their institutions have become increasingly complex. Originally organizations such as the UPU and ITU had a permanent administrative bureau with a policy-making meeting of member countries' representatives every few years and this seemed to be the most common pattern for the international service unions, although the International Union for the Publication of Customs Tariffs, established in 1890, only has a bureau supervised by the Belgian Ministry of Foreign Affairs, there being no provision for the meeting of member governments' representatives. Another pattern, clearly established with the creation of the League of Nations, was to have a secretariat, a plenary gathering of members' representatives and a body – the Council – which was drawn from a selected number of states. The International Labour Organization, set up in 1919, had two innovations in its structure: it included representatives drawn from non-governmental groups, in this case employers and employees, who sat together with governmental representatives at the General Conference and the meetings of the governing body. Separate organs representing economic and social groupings have become more common in organizations established post-1945 – as in the Economic and Social Committee of the European Communities. The ILO also established an administrative tribunal in 1927, an example followed by post-war institutions such as the UNO, NATO, OECD and the WEU. Juridical institutions dealing not so much with administrative disagreements within the organization but more with disagreements between members date back to the dispute-settling powers of the top bodies of the Central Commission for the Navigation of the Rhine and the Moselle Commission, to the peaceful settlement of disputes undertaken by the Permanent Court of Arbitration and the work of the Permanent Court of International Justice. There now exists a range of legal institutions attached to international organizations for the purpose of settling disputes or controversies: the UNO's International Court of Justice, the Court of Justice of the European Communities, The Council of Europe's Court of Human Rights and European Commission of Human Rights are perhaps the best known examples. A further institutional innovation has been that of parliamentary organs consisting of either a number of elected representatives from member states' parliaments – as in the case of the Consultative Assembly of the Council of Europe, the Nordic Council, the Assembly of the Western European Union or the Parliament of the European Communities previous to 1975 – or of directly elected members, the post-1975 European Parliament providing the one example.

As the number of international organizations has grown, so have the possibilities of institutional innovation. Some organizations have gone through their own process of institutional development during the past twenty years: the Nordic Council has obtained a secretariat and added a Council of Ministers to its original parliamentary base; the Commonwealth of Nations now has a permanent secretariat. Others have been attracted by simplicity: the South African–Botswana–Lesotho–Swaziland Customs Union has, under their 1969 Agreement, kept a Customs Union Commission composed of representatives of all the contracting parties meeting annually. At the other extreme, the United Nations Organization is now a network consisting of the Security Council, General Assembly, Economic and

Social Council, Secretariat, Trusteeship Council, International Court of Justice and the various commissions, committees, conferences, boards and specialized agencies attached to these principal organs.

On what basis can institutional structure provide a typology of international organizations? Three basic questions about the institutions, suggested by Reuter (1958, p. 248), help in providing an answer:

1   What provision is made in the organs to balance the interests of one member against those of another or one group of members against another group? How, then, is institutional power distributed?

2   How is the balance between the power and influence of the member states and that of the organization's institutions reflected in its structure?

3   What is the balance between governmental and non-governmental representation?

What is needed next is a scheme of the possible range of organs within international organizations to which the above questions may be applied. In his *International Institutional Law*, Professor Schermers (1972, pp. xiii–xvi) seems to divide the structure of organizations in the following way:

a	Policy-making organs –	1	plenary: General Congresses, Junior Congresses, Specialized Congresses, Plenary Commissions
		2	non-plenary: Executive Board, Governing Board, Commissions and Committees, President of the Organization
		3	secretariats
b	Organs of Control –	1	parliamentary
		2	judicial.

Klepacki has rightly criticized this division for its simultaneous or alternating use of three criteria – the function of organs (policy-making, control, general or specialized, executive, governing etc.); numerical strength (plenary, non-plenary) and legal status (secretariats). Also secretariats are not always policy makers, neither are judicial organs always ones of control. Klepacki (1973, pp. ix–x) introduces his own classification:

a	Legal status of members – of the organs	1	interstate organs
		2	organs of international functionaries (officials)
		3	parliamentary organs
		4	organs of the representatives of interest groups of economic and social life
		5	organs of mixed membership.
b	Function of the organs –	1	interstate: top organs executive-governing organs
		2	officials: executive-governing organs administrative organs for settling controversies, and assisting in solving disputes
		3	parliamentary
		4	representative of interest groups
		5	mixed membership
		6	subsidiary organs.

This seems a more logical, satisfactory division and one that is more helpful when applying the three original questions to the structure of international organizations. Examining each of these questions separately, it can be seen how the answers may help to provide a classification of organizations by their structure.

1   *Institutional power of members*

In looking at both the legal status of members and functioning of organs, the interstate organs are of crucial interest. How is power divided between deliberative, plenary organs on which all members are represented (top organs, by Klepacki's nomenclature) and executive-governing organs which do not always have representatives of all members on them? Klepacki (1973, p. 31) points out that both the constitution and practice of leading IGOs provides 'permanent representation in the executive-governing organs of states playing a leading role in the realm which constitutes the main sphere of action of a particular organization'. Examples are the permanent seats given to the Great Powers in the Council of the League of Nations and the UN's Security Council (though it is arguable whether these can be called 'executive-governing' organs without qualification), those given to the large capital subscribers of the IMF, the IBRD, the International Development Association (IDA), the International Finance Corporation (IFC) and the Bank of International Settlements (BIS), and the distribution of ten of the twenty-four seats on the governing body of the ILO to the major industrial states. On the other hand, an organization may have an executive-governing organ on which all members are represented equally or may only have plenary deliberative organs in the interstate section. The OAU has a Council of Ministers, which is responsible to the supreme organ of the Assembly of Heads of State and Government, but all members are equally represented on the Council. The WEU has only a Council (with all members on it) at intergovernmental level though a distinction is made between its three-monthly ministerial meetings and the ambassadorial gatherings in between.

Another structural way of affecting the distribution of power and influence between the members within an organization is by means of the voting mechanisms. One possibility is to allow parts of a state separate representation – this was the course adopted by the UN and its specialized agencies to allow the Soviet Union extra votes in the form of representation by two of its constituent republics, Byelorussia and the Ukraine. A more usual method is to weight the votes, something done within IMF, IBRD, IDA and IFC in accordance with the economic strengths of the members as reflected in their subscriptions to the capital of the organization. The representation of national delegations to the parliamentary and economic and social organs of certain organizations is frequently moderated by population size – in the European Community, Luxembourg has six representatives in the European Parliament whilst the Federal Republic of Germany, France, Italy and the United Kingdom have eighty-one each; the Danish, Finnish, Norwegian and Swedish delegations to the Nordic Council each have seventy-eight members although their populations are, respectively, about five, five, four and eight millions, but Iceland, with a quarter of a million people, has six seats.

Sometimes the majority needed for decisions within institutions can be varied. Before the First World War the UPU and other public international unions accepted two-thirds majorities. Although the League of Nations worked on the unanimity principle, it was accepted that a motion passed by a two-thirds majority, whilst not a decision, should be respected as an indication of the members' wishes ('*voeux*'). The UNO and many of its associated agencies have accepted majority voting – the General Assembly takes most of its decisions by a simple majority of members present and voting whilst 'important questions' are decided by a two-thirds majority (Article 18). Given that the USA and the USSR have only one vote each, they could find themselves being dictated to by a majority of much smaller states. To alleviate this position in the Security Council, while decisions are taken by the affirmative vote of nine of the fifteen members, the permanent members are given the right of veto.

It is difficult to reflect accurately the political reality of relationships in voting formulae. An elaborate system of weighted voting was devised for the Council of Ministers of the European Community to allow them to take majority decisions but this system has rarely been used because of the members' wish to protect their essential national interests by the use of the veto, if necessary, and the general acceptance that Community decisions are best taken with the support of all member states. Sometimes arrangements become outdated: the veto rights allowed the United Kingdom and France in the UN Security Council seem superfluous now they are no longer major colonial powers. In many cases institutional arrangements show little propensity to reflect power relationships: those of the Warsaw Treaty Organization and of NATO do not indicate the dominance in the organization of the USSR and the USA respectively.

To sum up this section: international organizations may be classified by whether their institutions differentiate between one member and another, whether some institutions have only limited membership, whether they have weighted voting, majority or unanimity decisions and whether certain members have veto rights. It can then be estimated whether the institutions of a particular organization are more or less egalitarian.

2   Member states/institutions

The bureaux of the early public international unions were often allowed a good deal of independence in the limited functional area of their competence. Whilst the periodic meetings of interstate organs could exercise sovereign control over general policy, the implementation of this policy and the day-to-day running of affairs had to be left to the bureaux – the secretariat. There was little or no tension between the organ representing the individual sovereign states and that embodying the collective needs. Once organizations started to deal with more than technical questions and once they obtained permanent bodies, meeting frequently, that represented the member governments, there was a greater possibility of a conflict between the demands of the individual members and those of the organization's institutions.

An important element in this equation is the extent to which the international functionaries or officials are controlled by the member states. In the early public international unions the bureaux were quite often run by one member state – Switzerland in the case of the UPU and ITU, Belgium for the International Union for the Publication of Customs Tariffs. The former two offices acted within the general policy limits set by the member states meeting at regular intervals whilst the latter was not inhibited in such a way – its task was so specific and obvious from the 1890 Brussels Convention (amended in 1949) that it needed no further control. The advent of the League of Nations brought the notion of an international secretariat to the fore – that is, civil servants with a loyalty to the organization rather than to their original home country. The UNO took over this concept in Article 100:

1.   In the performance of their duties the Secretary-General and the staff shall not seek or receive instructions from any government or from any other authority external to the Organization. They shall refrain from any action which might reflect on their position as international officials responsible only to the Organization.

2.   Each Member of the United Nations undertakes to respect the exclusively international character of the responsibilities of the Secretary-General and the staff and not to seek to influence them in the discharge of their responsibilities.

The UN Charter also gave, as well as executive and administrative responsibility, political powers to the secretary-general in Article 99:

The Secretary-General may bring to the attention of the Security Council any matter which in his opinion may threaten the maintenance of international peace and security.

In practice the secretaries-general have exercized a political role even without reference to Article 99. Both the first and second holders of the office – Lie and Hammarskjold – accumulated a great amount of responsibility using their own interpretation of their duties, sometimes in opposition to members of the Security Council.

However, there have been serious constraints on the independence of action of the UN secretariat. Members of the permanent staff have not always come up to the standard of Article 100 – East European and some Third World members have kept obvious connections with their home governments. Also short-term secondment of national civil servants has been used so that '[T]he UN Secretariat has gradually and painfully, evolved a series of compromises with the original concept of a largely international civil service' (R. R. James,

1971, p. 70). The earlier independent role of the secretary-general seems to have been moderated after the problems experienced by Dag Hammarskjold in the Congo from 1960 to his death in 1961. For example, the role of the secretary-general in the Cyprus peace-keeping operation was severely curtailed by the Security Council. This question is dealt with further in Chapter 4.

The European Community has, in the Commission, a body made up of international functionaries which has important executive-governing powers. Members of the Commission are obliged to act in the interests of the Community rather than any one country and they have at their service an international staff. Whereas the High Authority of the European Coal and Steel Community and the Commission of the EEC under its first president, Walter Hallstein, tended to consider the needs of the whole of the Community area – that is, to take a supranational view of their task – the French Government's stand against this independent attitude in 1965–6 brought a greater stress on satisfying national needs.

Both the secretary-general of the UN and commissioners of the EC have been open to another form of control by the interstate organs; their tenure is renewable and they are chosen by the member states. The opposition of the Soviet Union to both Lie and Hammarskjold limited the diplomatic and mediating role that they could perform between East and West and in the end Lie was forced to resign and Hammarskjold almost certainly would not have had his term of office renewed had he lived. Similarly, members of the High Authority of the ECSC in the past and of the Commission of the Economic and Atomic Energy Communities have been and are chosen by member states. It is accepted that every four years the government of each of the larger states names two commissioners and each of the smaller states names one. A past President of the Euratom Commission, Etienne Hirsch, did not have his term of office renewed in 1962 because he had incurred the displeasure of his home government – the French Government of President de Gaulle.

While there have been important developments in the creation of institutions that can take independent decisions in vital political areas in some international organizations – notably the UNO and the EC – this process has met resistance among key member states. Likewise the 'international' nature of the functionaries of these – and other – organizations has been held in check. Dag Hammarskjold described 'two of the essential principles of an international civil service: 1 its international composition, and 2 its international responsibilities', and it is the achievement of these that has been an uphill task in the face of criticism and opposition from members wishing to maintain the dominance of interstate organs. Even the international secretariats of the specialized agencies are feeling the strain of having to insure 'equitable geographical distribution' in their recruitment to satisfy new members though this may mean a decline in the standards of appointment (Symonds, 1971, p. 113).

3 Governmental/non-governmental

The major indicator here is the extent to which organs of an international organization contain non-governmental representation as opposed to governmental. At one end of the scale are those INGOs that have no governmental representatives on any of their institutions whilst at the other end of the scale are the IGOs without any non-governmental representation. In the middle but to the INGO side are those organizations such as the Inter-Parliamentary Union which have special links to governments and the Consultative Group on International Agricultural Research with governmental, foundation, bank and EC membership. To the IGO side are those inter-governmental organizations which have non-governmental representation in the institutions such as the European Community and the ILO.

A classification of international organizations by an examination of their structures would demonstrate whether the institutions are more or less egalitarian, what degree of independence the institutions have from their membership and the balance between governmental and non-governmental participation. A division using these elements produces examples as in Table 2.6. .

Table 2.6   A Division of International Organizations Based on Structural Characteristics

Membership organs	Governmental		Mixed		Non-governmental	
Organs dependence on members Egalitarian nature of institutions	More	Less	More	Less	More	Less
More ↑ ↓ Less	NATO	Arab League	ILO	EFTA	Salvation Army	Nordic Association
	IMF	League of Nations	EC	International Council of Scientific Unions	World Wildlife Fund	

Summary

This chapter has examined three of the most common classifications of international organizations: by membership, by aims and activities, and by structure.

When considering *type of membership*, a distinction was made between organizations made up of governmental representatives (IGOs) and those with non-governmental members (INGOs), though there are a number of international organizations with mixed membership (e.g. ILO). Also identified are international organizations between governmental actors that are not controlled by the central foreign policy organs – transgovernmental organizations (TGOs). Excluded by the definition of international organizations are the Business International Non-Governmental Organizations (BINGOs) and other multinational enterprises (MNES) partly on the grounds of their being based in one country but mainly because their aim is the making of profit. However, they are important transnational actors.

The *extent of membership* introduces the question of regionalism versus universalism. The definition of a region in itself presents problems, though it is generally agreed that the concept denotes more than geographical closeness – it normally indicates economic, social, cultural and political ties as well. This does not help in the task of defining any one region: certainly international organizations are best typified as being more or less regional rather than regional or universal. It is most helpful to refer to organizations with limited membership as opposed to those, such as the UNO, that have extensive membership. This also helps avoid some of the normative elements attached to the word 'regional'.

The *aims and activities* of international organizations show what they are meant to do and what they actually do, thus providing the fairest way to classify them. Both aims and activities may be ranged along a 'general–specific' scale and can also be divided according to whether they are oriented towards co-operative relations between members, lowering their level of conflict or producing confrontation between members (and, in some cases, specific non-members). International organizations may have elements of all three in their basic documents, though the co-operative aspect seems to be the strongest.

An examination of the *structure* of international organizations is the easiest method of classification. The historical growth of the numbers and complexity of international organizations has provided a wide range of structures. A study of these structures can examine how institutions differentiate between one member and another – whether they are more or less egalitarian in their treatment of members, the degree of independence the institutions have from the member governments and the balance between the governmental and non-governmental elements in the institutions.

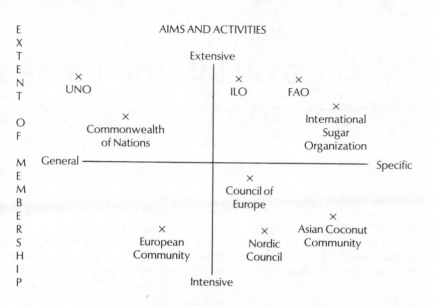

Figure 2.4   A Cross-Classification of IGOs

A combination of the above elements can be used to classify international organizations. For example, the extent of membership factor can be placed together with the general/specific range of aims and activities producing the sort of outcome seen in Figure 2.4. Whichever way types of international organizations are identified, the question to be asked is whether the classification helps in understanding the nature of international organizations. To do this, membership characteristics, behaviour or form should be disentangled in such a way that the factors that make for different international organizations are understood as well as those elements that unify institutions under the one heading of 'international organizations'.

3

Writings on International Organizations

The student of international organizations is not short of written material on the subject – most textbooks on international relations contain a chapter or section on them and, as shown in Chapter 1, there are a number of books and articles devoted exclusively to the phenomenon. There are also some bibliographies dealing with international organizations – Yalem (1966), Michael Haas (1971), Atherton (1976) – and two periodicals – *International Organization* and the *Yearbook of International Organizations* – provide a rich source of material and observation. The major problems are those of access – how to reach the necessary book or article – and of choice – which publications to leave out, which to read and note.

This chapter is by no means a comprehensive survey of the literature: it is bound to be selective not just because a full account would be indigestible for the reader but also because of the limitations on the author. This means that material is drawn from that originally written in the major European languages with English and American literature dominant. It does not mean that material written in other languages is of little value – clearly this is not the case. Because of the international nature of the political science community, important contributions originally written in, say, Rumanian or Chinese will normally filter through with translation into English or one of the other European languages. Despite this probability, the reader should note that linguistic constraints, the nature of publishing and what might be called the 'cultural imperialism' of the European and North American area all mean that ideas from the Third World fight an uphill battle to be widely disseminated in print. So this chapter is bound to have a built-in cultural bias however careful the author may be.

The literature covered is arranged into four major sections: that representing the more traditional view of international organizations based primarily on the state-centric model of international affairs; the newer ideas that accept the role and importance of non-state actors; the views of Marxist writers; and what are broadly called the 'Third World' approaches. These divisions should not be regarded as watertight – there is clearly some overlap between the first and second approaches and between the third and fourth, to take the most obvious examples. Within each section disagreement over the role and importance of international organizations may be found but the four sections represent distinct ideas as to the nature of international organizations. They are seen, respectively, as institutions between states and governments; institutions between societies as well as states; part of a political superstructure built on a particular economic base; and either instruments of exploitation used against the poor by the rich or potential tools of liberation. An attempt has been made to choose the major writers typifying these main lines of thought about international organizations and to include those authors who offer interesting points of dissent.

Traditional Views

Traditional views of international organizations consider them to be part of the institutionalized relationship between states and governments. They have a state-centric view of the political world and have little interest in INGOs. Notable contributions of this type have been made by international lawyers, by the more idealist thinkers of the interwar period and by the 'realist' commentators on international relations.

International Lawyers

Much of the literature about international organizations is descriptive, often dealing with several organizations and giving particular emphasis to the League of Nations and United Nations, sometimes dealing with one organization such as NATO, the OAU or the European Communities. Leading in this area are the works of the international lawyers who give particular consideration to the constitutions of international organizations, their legal personalities and to institutional problems. Indeed, it was probably the professor of law at Edinburgh University, J. Lorimer, who first coined the expression 'international organization' in 1867.

Noticeable contributions to the study of international organizations have been made by British legal experts and historians such as

Zimmern in his study *The League of Nations and the Rule of Law* and J. L. Brierly's comparison of the newly emerged United Nations with the structure and aims of the then dying League. Brierly demonstrated a strong preference for the intrusion of international law into economic and social affairs so that the generic grievances of states may be removed (1946, p. 93). Hersch Lauterpacht published *The Development of International Law by the Permanent Court of International Justice* in 1934 and this was later matched in the United States by Judge Manley O. Hudson's work *International Tribunals, Past and Future*. Wilfred Jenks, the Legal Adviser to the ILO, contributed not just on that organization (1962a) but also more general works on international organizations (1962b, 1945a, 1945b). He stressed the need to marry the craft of the international lawyer with the prudence of the politician to develop an effective system of international organization:

> Institutional development is primarily the responsibility of statesmanship; it must be guided and controlled by a true appreciation of political forces ... The greatest of legal traditions is still to be created; its texture will be largely determined by the quality of the craftsmanship which international lawyers place at the disposal of statesmen during the next generation. (1945a, pp. 71–2)

More modern international institutions textbooks have been provided by two European international lawyers. Henry Schermers, Professor of Law at the University of Amsterdam, in his two-volume work restricts himself to 'international institutional law' which '[b]y concerning itself with the structure and functions of international organizations ... tries to explain the present development and to promote the harmonious growth of international organization' (Schermers, 1972, p. 2). He deals with the participants in international organizations, the general rules for their organs and the activities of these organs from primarily a legal viewpoint. A similar approach is adopted by the British international legal expert, D. W. Bowett, whose book (1970) places greater emphasis on particular institutions – the League, the UN and its specialized agencies, the regional organizations, the juridical institutions – as well as dealing with general questions such as the international personality of the organizations and their impact on the doctrine of the sovereign equality of states. For a blend of sociology, history and international law, the work of Paul Reuter (1958), Professor of International Law at Paris University, is unsurpassed. It examines the phenomenon of international organization rather than just the organizations and institutions and therefore spends some time on the nature of international society, the origins and foundations of international institutions as well as the position of states in international society.

International lawyers have also given extensive consideration to particular institutions. The League of Nations attracted special attention as lawyers played an important role in its drafting and as it had as its aims the promotion of international co-operation and the achievement of international peace and security

> by the firm establishment of the understandings of international law as the actual rule of conduct among Governments, and by the maintenance of justice and a scrupulous respect for all treaty obligations in the dealings of organised peoples with one another.
> (Preamble to the Covenant)

Furthermore the central part of the Covenant dealing with the keeping of peace, Articles XII–XVI, adopts a legalistic approach in defining an act of war against all League members as being resort to war in disregard of Articles XII, XIII or XV (Article XVI (1)). In other words, the cardinal sin is the breaking of the legal agreement made with other states. International lawyers in particular were concerned with how international law might be agreed, judged and enforced and in the interwar period turned much of their attention to the activities of the Permanent Court of International Justice and the League of Nations. Judge Hersch Lauterpacht, for example, considered that all international disputes were justiciable and thus open to solution by the judicial process in international law. He considered the League to be a useful step in the development of international law and the sanctions allowed for in Article 16 of the Covenant as marking 'the first step' towards the collective enforcement of international law (E. Lauterpacht, 1970, p. 19).

The League had its advocates among other legal writers. Alfred Zimmern, writing in 1938, set the League's activities and institutions against the backdrop of the gathering storm in Europe and still found much to say for it: it had developed and expanded the old diplomatic system, had encouraged co-operation in many areas and at least represented an attempt to eliminate war even during a period of what Zimmern called 'earthquakes' (1939, pp. 491–509). Lord Robert Cecil, one of the founders of the League as well as a lawyer and Conservative politician, when writing in 1941 admitted the failure of the organization in preventing aggressive powers but hoped that it would be reformulated after hostilities with a core of a confederation of European states 'the central object of which should be the preservation of the European peace'. Peace in the rest of the world would depend pretty well on the then just-existing Covenant with some small changes. Cecil did admit that 'another piece of machinery' could do little unless the peoples and governments 'really put the enforcement of law and maintenance of peace as the first and greatest national interests' (pp. 349–51).

The hopes of those who yearned for legal solutions to international disputes clearly declined as the UN Charter, with its emphasis on political solutions to what after all were political disputes, replaced the optimistic legal formulas of the League Covenant. The UN Charter was not to be without its international legal commentators. Indeed, two standard books on the UNO are by distinguished lawyers: Kelsen (1950) and Goodrich and Hambro (1969), though the latter have admitted that when interpreting the Charter

> since the responsibility for interpretation is vested in organs and members alike, the process is more likely to be political than judicial ... Decisions tend to reflect the common interests of members in achieving certain results. (p. 15)

World Law School

Two American lawyers, Clark and Sohn, were not to be denied a legal solution for global disorder. In *World Peace Through World Law* they advanced two alternative plans, one for the revision of the UN Charter and one for a new world security and development organization to supplement the present work of the United Nations, the general aims of which would be

> to achieve and maintain total national disarmament, to enforce world law against international violence, and to promote economic and social development. (p. xiii)

This was seen as a practical prospect with the process of universal and complete disarmament well on its way by 1975 (though a later note postpones this to 1985) using either a revised UNO or a supplementary organization as the instrument of change. The riposte of the 'realist' school to such plans is noted below (pp. 120–31) but one comment should be mentioned here: if ever Clark and Sohn's plans were agreed by all governments, or even by all of the larger powers, it would seem that the very reason for their creation – the harmful political divisions in the world that so often lead to violence and warfare – would have substantially disappeared.

International Government

Another American legal authority, Clyde Eagleton, has given the United Nations a critical, though somewhat understanding, appreciation, summing up its dilemma as such:

> If the United Nations cannot do more than it has, the fault lies with the Members who made it and operate it, and who, it seems, still prefer the tooth and the fang to international law and order. (1948, p. 552)

Eagleton placed the record of the United Nations in the context of its predecessors in the history of the growth of international government, and of its legal and political background. He examined proposals to achieve the 'international government' that the UN has failed to reach but concluded that a change in the attitudes of states and their peoples is needed first (p. 583). Eagleton's work underlined the point made by Evan Luard in his *International Agencies* (1977) that with the existence of the UNO and its associated agencies, many of the world's problems are not without institutions exercising authority over them. The powers of this range of organization can be questioned, as can their standing in relation to their sovereign state members, but their existence in the post-war world – and their growth from their nineteenth-century beginnings – is a reality.

This interest in the growth in 'international government' is neither new nor restricted to the legal profession. One of the earlier publications on the subject was by the writer Leonard Woolf who was a founder of the Fabian Society, the reformist discussion group within the British Labour Party. Writing in 1916, he outlined the extent to which 'international government' had been accepted through diplomatic gatherings, the use of public and private international unions and the increase in commodity agreements, and he put forward plans for the further regulation of international activity. 'If war is to be prevented,' he claimed 'states must submit to some international control and government in their political and administrative relations' (p. 228). He advanced a Fabian Committee plan for 'the Supranational Authority that will Prevent War', elements of which found their way into the League Covenant and which, *inter alia*, recommended 'the establishment of an International High Court, an International Council of states' representatives and an International Secretariat'. Woolf and his Fabian colleagues hoped that with this machinery, legal, justiciable disputes would be submitted to the Court or a similar tribunal and other disputes to the Council for settlement, with the parties to the dispute constrained from warlike action for a period of a year. Provision was to be made for sanctions which all states should put into operation and all agreed 'to make common cause, even to the extent of war, against any constituent State which violates this fundamental agreement' (p. 233).

Woolf, together with jurists such as Hersch Lauterpacht and Alfred Zimmern and British political writers like Philip Noel-Baker, Lord Cecil and Gilbert Murray, represented both the practical and intellectual supporters of the League of Nations in the interwar period often classified as 'idealists' or neo-Grotians. Hedley Bull (1966, pp. 52–5) described the central Grotian assumption (named after the seventeenth-century legal writer Hugo Grotius) as being 'that of the solidarity, or potential solidarity, of the states comprising international society, with respect to the enforcement of the law' and Grotius's basic criterion of just war being fought in order to enforce rights – a notion clearly echoed in the Fabian Committee's 'The supranational authority that will prevent war'. Bull criticized the way this group lost sight of international politics in their preoccupation with international law, international organization and international society:

> In dealing with international morality, which they were inclined to confuse with international law, they contributed only a narrow and uncritical rectitude which exalted the international interest over national interests (but without asking how the former was to be determined), constitutional reform over revolution as the means of transcending the society of sovereign states (but without considering whether states could become the agents of their own existence), and respect for legality over the need for change (but without facing up to the fact that the international legal system, as they construed it, could not accommodate change). (1972, p. 36)

This is a telling enough assessment of the 'idealists' ' views, including their writings on international organizations. However, the background of the group should be remembered – they represented a generation devastated by the First World War and which was used to a national society (turn-of-the-century Britain) that had benefited through institutional change and in which the rule of law had not precluded reform. The League of Nations, the PCIJ and the ILO were for them part of 'A Great Experiment', to use Lord Cecil's phrase.

The Realists

Another group of writers on international relations with their intellectual roots in the 1930s, the Second World War and the Cold War was that of the 'realists', otherwise known as the Power Politics school, represented by E. H. Carr and Georg Schwarzenberger in Britain and Reinhold Niebuhr and Hans Morgenthau in the USA. Their starting point was the existence of the present state system in which there is no common authority over and above the sovereign state and where there is international anarchy in the sense of a lack of government at the international level. Naturally enough, this viewpoint has consequences for their appreciation of the role of international organizations in interstate relations.

E. H. Carr's writings reflect the disillusionment with the League of Nations in the 1930s over its – or rather its members' – failure to prevent the invasions of Abyssinia and Manchuria, and with the conquests by the Nazi and fascist states in Europe. He considered that it was misguided to suppose that a more rational – and more moral – mode of conducting interstate relations, such as by use of the League and the PCIJ, would necessarily lead to a more satisfactory world order, especially if it were not based on the realities of existing power relationships. The League, and the structure it purported to uphold, was only as strong as those countries willing to support it. As the most powerful League supporters – France and the United Kingdom – found an increasing number of states ranged against the League system – Germany, Japan, Italy – and the USA and the USSR either unwilling or unavailable to help, they compromised their support of the League to keep the wolves from their own doors. Indeed Carr was prepared to support such policies as the Munich Agreement of September 1938 as 'the nearest approach in recent years to the settlement of a major international issue by a procedure of peaceful change' and as a recognition of the preponderance of German power in central Europe (1939, p. 282). Furthermore he concluded that there were two major shortcomings in international morality, on which the League of Nations was supposedly based. First, there was discrimination in the international community between the way in which the cases of certain countries were treated: there was, for example, a different attitude by the British and French governments to Greece or Abyssinia being attacked – the former was unacceptable, the latter case only regrettable. Secondly there was 'the failure to secure general acceptance of the postulate that the good of the whole takes precedence over the good of the part' (Carr, 1946, p. 166). Without such acceptances it is hard to imagine an organization such as the League working unless based on the overwhelming predominance of power of its supporters. Carr's emphasis on power does not mean that he jettisoned the role of morality in international affairs. He recommended a judicious blend of morality and power, though compared with the national order '[I]n the international order, the role of power is greater and that of morality less' (ibid., p. 168).

The major work of Georg Schwarzenberger – *Power Politics* (1941) – also took the failure of the League and the interwar system as a point of departure. On the question of collective security, the rock on which the League of Nations was built, Schwarzenberger remarked, referring to bilateral pacts of mutual assistance:

> The very need for treaties of this sort proved that League members either assumed that the system of the Covenant would be inadequate, inoperative or too slow to be of use, or that the other members of the League would not honour their obligations under the Covenant. Thus they offer the most open refutation that can be imagined of the solution envisaged by the drafters of the Covenant in a world imbued with century-old traditions of power politics. (1941, p. 252).

During the latter part of the 1930s supporters of the League had turned their interest from the central question of peace and security to the more peripheral areas of the economic and social activities of the League and agencies such as the ILO. Such an interest is shown by Lord Cecil in the conclusion to his autobiography published in the same year as Schwarzenberger's book. Schwarzenberger was not convinced by the faith placed in such functional links:

> Organizations of a technical, commercial and professional kind, such as the International Postal Union, the Bank of International Settlements, white slave control or the Interparliamentary Union are, within a system of power politics, limited to that sphere of international relations which is irrelevant from the standpoint of 'high' politics. (p. 388).

Writing during uncertain times Schwarzenberger was not aiming to adopt a merely negative stance. Indeed he desired international relations to be based on a community spirit and founded on the rule of law but thought that nothing was more dangerous to this objective 'than the belief that half-way houses like the League of Nations or limited plans for economic co-operation are adequate to bring about this vital transformation' (p. 11). International order and the rule of law in interstate relations presupposed national communities based on 'Justice, freedom, truth and love', Christian virtues to which Schwarzenberger recommended Western states to return (p. 434).

A strong Christian element is also to be found in the works of the American writer Reinhold Niebuhr who, nevertheless, is to be counted amongst the 'realist' school. Writing in 1948, Niebuhr contrasted growth in man's technical achievement with the lack of advance in political areas:

Our problem is that technics have established a rudimentary world community but have not integrated it organically, morally or politically. They have created a community of mutual dependence, but not one of mutual trust and respect. (p. 379)

Niebuhr examined the case for world government noting that almost all the arguments for it rested on the 'presupposition that the desirability of world order proves the attainability of world government' (p. 380). He identified two faults which undermined arguments for world government – governments are not created by fiat but need a community for their base; governments 'have only limited efficacy in integrating a community' (p. 380). Given the absence of such a community of interest in the world, Niebuhr preferred the imperfections of the Charter of the United Nations to an international organization that would attempt world federation but would accomplish something a lot less spectacular. However he did note that 'the international community is not totally lacking in social tissue' (p. 386): he listed economic interdependence, fear of mutual annihilation and moral obligation as unifying factors in the modern world. Pitted against these were the economic disparities in the world, the negative effect of fear of destruction and the lack of common convictions on particular issues: 'in short, the forces which are operating to integrate the world community are limited' (p. 388). Writing during the initial night-frost of the Cold War, he tempered his realistic view of the world with an appreciation that satisfaction with the status quo is in itself dangerous: 'we might also gradually establish a genuine sense of community with our foe, however small. No matter how stubbornly we resist Russian pressures, we should still have a marginal sense of community with the Soviet Union' (p. 388). For this reason Niebuhr placed emphasis on international organizations such as the UNO not as being nascent world government but, in the Security Council, as being 'a bridge of a sort between the segments of a divided world' (p. 382). The Christian Niebuhr recognized that whilst individuals may be moral, the morality of groups is much inferior: 'it may be possible, though it is never easy, to establish just relations between individuals within a group purely by moral and rational suasion and accommodation. In inter-group relations this is practically an impossibility' (1936, pp. xxii–xxiii). Mankind might dream of peace and brotherhood but has to content itself with a more modest goal – 'a society in which there will be enough justice, and in which coercion will be sufficiently non-violent to prevent his common enterprise from issuing into complete disaster' (1936, p. 22).

Perhaps the most famous of the 'power politics' or 'realist' school is Hans Morgenthau, author of the classic *Politics among Nations* (1960), first published in 1948. Morgenthau was a German-born international lawyer who emigrated in 1937 to the United States where his post-war work had a deep influence on international relations thinking and practice. Although he did not specifically devote any book to the problems of international organizations, his works were so broad as to envelop the general problems of relations between states and the specific questions of interstate organizations. The three major elements that typify Morgenthau's writings – and indeed the Realist school generally – are the beliefs that nation states are the most important actors in international relations, that there is a clear distinction between domestic and international politics and that international relations is predominantly about the struggle for power and peace (Vasquez, 1979, p. 211). These basic tenets are reflected in Morgenthau's treatment of international organizations which are seen purely as interstate institutions important in so far as they are used in the search for power or in solving the problem of peace.

A crucial sentence in *Politics among Nations* points to a central idea in Morgenthau's work:

> The main signpost that helps political realism to find its way through the landscape of international politics is the concept of interest defined in terms of power. (1948, p. 5)

Thus '[i]nternational politics, like all politics, is a struggle for power' (p. 27) and '[w]hen we speak of power, we mean man's control over the minds and actions of other men' (p. 28). Furthermore:

> All politics, domestic and international, reveals three basic patterns; that is, all political phenomena can be reduced to one of three basic types. A political policy seeks either to keep power, to increase power, or to demonstrate power. (p. 39)

These policies are seen in three forms: the politics of status quo, the politics of imperialism and the politics of prestige. Morgenthau then evaluated 'national power' and limitations on it in the form of balance of power, international morality and world public opinion and international law. He considered world politics in the mid-twentieth century and the problem of peace. He examined attempts to obtain peace through limitation (disarmament, collective security, judicial settlement, peaceful change, international government), through transformation (into either a world state or a world community) and through accommodation by diplomacy. During his work Morgenthau touched on the role of international organizations especially in his sections on international law, on peace through limitation and on world community.

Morgenthau stressed that on the basis of international law there has been built 'an imposing edifice, consisting of thousands of treaties, hundreds of decisions of international tribunals, and innumerable decisions of domestic courts'. These regulated relations between states arose from

> the multiplicity and variety of international contacts, which are the result of modern communications, international exchange of goods and services, and the great number of international organizations in which most nations have co-operated for the furtherance of their common interests. (p. 277)

Whilst most international law has been respected, Morgenthau remarked that when rules are violated, they are not always enforced and even when enforcement is undertaken, it is not always effective. Mentioning the Briand–Kellogg Pact, the Covenant of the League of Nations and the UN Charter, he considered that

> These instruments are indeed of doubtful efficacy (that is, they are frequently violated), and sometimes even of doubtful validity (that is, they are often not enforced in case of violation). They are, however, not typical of the traditional rules of international law. (p. 277)

In the section on international government Morgenthau noted that since the start of the nineteenth century each of the three world wars (the Napoleonic War, The First and Second World Wars) have been followed by attempts to establish international government: the Holy Alliance, the League of Nations and the United Nations. The first two attempts foundered because of the varied interests of states involved, in particular because of disagreements about the status quo they were supposed to be supporting. According to Morgenthau

> conflict between the British and French conceptions and policies did not, however, wreck the League of Nations, as the conflict between Great Britain and Russia had the Holy Alliance. It rather led to a creeping paralysis in the political activities of the

League and to its inability to take determined action against threats to international order and peace. (p. 469)

The League could only be said to have exercised governmental functions in the area of the maintenance of international order and peace 'in the rare instances when either the interests of the great powers among its members were not affected or the common interests of the most influential among them seemed to require it' (p. 471).

The United Nations was also seen by Morgenthau as being based on unsure foundations, but for a different reason than for the League: after the Second World War the victorious powers 'first created an international government for the purpose of maintaining the status quo and after that proposed to agree upon the status quo'. However: 'Since such agreement has never existed during the life span of the United Nations, the international government of the United Nations, as envisaged by the Charter, has remained a dead letter' (pp. 493–4). He referred to a 'paralyzed' Security Council with the General Assembly and Secretary-General of the UN both displaying 'weakness' (pp. 492–3) with the whole organization achieving 'little enough' (p. 496). In his view

The contribution the United Nations can make to the preservation of peace, then, would lie in taking advantage of the opportunity that the coexistence of the two blocs in the same international organization provides for the unobtrusive resumption of the techniques of traditional diplomacy. (p. 497)

In examining the possibility of creating a world community based on a range of international organizations such as UNESCO and the other specialized agencies, Morgenthau made the point that the creation of such a community 'presupposes at least the mitigation and minimization of international conflicts so that the interests uniting members of different nations may outweigh the interest separating them' (p. 536). On the UN agencies, Morgenthau considered that

the contributions international functional agencies make to the well-being of members of all nations fade into the background. What stands before the eyes of all are the immense political conflicts that divide the great nations of the earth and threaten the well-being of the loser, if not his very existence. (p. 528)

In summary, Hans Morgenthau accepted that international organizations have a place in international relations though he was careful not to overstate their importance in the search for power and peace in the world. He saw their contribution as being modest and as part of the general intercourse between states and their governments and he gave no real consideration to international non-governmental organizations. Furthermore functional international organizations, whilst recognized as being useful, were not given any particular role in solving the problem of peace. Even the United Nations was only given credence in this context as 'the new setting for the old techniques of diplomacy' (p. 497).

The realist 'power politics' school's view of international organization is open to three major criticisms.

First, it could be claimed that from a moral viewpoint the power politics school is greatly lacking as it accepts too easily the status quo in international politics and does not allow international organizations a positive role in creating a better world. However, this is to forget that in the writings of a number of the realist school – Carr, Schwarzenberger and Niebuhr – there is a moral and often Christian aspect. Hans Morgenthau was just as concerned with the moral aspects of politics as his contemporaries who rejected the power politics precepts. The depth of his concern can be seen in his 1970 book *Truth and Power: Essays of a Decade 1960–70*.

Secondly the whole realist school, typified by the works of Morgenthau, can be challenged exactly on its major claim – its realism. To what extent does the school offer a useful description and explanation of international relations? Vasquez (1979) has outlined how international relations articles published previous to 1970 were dominated by the realist paradigm, yet their hypotheses proved to be inaccurate and even did less well than 'non-realist' hypotheses in their predictive power. Such findings tend to undermine the strength of what has been the dominant international relations school in Western academia and suggest that alternative paradigms – for example, the Marxist and the transnational – should be given more time and consideration than previously. This questioning of the power politics school's work must then also raise doubts about their rather dismissive treatment of international organizations as being marginal in international relations.

Indeed one of the major criticisms of the school's treatment of international organizations has been its emphasis on 'high politics' – the question of peace and war – to the neglect of 'low politics' such as economic, technical and cultural relations. International organizations are seen just as instruments of policy for states and international non-governmental organizations are hardly considered. Nowadays a neglect of economic relations and INGOs seems an even greater omission.

In defence of this attitude it should be remembered that most of the power politics writings were before the massive expansion of INGOs in the 1960s and 1970s. The school is rooted in the reaction to the infirmity of the Western democracies when faced by Hitler and Mussolini in the 1930s and it found its feet in the immediate post-war Cold War period. It is therefore understandable that it stresses 'high politics' and is antipathetic to international organizations which were seen to be connected with the discredited League of Nations and its intellectual supporters or with the original intentions of the United Nations Organization before these were stalemated by Great Power dissension.

Revisionist Views

The traditional writers, despite their differing evaluations of the worth of certain international organizations, have in common a state-centric approach to international relations. Though some were concerned that governments should reflect more the (inevitably) good intentions of their citizens in international affairs or that world organizations should have more power to deal with warlike or renegade states, their focus of attention is the international govern-mental organization – the IGO. A noticeable development in the international relations literature since the Second World War has been the movement away from this state-centred view towards one that admits the importance of international actors other than the sovereign state – IGOs in their own right (rather than as meeting places for or instruments of their member states), INGOs, transnational organizations, political groups and individual citizens. Although many publications just describe these new phenomena which have become more active in the last forty years, there is also a prescriptive element to some of the writings: they tend to prescribe increased non-state activity in international relations as a way of underpinning closer relations between states and societies or undermining hostile attitudes by governments. Taken to its logical conclusion there is the belief that the division of the world into sovereign states is both futile and costly for mankind and that transnational activities help to stress the 'wholeness' of 'only one earth'. Whilst this general 'revisionist' viewpoint is similar to Marxist approaches (dealt with in the next section) in stressing non-state relations in international politics and in viewing the globe as an entity, it does not adopt a Marxist analysis of mankind's situation and will therefore be dealt with separately. The 'revisionist' approach to the study of international relations has consequences for the consideration of international organizations and it has made a noticeable contribution to the literature on the subject, especially since the 1950s.

Functionalists

An early break with the traditional view of international organizations based on the state-centric model can be seen in Leonard Woolf's book *International Government*, published in 1916. Although still primarily concerned with interstate relations and the questions of peace and security, a sizeable section of his writings covered governmental technical and economic co-operation and INGOs:

> We are accustomed to regard the world as neatly divided into compartments called states or nations . . . But this vision of the world divided into isolated compartments is not a true reflection of facts as they exist in a large portion of the earth today. (pp. 216–7)

Such a step placing greater emphasis on non-state international relations was taken further in the writings of the Rumanian-born author David Mitrany. Though Mitrany's ideas, known as the functionalist approach to international politics, were inspired by his early life in the Balkans, he found much intellectual stimulation after coming to London in 1912 and working together with Leonard Woolf, among others, in the League of Nations Society, the Labour Party's Advisory Committee on International Affairs and the Fabian Society. His two major early works were *The Progress of International Government* (first published 1932, reprinted in Mitrany (1975)) and *A Working Peace System* (first published in 1943, republished in 1966), though he also made a substantial contribution in articles until his death in 1975. Many of his writings together with an autobiographical piece and an introduction are gathered together in *The Functional Theory of Politics* (1975). In his 1932 work he outlined the nineteenth-century growth in international government along similar lines as Woolf:

> The nineteenth century produced that amazing growth in the material equipment of civilization which welded the world together into one organic whole, making each people a partner in the fate of all. The outward expression of that change was the appearance of world-wide popular movements and the making of innumerable private and public international agreements. (1975, p. 89)

Mitrany was concerned that the rise of the nation state and the insistence of new states on the doctrine of sovereign equality when they were clearly weaker and smaller than the Great Powers hindered international co-operation in, for example, the economic sphere. However, he saw that the force of events was working against 'statism':

> No matter what the size and shape of the particular community, its functions are such that they have to be organised; and the forces and factors now at work no longer have any true relation to the old political divisions, within or without the state. The new functions imposed upon our political institutions are compelling a complete reconstruction of the technique of government, on a purely practical basis. I reach that conclusion by asking at the outset not, 'what is the ideal form for an international society?'; but rather, 'what are its essential functions?' (1975, p. 99)

He claimed that essentially the aims of international government were no different from those of municipal government – to create equality before the law for all members of the community and to promote social justice. To expect to achieve the first aim in international society where states were neither equal nor unchanging units would be unreasonable. It would be far more practical to compromise this aim and establish a League of Nations in which Great Powers would be directly represented. Secondary states would have group representation and smaller states would have 'panel representation'. At the same time secondary bodies would be set up in various parts of the world as organs of regional groupings of states and these bodies would be connected with, and subordinate to, the new central League organs. They would also be able to deal with problems more readily, especially as the unanimity of all states would not be needed for a settlement.

These suggestions are not the novel aspects of Mitrany's work. They are important in changing the emphasis away from the rights of states towards the duties – or at least the activities – of states. Still the concern was with arranging relations between states. In a paper submitted to the British Foreign Office in 1941 and in his study *A Working Peace System* (1966), Mitrany concentrated on how the functions of government might be carried out more expeditiously. He recognized that within liberal democratic states the line between which functions are carried out by public and by private action was shifting and this line 'under the pressure of fresh social needs and demands . . . must be left free to move with them'. A similar demarcation existed in the territorial sphere internationally: some functions (e.g. railway systems) could best be organized continentally, some intercontinentally (e.g. shipping) and some universally (e.g. aviation). However there would be no need for rigid patterns except perhaps in the exercise of negative functions – those related to security where more formal, static institutions would be needed. In the field of positive functions – those related to economic, cultural and social affairs – the dimensions, organs and powers of any organization would be determined by the nature of the function and would be fairly flexible. Mitrany foresaw the establishment of functional bodies 'with autonomous tasks and powers' which would 'do things jointly'. This would link 'authority to a specific activity' thus breaking away 'from the traditional link between authority and a definite territory' (p. 125). This move would avoid the sterility of many of the wartime suggestions for post-war federations or constitutional innovations in the United Nations which foundered on the opposition of sovereign state resistance. Mitrany hoped that the number of international agencies that had existed before the Second World War, augmented by the Allied boards during the war itself, would serve as the basis for the network of international government. He quoted with obvious approval the words of an American scholar, J. Payson Wild, Jr, on the various wartime experiments:

> The lines between domestic and international activity are blurred, and national administrative agencies of the Powers concerned sometimes engage in domestic business, and at other times extend their functions into the international sphere. The result is a conglomeration of international board and domestic staff whose duties intermingle. Administrative officers of national units deal directly with their opposite numbers in other states without benefit of diplomatic intermediaries, and simultaneously perform both national and international tasks. So far no attempt has been made to establish a super-state. (p. 167)

Mitrany's vision is of a world in which the functions of everyday social life – transport, health care, communications, agriculture, industrial development, scientific development and so on – are no longer assiduously carried on within the confines of each sovereign state but are undertaken across frontiers on a regional, continental or universal basis. These activities would be overseen by international organizations which would be more like boards of management. The functional agencies of the UN – the ILO, WHO, FAO etc. – already undertake such co-operative tasks, as do some non-governmental groupings of specialists – League of Red Cross Societies, World Scout Movement etc. – but the line between what is now done internationally and what is still done domestically is drawn very much to the benefit of the latter and even international activities are riddled with political disputes, many of which have little to do with the good management of the function involved. Mitrany's scheme would gradually lower the line to allow more functions to be carried out at the level where they work more efficiently and would provide *management* of these functions rather than political interference. Not only would this development benefit the general social welfare of the world, it would also help to solve the problem of peace and security. The Lilliputian ties of international functional co-operation would pin down the giant of conflict, weakening the urge to destruction and warfare by the promise of construction and co-existence.

The functional approach does not focus just on intergovernmental organization but allows for a network of specialized agencies many of which could be non-governmental. It differs in emphasis from the mainstream traditionalist writings, and Mitrany's work presaged a move away from interstate relations to world politics. Whilst 'the functional approach does not offend against the sentiment of nationality or the pride of sovereignty' (Mitrany, 1965, p. 139) there is no doubt that it is meant to weaken the importance and power of the 'middle man' between the individual and a world community – the sovereign state. The feeling of solidarity encouraged by functional links is not between states but between people or associations of individuals:

> Each of us is in fact a 'bundle' of functional loyalties; so that to build a world community upon such a conception is merely to extend and consolidate it also between societies and groups. (p. 143)

Such an imaginative approach to world problems and the mundane, hard-working, apolitical role it implies for international organizations has its faults. To criticize Mitrany's functionalism as being impractical is unfair both because international functional links *have* grown, especially since the Second World War, and because Mitrany's approach is a gradual one – he did not expect it to be adopted overnight. Even so it does have certain ambitious aspects which should be critically examined.

First, despite the reference to possible regional functional arrangements, Mitrany's plans run counter to the notion of all-embracing regional organizations such as the European Community. Whilst these organizations may link their 'authority to a specific activity' such as the conditions for running the coal and steel industries or the agriculture of the EC's member states, they still hold to 'the traditional link between authority and a definite territory' as the coal and steel policies or the Common Agricultural Policy are not extended to the industries and farmers of other countries who may wish to participate in their schemes. Yet it can be argued that it is precisely in these limited geographical blocs that functional arrangements are best executed, with limitations on membership. To work properly, schemes must encompass defined areas with a good deal in common – the flexibility of Mitrany's proposal could lead to such fluidity in membership that the proposals would soon break down or the members would have so little in common in, for example, the running of agriculture that co-operation would be difficult or non-productive.

Secondly, Mitrany did not really envisage any political control of the functional ties between countries – thus distinguishing him from the more traditionalist approach to international organizations. He was hopeful that the problems of co-ordination between functional agencies could be worked out as they arose and wrote:

> To prescribe for the sake of traditional neatness something more definite than the guidance and supervision of, e.g., the Economic and Social Council, would be to distort the whole conception from the start ... to impose upon them [functional bodies] a 'co-ordination' authority, with anything like controlling status, would be to move again towards that accumulation of power at the centre. (1965, p. 143)

Thus the institutions of the European Community – the Council of Ministers, the Commission, the Court of Justice, the European Parliament, the Economic and Social Committee – were an anathema for Mitrany. They were just mirroring the political controls of the nation state at a part-continental level and, according to Mitrany, 'Continental unions would have a more real chance than individual states to practice the autarky that makes for division' (1966, p. 27). This may offend against the functionalists' hope for a universal approach to problems but the abhorrence of political institutions is strange, when the functional agencies will, after all, be making political decisions – decisions concerning the authoritative allocation of resources. Not only will international functional transport organizations, established according to Mitrany, have to decide that certain areas will be well served by railways and roads, others not, some ports built up, others left to decay, some airlines expanded while others are allowed to contract, but decisions will have to be made on how to distribute scarce resources between either investment in transport or building more hospitals or restructuring the steel industry throughout the area covered by the organizations. These are political decisions. In a period of economic growth and plenty, their political nature may be less obvious as resources are available for almost every plan advanced by world or regional shipping, aviation, health or steel organizations. Otherwise there must surely be a system by which scarce resources are allocated. This problem was faced squarely by Mitrany's successors in the neo-functionalist school, dealt with below.

A third problem in Mitrany's approach is brought out in a comment by Inis Claude:

> The functional theory of international organization ... is ultimately concerned with the issue of political and military struggle; functionalism treats the promotion of welfare as an indirect approach to the prevention of warfare. (Claude, 1968, pp. 34–5)

Mitrany quoted Claude with approval implying that functionalism would indeed make a positive contribution (albeit indirectly) to the prevention of war. This proposition is open to several criticisms. Given the level of armaments in the world and the potential for conflict, the contribution to peace made by functional activities may come too late. A youth group exchange between the USA and the Soviet Union may bode well for the future but will be of little use if the respective parties are beaten to their destinations by inter-continental ballistic missiles. Furthermore the promotion of welfare may increase international conflict by increasing expectations. Especially if social and economic changes are brought about by inter-national functional agencies, developing countries' political leader-ships may find it increasingly difficult to meet their populations' demands for more economic benefits, for a fairer distribution of benefits or, in some cases, for a control of the social consequences of economic growth. Internal strife and unrest may then spill over into international conflict. Finally Mitrany claims that '[T]he functional approach circumvents ideological and racial divisions, as it does territorial frontiers' (1975, p. 226). There is good evidence that the opposite has been happening – that the existing functional organiza-tions such as UNESCO, WHO and ILO have been riddled with ideological and racial (or at least North–South) divisions which have reflected political arguments outside the organizations but have nevertheless adversely affected their basic work.

Neo-functionalists

The move away from the state-centric view of international organization started by Woolf and Mitrany was continued in the immediate post-war period by social scientists applying aspects of functionalist theory to European and Atlantic institutions. This new functionalist approach showed particular interest in the European Communities which arose in the wake of the Schuman Plan. In May 1950 Robert Schuman, the French Foreign Minister, advanced the idea that West European states should establish a 'High Authority' with powers to administer their coal and steel industries. Negotiations on the details of this plan led to the signing of the Treaty of Paris in April 1951 by France, West Germany, Italy, the Netherlands, Belgium and Luxembourg ('the Six') thus giving substance to the idea that functional activity could be managed across frontiers by an organization over and above the governments of the member states – a supranational authority. The idea was widened to cover an expanded range of economic activity when the Six established the European Economic Community (EEC) with the Treaty of Rome in March 1957. An Atomic Energy Community (Euratom) was established at the same time. However the element of supranationality was diluted in the High Authority's successor – the Commission of the EEC – having only limited decision-making powers and having mostly the task of proposing action to the representatives of the member states sitting in the Council of Ministers. Despite this, other Community institutions contained the germ of supranationality – the Court of Justice employing Community rather than national laws; a European Parliament which was eventually to be elected by direct elections amongst a Community-wide electorate voting for Community-based parties; and interest groups representing farmers, consumers, trade unions and businesses on a Community rather than a national basis.

These innovations in Western Europe triggered a spate of literature - primarily in the United States – which examined the nature and purpose of the Community institutions. The dominant strand amongst this writing was that of the neo-functionalists, specifically Ernst Haas, Leon Lindberg and Joseph Nye whose works are of importance in the study of international organizations. In contrast to Mitrany, the new functionalists tended at first to limit their study to developments in Western Europe (Haas's *Beyond the Nation State* (1964) being a noticeable exception), especially the European Communities, although later comparisons were made with the growth of common markets in Africa, East Europe and Latin America. On the whole the neo-functionalists had retreated from Mitrany's world view.

The neo-functionalists also realized the dilemma faced by Mitrany in dealing with political decisions (pp. 87–8 above) and did not flinch in introducing a method of making necessary choices at the international level. Indeed this was the kernel of their ideas: that not only specific functions would be carried out at the subcontinental rather than the national level but that the decisions concerning these functions would be made at that level – with important consequences. It would have consequences for those groups interested in the decisions and would also affect other areas of policy. For example, suppose the ECSC required that the steel industry be organized as a West European entity instead of a number of national industries all controlled by different regulations, and that a supra-national authority be created to decide on the policy for the running of the West European steel industries. In consequence those involved in, say, the French steel industry would switch their attention away from Paris, where policy was previously made, to Brussels where ECSC policy is made. Furthermore a Community, rather than national, policy on steel could spill over into creating a Community policy for coal, transport and other associated activities. As the number of functional policies decided at a Community rather than a national level expanded, so the need for political action at this higher level would grow, and the political systems of the countries involved become inexorably interwined. This was the logic of the innovator of the Schuman Plan idea, Jean Monnet, who considered that the establishment of a Coal and Steel Community followed by similar organizations dealing with other functional areas – agriculture, transport, trade, defence – would be steps on the way to 'building Europe'. The end would be an economically and politically integrated Europe – in Monnet's scheme a federal West European state. The means would be functional but with a political content.

In his study of the European Coal and Steel Community, Ernst Haas examined this strategy and also defined political integration in its ideal type as being

the process whereby political actors in several distinct national settings are persuaded to shift their loyalties, expectations and political activities toward a new centre, whose institutions possess or demand jurisdiction over the pre-existing national states. (1958, p. 16)

This 'new centre' would be the power-house managing the political problems of functional co-operation – the High Authority of the ECSC and the institutions of the EEC. The 'political actors' involved would be those elites leading the political groups habitually concerned with the public decision making and would include trade union officials, business and trade representatives, higher civil servants and active politicians. As these elites turned their attention to the new political centre, they would find that Community policy in one area 'can be made real only if the task itself is expanded' (1961, p. 368) by way of a 'spillover' of activity into another policy area. Eventually Community policy-making would take over from state policy-making in all the crucial areas and the new centre would emerge as being potentially more powerful than the member states' governments which had been drained of their most meaningful political activities.

At this stage it can be queried whether Haas was describing an international organization or a potential federal state. In discussing this question in his book on the ECSC, Haas concluded that

> The balance of 'federal' as against 'intergovernmental' powers seems to point to the conclusion that in all matters relating to the routine regulation of the common market, the High Authority is independent of government... (p. 55)

and that

> Supranationality in structural terms, therefore, means the existence of governmental authorities closer to the archetype of federation than any past international organization, but not yet identical with it. (p. 59)

However this supranationality 'in practice has developed into a hybrid in which neither the federal nor the intergovernmental tendency has clearly triumphed' (1958, p. 527). It is also clear that the original Coal and Steel Community was much more functional–federal than the later Economic Community and the unified and expanded Community has seemed to play down the elements of supranationality in favour of its intergovernmental institution, the Council of Ministers. This and other developments have led Haas to reconsider his original view of Community institutions.

In the 1968 preface to *The Uniting of Europe* (which was written in 1958), Haas already identified factors that had changed the nature of the European Community experiment in the previous ten years. He observed that during this period 'various spill-over and adaptive processes still had not resulted in a politically united Europe' and in answering the question 'what went wrong?' outlined four considerations: the new functionalists had failed to distinguish between background variables, conditions prevailing at the time when the Community was established, and new aspirations and expectations that had developed after establishment which had run counter to the Community spirit; the impact of nationalism had been underestimated; factors within the Community had been stressed to the detriment of those coming from the outside world; the massive transformation of Western society taking place independent of European integration had been underestimated (1968, pp. xiv–xv).

Haas's definition of integration had also become somewhat more negative, more state-centric than his original 1958 emphasis on national actors shifting 'their loyalties, expectations and political activities toward a new centre'. By 1970 Haas considered the study of regional integration to be concerned

> with explaining how and why states cease to be wholly sovereign, how and why they voluntarily mingle, merge, and mix with their neighbours so as to lose the factual attributes of sovereignty while acquiring new techniques for resolving conflict between themselves. (1970, p. 610)

By 1975 Haas considered regional integration theory 'obsolete in Western Europe and obsolescent – though still useful – in the rest of the world' (1975, p. 1) and by 1976 he had carried out a major reinterpretation of new-functionalist theory as it applied to the European Community. The definable outcome of integration in Western Europe was seen either in traditional federalist terms – a West European federal state created out of years of functional activity has led to a transfer of political activity away from the old nation states towards a new structure – or as the institutionalizing of some intermediate stage such as the present status quo whereby authority is distributed unequally between several centres with the old nation states losing their previous authority but with no new federal government in prospect. Whilst the original aspects of the European Community – the customs union and the Common Agricultural Policy – have become entrenched, the 'spillover' into other policy areas has not occurred as the neo-functionalists predicted. Also common policies have been developed in different organizations – the OECD, the summit of industrialized countries, the Group of Ten – rather than within the EC. The problem, according to Haas, has been *turbulence* whereby those involved in politics have found themselves 'in a setting of great social complexity . . .' where '[t]he number of actors is very large' and '[e]ach pursues a variety of objectives which are mutually incompatible; but each is also unsure of the trade-offs between the objectives'. He continued:

> This condition implies the erosion of such interorganizational patterns of consensus, reciprocity, and normative regularity as may have existed earlier . . . Everything is 'up for grabs'. (1976, p. 179)

Haas suggested that in the European Community 'policies and the institutions devised to implement them *illustrate the attempt to deal with the turbulence rather than achieve regional political integration*' (p. 180).

A similar shift away from the earlier aspirations is seen in the works of Lindberg and Nye. Lindberg, whose 1963 book *The Political Dynamics of European Economic Integration* had followed on closely from Haas's work, was by 1966 showing that moves towards integration within the European Community could cause stress within the system and increase the barriers to further integration (p. 254). Together with Scheingold in 1970 he was describing a European Community that had not developed into a federal structure, had different levels of integration for different functions and was still susceptible to crisis. It was 'an unprecedented, but curiously ambiguous "pluralistic" system . . . there seem to be no satisfactory models or concepts in the social science vocabulary to adequately define it' (Lindberg and Scheingold, 1970, p. 306). In a 1970 article Joseph Nye considered that despite these and other revisions, 'the neo-functional approach still embodies a number of faults that reflect its origins in the 1950's' (Nye, p. 797). He proposed a number of changes stating the dependent variable less ambiguously, adding more political actors, reformulating the list of integration conditions and, perhaps most significantly, dropping 'the ideas of a single path from quasi-functional tasks to political union by means of spillover' (ibid.). He concluded that, short of dramatic change, 'the prospects for common markets or microregional economic organizations leading in the short run (of decades) to federation or some sort of political union capable of an independent defense and foreign policy do not seem very high' (p. 829).

All this is a long way from the functionalist–federal hopes of Jean Monnet back in 1950, but it demonstrates the evolution of not only the Community institutions and policies but also neo-functionalist thinking. The 'logic of integration' has given way to coping with crises; institutions mixing federalist and intergovernmental elements are replaced by a Western Europe in which 'institutional tidiness is best forgotten' (Haas, 1976, p. 211); and the federal elements are, at most, dormant. The hopes of the 1950s have been replaced by the uncertainties of the 1970s and 1980s.

Indeed these developments in neo-functionalist writings on international organizations point up some of the criticisms of the school.

First, despite the best efforts of Haas, Schmitter and Nye, it remains a theory overwhelmingly dominated by an interest in the European Community. In 1964 Haas and Schmitter tried to extend some of the lessons of economic union in Western Europe to Latin America. Drawing on Haas's 1968 preface to *The Uniting of Europe*, they discerned nine variables, four related to background conditions (similarity in power of members, rates of transaction, pluralism in member states, complementing elites); two referring to conditions at the time of economic union (similarity of governmental purpose, powers of the economic union) and three to process conditions (decision-making style, transactions rate, the adaptability of governments) (Haas and Schmitter, 1964, pp. 711–19). They looked at the 'chances of politicization', that is the possibility 'that the actors seek to resolve their problems so as to upgrade common interests and, in the process, delegate more authority to the center' (p. 707). Nye in his article 'Comparing common markets' tried to modify the 'Europocentric' nature of the neo-functionalist approach and drew on a wide range of cases of economic integration – Latin America, Central America, the Caribbean, Eastern Europe and East Africa as well as EFTA and the EEC. He concluded that

> The original neo-functionalist model was close to its origins in the strategies of European integrationists in the 1950's and thus might be seen as a tempting and misleading guide for policy in other areas. The revised neo-functionalist model is not something to be imitated but is simply a tool for making comparisons. We want to know what difference it makes if a group of states form a common market. (Nye, 1970, p. 830)

However, by the end of the 1970s there were few places to be found outside Europe where the process of forming a common market had continued. Events had once again forced neo-functionalism back to its European roots. Will future events force the neo-functionalists to revise, renovate and update their ideas again?

Secondly, it is clear that the neo-functionalists have had trouble with institutional formats. They have retreated from being 'functional federalist' almost back to Mitrany's eclectic approach towards institutions. They have also accepted the durability of the nation-state in resisting 'the logic of integration' and have sought compromise formulas which at least continue to place emphasis on non-state activities even if institutions above the state (supranational) are now seen to be susceptible to state interference.

A third criticism concerns the sort of non-state actors favoured by the neo-functionalists. They have constantly emphasized the importance of political activists, the elites of interest groups and technocrats. This may have partially blinded them to a weakness in the European Community that could have affected neo-functionalism's earlier prognostications from being fulfilled: its institutions cannot draw on the day-to-day political resources available to the national political actors. This has led to a gap, most noticeable in the new members, between perceptions of the Community by the representational elite and those of the ordinary voter or consumer. Whilst some earlier studies of opinion in the European Community did include opinion polls, these often dealt only with easy questions (showing one's European identity) or soft options (whether there should be, say, a more active EC industrial policy). Since the first expansion of the Community in 1973 and the first major oil price increase which coincidentally happened a year later, European voters have been faced increasingly with much harder options – inflation versus employment, trade union rights against consumer interests – and with the possibility that 'being a good European' may mean allowing some other country's nationals to exploit one's fish or oil.

In summary, the neo-functionalists took up Mitrany's study of the relations between groups and individuals in different states as well as the states' representatives. They tried to grapple with the question of political control of such institutionalized functional relationships and to understand how it would affect the nature of the nation state. They attempted to define the status of these newly created institutions though they were not helped by developments in the European Community, the focus of their studies. Their works have demonstrated that the Community institutions are by no means just ordinary intergovernmental ones. They have also provided a mirror of the history of events in Western Europe in particular – moving from 'uniting' and 'political dynamics', through 'stress', 'joys and anguish' to 'obsolescence' and 'turbulent fields'.

Transactionalists

Another American writer whose work dealt with the question of integration is Karl Deutsch. Although not a neo-functionalist, his transactionalist approach has dealt with some common themes. He has been concerned with more than intergovernmental relations and indeed stressed relations between peoples rather than just the elites favoured by many neo-functionalists. Deutsch concerned himself with 'the absence or presence of significant organized preparations for war or large-scale violence' between international political communities. It was the 'security communities' that had eliminated 'war and the expectation of war within their boundaries' that Deutsch and his Princeton colleagues examined in *Political Community and the North Atlantic Area.* A security community was defined as 'a group of people which has become "integrated" ' in the sense that 'there is real assurance that the members of that community will not fight each other physically, but will settle their disputes in some other way' (Deutsch *et al.*, 1957, p. 5). Integration does not necessarily mean 'the merging of peoples or governmental units into a single unit' that is explicit in federalist thinking and implicit in much functionalist writing. Instead, two sorts of integrated security communities are identified: the amalgamated where previously independent units have been formally merged into a larger unit with a common government (e.g. the USA) and the pluralistic where separate governments maintain their legal independence (e.g. Canada and the USA). In studying a number of cases of attempted or actual integration in the North American and West European area, Deutsch concluded that there were twelve conditions essential for the success of an amalgamated security community and three were necessary for its pluralistic counterpart. These three consisted of 'the compatibility of major values relevant to political decision-making', 'the capacity of the participating political units or governments to respond to each other's needs, messages, and actions quickly, adequately, and without resort to violence', and the 'mutual predictability of behaviour' (Deutsch, *et al.*, 1957, pp. 66–7). In Deutsch's work, emphasis was placed on communication between political units: increased transactions between them such as political exchanges, tourism, trade and transport brought increases in mutual dependence. For a community to be created, this high level of transactions must be accompanied by mutual responsiveness so that the demands of each side on the other can receive adequate and sympathetic treatment. This not only precluded the need for aggressive action to achieve ends but also built up a feeling of trust and security in the relationship.

Deutsch does not have an obsession with international organizations: although his 1957 book is in the end concerned about the creation of a security community in the NATO area, there are few references to international organizations. Many of the case studies are set in the period before the post-war expansion of such organizations and almost all deal with bilateral relationships. Deutsch's work has consequences for the study of international organizations – governmental and non-governmental international organizations can be created as a result of a pluralistic security community, the integration of which may eventually become institutionalized as happened when the Scandinavian states created the Nordic Council. There can also be forms of institutionalized communications between societies which provide the transactions and understanding that help create a security community. Deutsch wrote:

> If the way to integration, domestic or international, is through the achievement of a sense of community that undergirds institutions, then it seems likely that an increased sense of community would help to strengthen whatever institutions – supranational or international – are already operating. (1957, pp. 7–8)

Interdependence

Further emphasis on the growth in transactions between societies can be seen in the works of Keohane and Nye who have been in the forefront of the interdependence school in the United States. They have pointed out the consequences of the increase in transnational actions to the study of international relations. Their starting point was summarized thus:

> Transnational relations are not 'new', although . . . the growth of transnational organization in the twentieth century has been spectacular. Yet, our contention is not only that the state-centric paradigm is inadequate . . . but also that it is becoming progressively more inadequate as changes in international relations take place. (Keohane and Nye, 1971, p. xxv)

They listed five consequences of this growth of international interactions and organizations for interstate politics: the promotion of attitude changes amongst citizens; an increase in international pluralism – 'the linking of national interest groups in transnational structures, usually involving transnational organizations for the purpose of coordination' (p. xviii)which has been the basis for much neo-functionalist writing; 'the creation of dependence and inter-dependence, is often associated with international transportation and finance' (p. xix); 'creating *new instruments for influence* for use by some governments over others' (p. xx); and finally 'the emergence of autonomous actors with private foreign policies that may deliberate-ly oppose or impinge on state policies' (p. xvii).

In a later book (1977) Keohane and Nye dealt with the question of interdependence in world politics in greater depth. Interdependence since the Second World War has often resulted from increased transnational activities and is divided into two sorts – sensitivity interdependence (the costly effects of changes in transactions on societies or governments) and vulnerability interdependence where the actors' liability to suffer costs imposed by external events is taken into account (Keohane and Nye, 1977, pp. 12–13). In contrast to the realist view of world politics, Keohane and Nye put forward the ideal type of complex interdependence which, they claimed, 'sometimes comes closer to reality than does realism' (p. 23) and which has three main characteristics: it allows for multiple channels – interstate, transgovernmental and transnational – connecting societies; there is an absence of hierarchy among the many questions at issue between states, with military security no longer dominating any agenda; and '[m]ilitary force is not used by governments toward other governments within the region, or on the issues, where complex interdependence prevails' (p. 25).

These three conditions are said by Keohane and Nye to typify fairly well some issues of global economic and ecological inter-dependence and 'come close to characterizing the entire relationship between some countries' (p. 25). Complex interdependence gives rise to distinctive political processes: a state's goals will vary by issue area with transgovernmental politics (see above p. 41) making goals difficult to define as transgovernmental actors (for example, ministries of agriculture, intelligence agencies, national weather bureaux) pursue their own goals; in each issue area the resources of a state for that particular area are most relevant rather than the state's overall military strength, and international organizations and trans-national actors will be manipulated as major instruments of state policy; the agenda of issues will be formulated by changes in the power distribution within the issue areas, by the position of inter-national regimes, by changes in the importance of transnational actors and by linkage from other issues; linkage between issues will be more difficult for strong states to undertake if force is downgraded, whilst linkage by weak states through international organizations sets agendas, helps coalition-forming and provides arenas for the political activity of weaker states which can use the choice of organization forum for an issue and the mobilization of votes as a political resource (p. 37).

Thus Keohane and Nye gave international organizations an important role in their complex interdependence model of world politics, a model which whilst not used to explain all world politics, was one that they claimed to have increasing relevance in a large and growing area. They used an international organization model as one of the explanations for international regime change, that is the change in the sets of governing arrangements affecting relationships of interdependence. In this case, international organization referred to 'multilevel linkage norms and institutions' (p. 54) which, once established, are hard to eradicate. Because of this, they may stand in the way of states using their capabilities in order to change regimes. Instead, power outcomes will be more affected by voting power (in the UN General Assembly for example), ability to form coalitions and to control elite networks (such as that found in the institutions of the European Community). Whilst the complex international organization model was only one of four advanced by Keohane and Nye to explain regime change, they did expect it to contribute to such change in a world where complex interdependence conditions pertain.

The contributions by Keohane and Nye demonstrate both the concern of American writers in international relations in the 1970s with alternatives to the state-centric model and their willingness to draw from more than one approach, bringing together elements from the more traditional approaches with economic models and non-state-centric elements. Their work does, however, have certain weaknesses. Perhaps the most serious is the use of the term 'interdependence' and its division into sensitivity and vulnerability interdependence. Accepting that interdependence means 'mutual dependence' (and this leads to discussion as to how mutual many relationships are), the phrase 'sensitivity-interdependence' scarcely warrants the use of the term 'interdependence'. The fault lies with the authors' loose definition of dependence as 'a state of being determined or significantly affected by external forces'. The inclusion of 'significantly affected' weakens the utility of the term so that the notion of sensitivity interdependence seems to refer to any noticeable effect of one state and society on another. A person may be significantly affected by taking drugs but without being dependent on them. David Baldwin showed that this use of the term 'interdependence' ran contrary to the stricter understandings of the concept found in Machiavelli, Montesquieu and Rousseau as well as in the works of twentieth-century writers such as Norman Angell, Francis Delaisi and Ramsay Muir (Baldwin, 1980, pp. 7–8). He suggested the use of the terms 'mutual influence', 'mutual responsiveness' or 'mutual sensitivity' instead of sensitivity interdependence (p. 19).

A second criticism of Nye and Keohane's books also concerns their terminology. In dealing with transnational influences '[t]hey lump together . . . all types of relations in which non-governmental actors participate' thus making the components of their new paradigm 'shifting and poorly defined' (Wagner, 1974, pp. 440–1). Wagner questioned whether their work just demonstrated a shift in interest to new areas of international politics – especially economic ones – and whether the world has really changed 'or whether we have just over-looked some things all along' (p. 441). The extent of interdependence has also been challenged: by Waltz (1970) and Rosecrance *et al.* (1977) in the USA and by Little and McKinlay (1978) and Sullivan (1978) in the British literature.

Despite any failings, Keohane and Nye have provided insights into transnational politics, they have shifted attention away from purely governmental actors in interstate relations and they have pointed out the importance of international organizations in the interdependence or, at least, mutual responsiveness of states.

Globalists

The next stage from the functionalist, neo-functionalist and inter-dependence writings, with their decreasing emphasis on the nation state and their stress on links between groups and individuals, is an approach that starts from a world view. It is 'the next stage' in the sense that, like the three approaches mentioned, it places emphasis on what unites people and has little time for the demands of power politics and state-centric organizations. It goes further by not limiting its view either to parts of the world or to relations between particular politics or indeed just to the economic, social and political demands of mankind. Paradoxically it can be seen as an approach the very opposite of the functionalist, with whom there is much in common. In contrast to the functionalist – or neo-functionalist or inter-dependence school – and certainly to the power politics writers, the 'whole world' approach places emphasis not on the discrete require-ments of groups, states or individuals, but on the well-being of the ecosystem in which these function – the planet Earth. The concern of this approach, which is reflected in its treatment of international organizations, is for the survival of the planet, for its efficient functioning in its widest sense and for the survival of the myriad of species – only one of which is *homo sapiens* – that inhabit the globe.

Since the 1960s a number of writers on international affairs have expounded on this view and have consequently considered the implications for international organizations. John Burton in his *World Society* considered interstate relations to be only a part of world politics and wrote:

If we employ the term 'world society' instead of 'international relations', if we approach our study in this global way instead of the more traditional 'national' way, we will tend to have a wider focus, to ask questions that are more fundamental and important to civilization, and be able to assess better the relevance of our own national behaviour to the wider world environment. (1972, p. 21)

Richard Sterling posed the problem more specifically:

Nuclear escalation, the population explosion, the pollution of the environment, the communications revolution, the world-wide concentration of wealth and world-wide expansion of poverty are all essentially global and not local phenomena. They have given rise, in turn, to earth-spanning and revolutionary demands for mass education, mass health, mass welfare, and mass participation in the decisions affecting man's fate. (1974, p. 322)

This world view of the problems of 'the spaceship Earth' begged for global solutions. It suggested that not only is the system of sovereign states as yet unable – or unwilling – to come to grips with the above-mentioned problems but that a network of intergovernmental organizations based on the rights of state sovereignty will also be hamstrung. Global problems needed global solutions based on institutions that can take a global perspective. Thus Sterling considered that 'it is not unreasonable to anticipate that the member states will be moved to consider equipping the United Nations with more comprehensive powers as global pressures build' (p. 323). A more compelling call was issued by Barbara Ward and René Dubos in their book prepared for the UN Conference on the Human Environment, *Only One Earth: The Care and Maintenance of a Small Planet.* They stressed the unit of the Earth and its environment and the problems faced by its inhabitants – essentially those outlined by Sterling. The authors pointed out that the environmental question had, by 1972, already had some impact on governments and international organizations but the effect was somewhat unco-ordinated and unfocused. In three particular areas – the global atmosphere, the oceans, the world's weather systems – they saw the immediate need for common policy and co-ordinated action 'where pretensions to national sovereignty have no relevance to perceived problems'. But there was a need to go further and deal with other global problems – disease, starvation, illiteracy, unemployment, overcrowding. International policies were at the stage reached within the developing states of the nineteenth century: 'Either they will move on to a community based upon a more systematic sharing of wealth . . . or they will break down in revolt and anarchy' (Ward and Dubos, 1972, pp. 295–6). They looked forward to a sense of global community based on the hope of protection – from war and disaster – and the hope of enhancement – ecological as well as economic. The 'practices and institutions with which we are familiar inside our domestic societies would become, suitably modified, the basis of planetary order' (pp. 297–8). This would include 'non-violent settlement of disputes with legal arbitral and policing procedures on an international basis'; it would mean the transfer of resources from rich to poor and increased co-operation in areas such as health and education, farming, urban planning and pollution control. As there has been a shift of loyalty from family to clan, from clan to nation and from nation to federation, there was hope, claimed Ward and Dubos, for 'an ultimate loyalty to our single, beautiful and vulnerable Planet Earth' (p. 298).

Whilst the institutional framework and organizational structures remain, of necessity, vague in *Only One Earth*, it is clear that the authors were aiming at a network of world-wide, functionally-based organizations (both IGOs and INGOs) that could take on much of the work presently done by governments – or rather, which ought to be done by governments. It is a vision that stressed unity and common cause rather than disagreement and confrontation and could therefore foresee disputes being solved internationally, very much in the way that they are presently solved within many nation states – by resort to arbitration and law and by enforcement, if necessary. In this, they have much in common with the international lawyers and idealist writers of the early twentieth century mentioned at the beginning of this chapter (pp. 69–74). The globalists are inspired in their thinking more by fear of a nuclear holocaust and by environmental break-down than by the direct experience of war that affected the writings of Woolf or Brierly.

The globalist approach is open to the criticism of being too idealistic in a cynical world and too impractical in its institutional suggestions. But the dismissal of these works as 'globaloney' does not rid the world of the problems which they have so effectively publicized. They have tried to add another dimension to what is possible by showing that it is necessary for the survival of the planet.

Marxist Views

There is no one Marxist interpretation of the role of international organizations in world politics. But Marxist approaches have certain elements in common and form a distinctive school of thought about international relations generally and therefore about international organizations. These approaches are based on the writings of Karl Marx (1818–83) in co-operation with Friedrich Engels (1820–95) with perhaps the greatest later contribution being made by V. I. Lenin, leader of the 1917 Bolshevik revolution in Russia.

Neither Marx nor Marxists have taken the state to be the 'currency' of international relations. Unlike the traditional viewpoints they have not considered interactions between sovereign states to be of over-riding importance. Unlike the functionalists and other modern Western views that stress non-state actors, the Marxists have in particular emphasized *class* relationships both within states and across state boundaries. Indeed it is difficult to talk only of a Marxist view of international relations, let alone international organizations, as this separates one particular aspect of human behaviour for Marxist treatment, divorcing it from the underlying tenets of Marxist beliefs. Marxism provides a framework of understanding by which, it is claimed, society past and present can be explained and the future development of mankind determined.

Marx and Engels

According to Marx, relationships between people, and the forms that institutionalized those relationships, depended on the 'economic structure of society', the way that production was organized. He traced the history of civilized mankind through five historical stages – Asiatic, ancient, feudal, capitalist and socialist – which have different dominant methods of production leading to 'a complicated arrangement of society into various orders, a manifold graduation of social rank' (Marx and Engels, 1965, p. 40). Each form of society has contained the conflictual divisions which help to transform the nature of that society: contradictions in the mode of production placed strain on the existing social order, sharpening the divide between economic classes and eventually leading to a revolutionary change in the economic foundation of society and a rapid transformation of its superstructure, its legal, political and religious institutions. Thus by a confrontation of class contradictions one historical form of society was transformed into a higher stage of social development – 'the history of all hitherto existing society is the history of class struggles' (p. 39). Marx and Engels were particularly concerned with capitalist society – at its heyday during their lives – and its transformation into socialist society within which there would be no division of labour, and no classes and no states; no expropriation of labour's surplus value, and thus no private property; no exploitation of one class by another, with no need for war.

For Marx and Engels 'Classes then, and not nations or states, are the basic units in history, and the struggle between classes, instead of interstate conflict, occupies the center of attention' (Berki, 1971, p. 81). From the nineteenth century onwards this struggle, seen in Marxist terms, has been primarily between the capitalist class, the bourgeoisie, and the labouring class, the proletariat. As the transformation from capitalist society to socialism to communism took place, then the superstructure of bourgeois society – religion, national divisions, bourgeois political institutions, the state – would be swept away and in Engel's famous phrase 'the government of persons is replaced by the administration of things' (Feuer, 1969, p. 147) with the state relegated to the museum together with 'the spinning wheel and the bronze axe' (p. 433).

Marx saw the European states of his own time as being means by which the ruling class could oppress the working class by using the agents of the state such as the judiciary, the police, the army and the church. The external activities of the state were also determined by its class nature. The national bourgeoisie of Britain, France, Germany and other European states undertook imperialist expansion in pursuit of greater profits. Meanwhile transnational relations of a more meaningful kind would be created by trade, the movement of capital and increased contact and solidarity between the proletariat of various nations. In this context it is worth noting that the international organizations of which Marx and Engels had direct experience were the First International and, for Engels, the Second International, both of which attempted to organize the representatives of working people across frontiers. Once again this stresses the Marxist emphasis on transnational class relations rather than on interstate relationships.

Yet it is not possible to write off intergovernmental organizations in Marxist terms as just being part of the superstructural froth on bourgeois society. The development of a Marxist state – the Soviet Union – in a world dominated by capitalist states and the emergence of the Third World are two factors that have led to major developments in Marxist views of international relations and consequently of international organizations.

Marxism – Leninism

A major contributor in both of these areas was V. I. Lenin. He gave Marxism a practical as well as a theoretical cutting edge by his advocacy of the leading role of the Communist Party as the vanguard of the proletariat in its struggle against the forces of capitalism. He also made a major contribution in developing Marxism in his consideration of imperialism and in his writings concerning the existence of the Soviet state in a hostile capitalist world. Both these areas have implications for any Marxist interpretations of the role of international organizations.

Lenin in *Imperialism: The Highest Stage of Capitalism* (1966) summed up imperialism as 'capitalism at that stage of development at which the dominance of monopolies and finance capital is established, in which the export of capital has acquired pronounced importance; in which the division of all territories of the globe among the biggest capitalist powers has been completed' (pp. 82–3). Lenin thought that the gains enjoyed by the imperialists would be used as bribes for sections of the European working class – 'opportunists'. However the damage would be done: the extension of capitalism to the rest of the world in order to prolong its life would forge links between the oppressed peoples of the exploited areas and the proletariat of the developed countries.

On the question of the existence of the Soviet state, Lenin, in his writings from 1917 to 1920, considered that imperialist states were the instruments of class dominance and were nowhere near 'withering away'. The dictatorship of the proletariat, existing in the USSR after 1917, was threatened from the bourgeoisie within and imperialists outside. The Soviet state was seen by Lenin as a proletariat class state acting to repress the Russian bourgeoisie, repel foreign invaders as well as taking on administrative and proselytizing functions. The Bolsheviks also had a duty to encourage the socialist revolution in countries outside Russia – this was the task of the Communist International established in 1919 when Lenin considered world revolution imminent (Kubalkova and Cruickshank, 1980, pp. 107–8). Over the following two years, as fervour in Europe cooled or was suppressed, Lenin wrote about the delay of the revolution outside Russia and turned his mind to the question of relations with capitalist states: 'we have entered a new period, in which we have, in the main, won the right to our international existence in the network of capitalist states' (Lenin, 1970, p. 264).

Lenin's approach to the questions of imperialism and the Soviet Union's 'co-existence' with capitalist states provided the basis for further Marxist writings on international relations and helped to explain Marxist views of international organizations. There were three important elements. In his writings on imperialism, Lenin, like Engels and Marx, stressed the exploitative class nature of imperialism rather than any formal colonizing policy of the European states. He admitted that this exploitation could take various forms and thus opened up a rich vein for later neo-Marxist students of the relationship between industrial and developing nations and the institutions used in this relationship. Lenin also stressed the potential for solidarity amongst those oppressed by imperialism, regardless of which state or colony they lived in. The emphasis was placed on transnational relations in international relations – relations between the proletariat of all countries. This line was taken up in Lenin's writings even after the creation of the Soviet state (and in practice with the establishment of the Communist International) and remained as an important motivating factor in the later establishment of communist international non-governmental organizations. Finally, Lenin's later consideration of the Soviet Union's relations with capitalist states provided a Marxist–Leninist approach which, again, was built on by later writers and which gave some guidance to Marxist – and in particular Soviet Marxist – views of international organizations.

Other Marxist writers whose works have had consequences for the study of international organizations can be divided into those which have followed the predominant Soviet orthodoxy and others who have taken a line more independent of Moscow.

Soviet writers on the subject since the time of Lenin have on the whole kept closely to the line dictated by the Communist Party of the Soviet Union. This has not prevented disagreements from surfacing, especially on the more technical aspects of international organizations. Since the death of Lenin, Soviet commentators have come to terms with the continued isolation of the Soviet Union within a capitalist-dominated world, yet they have also had to deal with the increasing importance of the ex-colonial 'Third World'.

Stalin, as the leader of the Soviet Communist Party – and in effect the Soviet Union – from 1924 to 1953, contributed little directly to Marxist thinking on international organizations. However, as Soviet leader he had to respond to the failure of the rest of the world to follow the Russian example of moving towards communism. Faced with 'capitalist encirclement' he adopted a policy of 'socialism in one country' – the building up of a socialist state in the Soviet Union – and of peaceful co-existence between the two camps – 'the camp of imperialism and the camp of socialism'. This survivalist view meant that the move Marx and Engels had made away from international relations to world politics and the stress on class rather than state relations was reversed and the focus was again on interstate relations. The two sets of relationships important for Stalin were those between the capitalist states (their colonies being regarded as mere appendages) and those between the two camps – capitalist and socialist. Because of the precarious nature of the Soviet Union's existence in the decades after its establishment, it was necessary to gain a 'breathing space' by peaceful co-existence with the capitalist world. Intercapitalist state relations were crucial for the Soviet Union as these determined the nature of the threat to its survival: the capitalist states united could lead to an attack on the USSR as in the War of Intervention of 1918–20; the capitalist states divided could lead them to destroy each other rather than the USSR as eventually happened in the Second World War. During the Stalinist period little theoretical consideration was given to the class nature of world politics, the struggle of oppressed peoples in the non-European world or indeed to the question of relations between two or more socialist states. The major question was that of the Soviet state's relationships with advanced Western countries.

Soviet writing on these problems reflected official concern with the prospect of Western nations uniting against the Soviet Union and offered a framework for organizing peaceful relations between the 'revolutionary' Soviet state and their avowed deadly enemies.

It is noticeable that the University of Moscow school of international law which predicated its arguments on the need to destroy national sovereignty in the expectation of the world revolution was disbanded in Stalin's time. The major theoretical debate centred around the Korovin school and that of Pashukanis, with A. I. Vyshinsky, Rector of Moscow University and later Soviet Chief Prosecutor, intervening when state policy demanded. Korovin saw Soviet–capitalist relations as being of a new type which, while neither totally capitalist nor totally socialist, would inevitably drift towards socialist dominance. Custom and precedence in international law, being based on capitalist practice, were to be rejected and treaties of mutual consent which allowed the Soviet Union to retain its own principles would be the only meaningful source of international law. Pashukanis, however, saw treaties and custom as being on a par. They merely provided an outline of an international relationship; the context was provided by each system according to its values. It was up to the Soviet Union to fill these capitalist institutions with socialist content (Kubalkova and Cruickshank, 1980, pp. 107–8).

Whilst Soviet writings on international organizations were fairly desultory in Stalin's reign, they did herald the move towards peaceful co-existence and foreshadowed the later rather restrictive view of such organizations by Soviet commentators.

In the post-Second World War period and in particular in the post-Stalin era, Soviet literature on international organizations has blossomed. This has reflected Soviet membership of many post-1945 organizations, the emergence of a socialist bloc of states and the increase in the number of sovereign states, all factors demanding a more sophisticated Soviet view of interstate relations than the survivalism of Stalin's period.

After the demise of Stalin, his successor, Krushchev, developed a revised view of international relations which gave a position to the emerging Third World. Peaceful co-existence between socialist and capitalist states was still considered necessary but this did not preclude the ideological struggle between the two camps: indeed, the Soviet international lawyer Professor Tunkin wrote: 'peaceful co-existence of states representing the two different social systems is a specific form of class struggle between socialism and capitalism' (Osakwe, 1972, p. 37). The Soviet Union also developed relations with the newly emerging ex-colonial countries and Soviet writings had to take account of this development. With the end of 'capitalist encirclement' enunciated at the Twentieth Congress of the Communist Party of the Soviet Union, there came a recognition of a third group of states between the capitalist and the communist – that of potentially friendly independent states in Europe and Asia such as India, Egypt, Indonesia and Yugoslavia, which would form a 'zone of peace'. Although the relations with the capitalist states still remained embedded in peaceful co-existence, there was an increased emphasis by post-Stalinist Soviet writers on the class element in the relationship – that is, the contact with 'progressive' elements in Western society such as the labour movement. Neither did peaceful co-existence rule out support of 'just wars of national liberation' – indeed it was seen as a strategy for world revolution. Finally, the relationships between the Soviet Union and East European countries were deemed to be based on socialist internationalism, postulating a harmony of national and community interests and concluding that 'independence and sovereignty of a socialist state means above all independence from capitalism' (*Red Star*, 1 December 1968).

Two noticeable Soviet writers on international organizations in the post-Stalinist period have been Professors G. I. Tunkin and Grigorii Morozov.

Professor Tunkin underlined traditional Soviet thinking that the constituent instrument of an international organization (for example the Charter of the UNO) was all-important in determining the extent that the organization had an international legal personality, that is, a standing in international law similar to that of a sovereign state. Examining the question of the autonomous will of international organizations, Professor Tunkin allowed that they need not just act as agents for member states:

In international practice treaties concluded by international organizations take their special place as treaties by which international organizations acquire rights and take upon themselves certain obligations. International organizations are created by states; they are brought into being by states but the actions of international organizations are not in any way, de facto or de jure, to be equated to the actions of states (Osakwe, 1972, p. 23).

This did not mean that an international organization was 'an entity independent of its member states' as any powers that they had were delegated by the members. In line with the Soviet doctrine of peaceful co-existence, Tunkin placed stress on the nature and the membership of an international organization – those which drew their membership from communist, capitalist and Third World states could expect to be generally recognized as having an international personality. He wrote:

The nature of contemporary international organizations is to a very great extent determined by the existence of states belonging to different socio-economic systems and the inevitable struggle between them. That is why peaceful coexistence is now the basic condition of the development of general international organization. (Osakwe, pp. 28–9)

Because of the mixed nature of such organizations, their founding documents not only reflect 'the coordinated will of the founding members' but 'are equally considered as embodiment of some uneliminated antagonisms between the contracting powers' (Osakwe, p. 30). Certainly this meant that the means used by organizations such as the UN to implement their original aims should not go beyond the limits originally agreed without the consent of all parties, although Tunkin did allow for 'implied competence' in limited areas and he granted the UN Charter a special position in international law: 'The Charter is above all other Treaties concluded by the members of the UN' (Osakwe, pp. 32–3). Central to Tunkin's thinking on international organizations was his Leninist belief that they were part of the peaceful co-existence between two different social systems which was 'a specific form of the class struggle' because 'socialist and bourgeois ideologies are incompatible' (Osakwe, pp. 37–8).

Although a more contemporary writer than Tunkin, Morozov nevertheless supported the basic aspects of his work but he did contribute some extra points of interest. First, he included INGOs in his study. He wrote:

International organizations have, as a rule, at least three member countries. These may be governments, official organizations or non-governmental organizations. (Morozov, 1977, p. 30)

In a later section on NGOs, they were identified as the largest group of international organizations, with two aspects that concerned socialist commentators – the NGOs' attitude towards the preservation of peace, with the World Federation of Trade Unions, the World Federation of Democratic Youth and other members of the World Peace Council gaining special mention, and the specialized character of some NGOs such as the International Council of Scientific Unions and the Scientific Committee on Antarctic Research. Morozov mentioned how NGOs can help establish a social climate, citing their contribution to the settlement of a number of international conflicts such as that in Vietnam. He also dealt with the role of the NGOs in the UN and the consultative status they have with IGOs, saying that

> students of international affairs in the socialist countries are critical of many aspects of this system, for the consultative status arrangements still fall short of what the development of modern international relations in fact calls for. (1977, p. 43)

This seems to suggest a more radical view of at least certain NGOs than is allowed for by a number of Western writers. The 'specialized nature' of NGOs was attributed by Morozov to

> the increased influence of the public at large on foreign policy, the greater impact of public opinion in international relations and the greater importance of the ideological factor in such relations. Account should also be taken of the processes of economic development and the consequences of the scientific and technological revolution, which has also led to a greater number of specialized NGOs. (1977, p. 42)

Secondly, Morozov, by virtue of writing in the late 1970s, was able to make more positive references to the role of Third World states in international organizations. He noted that 'the emergence of a large number of young national states have led to the emergence of international organizations among developing countries' (1977, p. 29) and claimed that the

> socialist conception of international organizations attributes great importance to the role of the young States in IGOs, for whom participation in these organizations is part of the process of consolidating their sovereignty and national independence and of solving their pressing economic and other problems. (1977, p. 31)

Finally, Professor Morozov (1977, pp. 31 and 34) developed the point made by Tunkin about the limited nature of international organizations – 'second class members' of the international system as opposed to the first-class members, sovereign states – by reference to their decisions. These have resulted from the interaction of political forces within the organizations and

> [t]he combined will of these IGOs is distinct from the wills of their individual members in its essence and in its nature ... The various wills in this case are not aggregated arithmetically: each one exists independently or inside a homogenous socio–political group, within whose framework they can be combined.

Soviet commentators also have a specific contribution to make in two other areas of international organizations – that of socialist organizations and that of Western-dominated IGOs.

Relations within the socialist bloc have been based on the principle of proletarian internationalism and have been characterized, according to Morozov (1977, p. 39)

> by disinterested mutual aid, friendship and co-operation, and the voluntary pooling of forces in the struggle for the victory of socialism. Such general democratic principles of international law as the principles of respect for state sovereignty, equal rights and self-determination of peoples, mutual benefit and non-interference, are reflected in the relations of the socialist countries.

These major international organizations seen by Soviet writers as displaying these worthy attributes were the Warsaw Treaty Organization and the Council for Mutual Economic Assistance, their members having a duty to protect the 'achievements of socialism'. This may involve some member states offering another, as in the case of Hungary in November 1956 or Czechoslovakia in August 1968, 'fraternal assistance' which, according to the Soviet theorist Sanakozev, represented 'defence of the socialist system and efforts to counteract attempts of bourgeois counter-revolutionary forces' (Kubalkova and Cruickshank, 1980, p. 226).

Western-dominated international organizations have been treated with suspicion and criticism by Soviet writers. Western 'military and political blocs and economic groupings', according to Morozov (1977, p. 30), have enhanced the threat of world war and disrupted the process of internationalizing world economic relations and have resulted in discrimination between states of different social systems.

Soviet views of international organizations have been criticized for emphasizing the differences between states rather than their common bonds and for being the basis of attempted hegemony over certain specialized agencies (Osakwe, 1972, p. 42). The former criticism seems just to be a condemnation of what Western as well as Soviet observers admit is a reality of international relations, whilst the latter point is more a criticism of the failure of Western policy in certain specialized agencies – particularly in relation to the Third World – rather than of Soviet doctrine. One need not agree with their ideology to admit that Soviet writers on international organizations have clearly based their works on their system of beliefs and have set out how they see both IGOs and INGOs playing a role in the triumph of communism over capitalism. Also Soviet writers have in their treatment of international organizations avoided many of the failings of certain Western writers. They have, for example, eschewed the regionalism/universalism dichotomy for an emphasis on more or less extensive membership and they have placed heavy emphasis on the aims and actions of organizations, stressing what they have regarded as the co-operative as against the conflict-producing institutions. Too often Western writers have dismissed Soviet writers on the subject as just hiding a 'power politics' view in Marxist–Leninist verbiage or being disingenuous in their writings. This is unfortunate as it misses the ideological element in Soviet writings, which may help partly in explaining Soviet actions, and it can gloss over crucial differences from the state-centric, power politics model of international relations, such as the introduction of the class element and thus the stress on non-governmental and transnational activities as well as interstate relations. It also supposes that the study of international organizations in the Soviet Union is still in the infancy of the 1950s and 1960s when Western writings on the subject were burgeoning. Whilst Soviet writers may have taken time to absorb the impact on international organizations of the newly-independent Third World states and the rise of INGOs and may lack the sophistication of US political scientists, their present diligence in studying international organizations matches the increased importance given these organizations by the Soviet Government. Western observers should perhaps look to their laurels.

Neo-Marxists

Non-Soviet Marxist writers on international organizations are more difficult to classify. The neo-Marxist 'dependency' school will be covered in the next section as it belongs more fittingly with Third World views. This leaves two other major groups – that of the

Western neo-Marxists and that of the Chinese Communists. It is somewhat paradoxical that the writings of the former are mainly concerned with the faults of Western society whilst Chinese Marxists are more critical about the behaviour of their Soviet neighbours.

The Western neo-Marxists are by no means a homogenous school: they are noted for their fissiparous nature. However they do have certain elements in common which mark out a particular contribution to writings on international organizations. They are not concerned with the mechanics of these organizations in themselves but as 'products of the present system' which 'therefore reflects its characteristics' (Jenkins, 1971, p. 189). Most neo-Marxists would agree with the distinction between international organizations which 'link national governments', mostly bringing together rich nations, and 'world organizations which penetrate nation states and cut across national boundaries' (Jenkins, 1971, p. 190). In the latter group multinational corporations and anti-imperialist revolutionary movements are included and this aspect of neo-Marxist writing will be covered in the next section on Third World views.

In dealing with international organizations the British neo-Marxist writer Robin Jenkins (1971, p. 189) claimed that they served three functions – the balancing, regulation and distribution of power. Military alliances, such as NATO and the Warsaw Treaty Organization, have been oriented towards balance of power but also have aimed at limiting power to themselves:

> As to the regulation of power . . . [m]ost international organizations do not help to distribute power more evenly in the international system; on the contrary, many of them serve to accumulate more power where the power already lies.

The Belgian Marxist Ernest Mandel gave further consideration to the institutions of the Western industrialized world. He rejected the 'Third Worldism' of some of his contemporary colleagues and instead stressed the complexity of the pattern of economic development throughout the world – exploitation is seen as being universal but not homogenous. Mandel stressed in particular the difference between American, Japanese and West European capitalism. He identified a permanent crisis within NATO and between the EEC and the USA as a result of the contradiction between the military dependence of Western Europe on the Americans and the decline of the US economically (Mandel, 1970a, p. 32). The weaker European industries were bought up or integrated into their American counterparts whilst the more resilient European enterprises pressed for a stronger European Community identity. Writing in 1970 Mandel claimed that 'Economic necessity forces British big capital to turn to Europe' (1970b, p. 70). A more historical Marxist account of the genesis of the European Community (Cocks, 1980, p. 15) labelled integration as 'a method of resolving certain actual or potential crises intrinsic to capitalist development'. The simpler ring of inevitability is avoided when dealing with the economic foundations of the Community:

> national governments were willing to support the Common Market, and thus legitimate its institutions, provided that its policies coincided with what national elites thought best for their own interests. Each individual state and its administrators, acting as defenders of the collective capitalist interests (and therefore acting against the interests of some capitalists) judged the EC according to whether in their view it forwarded their interest or not. (p. 32)

This quotation, excized of any reference to 'capital interests', could well be written by any traditionalist commentator on governmental action within international organizations. The neo-Marxist addition is the explanation of action by reference to the wishes of big business, an understandable Marxist approach drawn from the belief that the superstructures of society, such as international organizations, are based on economic relationships. The neo-Marxists have moved away from the crude lumping together of the USA and Western Europe as being like-minded capitalists with institutions such as the European Community being seen as a US capitalist stalking horse. Instead they have placed emphasis on the differences between one group of capitalists and another – American and West European, British and continental, small and large, traditional and innovatory.

The neo-Marxist commentators can be criticized for having a rather grand view of international organizations which often precludes an examination of detail. More seriously their stress on economic motivation sometimes clouds over important non-economic factors such as nationalism and religion. A sort of pluralism amongst capitalist interests is allowed in so far as it shapes government policy towards important international organizations such as the European Community, but the pluralism of the representational system and of interest and pressure groups is ignored or is only seen to reflect 'capitalist' or 'working class' interests.

Chinese Marxists

Chinese Marxist writers have largely reflected the views of the leadership in China since the coming to power of the Communist Party in 1949. Until the 1970s Communist China was excluded from almost all international organizations and it is not surprising that what little writing there was on the subject was fairly dismissive, usually consisting of condemnations of the UN for its action in Korea and the security alliances for their 'hegemonic' nature. Chinese Marxist thinking has divided the modern world into three groups: the First World consisting of the two imperialist superpowers, the USA and the USSR; the Second World consisting of other areas of advanced industrialized countries, primarily Europe and Japan, which were open to domination by the superpowers but which could start a dialogue with the Third World; and the Third World itself, consisting of the Afro–Asian–Latin American states supported in their struggle against First World imperialism by China. This view of the world has coloured Chinese writings on international organizations. The super-powers were seen as cynical manipulators of international institutions. Mao Tse-tung wrote of US policy towards such institutions: 'It makes use of them when it needs them, and kicks them away when it does not' (Society for Anglo-Chinese Under-standing (SACU), 1979, p. 42). US-dominated pacts such as SEATO and 'imperialist groupings' like the Alliance for Progress were derided. Special vitriol was saved for the Warsaw Treaty Organization which in one article was described as 'Soviet social-imperialism's tool for aggression' (Ming Sung, cited in Chen, 1979, p. 194). The Soviet Union was accused of trying to manipulate the Pact and negotiate with Western countries through the European Security Conference to consolidate its hegemonic status in Eastern Europe at the same time as dividing Western Europe, squeezing out the USA 'so as to make way for its expansion and infiltration into Western Europe' (Ming Sung, cited in Chen, 1979, p. 197).

Chinese writers regarded the Second World, especially Western Europe, as being a spent force in terms of imperialism, which now responded to the Third World with dialogue as in the Lomé Convention between the European Community and African, Caribbean and Pacific states. Furthermore, the defensive aspects of NATO were stressed and 'with growing European cohesion the trend is likely to be towards a force in which the American element is seen as a temporary necessity, eventually to be phased out' (Society for Anglo-Chinese Understanding, 1979, p. 90).

The countries of the Third World were seen as constituting 'the main force combating imperialism, colonialism and hegemonism', referring not only to the vestiges of West European colonialism but also to US imperialism and growing Soviet 'social-imperialism'. The Third World could help to exclude the great powers by banding together in such organizations as the OAU and they could work to correct unequal trade and economic relations with the superpowers through UN agencies and conferences such as UNCTAD and UNCLOS. Also raw material and exporting organizations like OPEC, the International Bauxite Association and the Union of Banana Exporting Countries were praised as changing the old international economic order and 'battering the biggest material plunderers in the world, the United States and the Soviet Union' (*Peking Review*, 26 September 1975 cited in Chen, 1979, p. 309).

Criticisms of the views of Chinese Marxist writings on international relations generally and international organizations specifically can be made from several standpoints. That of Soviet writers is implicit in each side's view about the other's country. A more unusual critical attitude from within the communist world comes from China's long-time ally – Albania. As well as criticizing Chinese policy, the Albanians have questioned the theory underlying the Chinese Communist view of the world. Specifically they have challenged the Chinese notions that the USSR is more threatening than the USA, that the West Europeans are more divided from the USA and are not exploiting the Third World and that the governments of the Third World are a revolutionary force. They therefore opposed the Chinese belief that West Europe should unite itself in the European Community and should be more active within NATO and they considered that Chinese endorsement of UN negotiations for a New International Economic Order (NIEO) only supported those in the Third World who collaborated with imperialism. In short, the Albanian criticism was that the Chinese view of international relations and of international organizations had placed too much emphasis on opposing the domination of the two superpowers rather than opposing imperialism: it was more concerned with the balance of power than the class struggle throughout the world (O'Leary, 1980, pp. 278–84).

A more Western criticism of Chinese views of international organizations would be that they have slavishly followed an official line and have done little to analyze institutions, preferring dogma instead. There is some evidence that the poverty of Chinese study of international organizations, no doubt caused by the lack of Chinese membership of such organizations until the 1970s and the turmoil of the Cultural Revolution, is coming to an end. The 1980s have brought detailed studies of the European Community, amongst other organizations, in Chinese universities.

There are some signs that the Marxist perspectives on international relations are finally receiving serious treatment amongst Western scholars, including those who do not accept the precepts of Marxism.

It would be no bad thing if writings on international organizations were included in the Western critical scrutiny of Marxist literature.

Third World Views

Many Third World – Afro–Asian and Latin American – writers on international organizations have adopted a Marxist framework and are particularly concerned about how institutions can be used as tools of exploitation of the Third World and how some can be used as agents of liberation. They have not been included in the section on Marxist views for three reasons: not all of them are Marxist; those who are Marxist place particular stress on the position of the Third World; and as Third World citizens they have, through their own experience, another perspective than that of writers from industrialized states.

Yves Tandon (1978, p. 377) has identified three Third World perspectives on international organizations. First there is that of the bourgeois or petty nationalists who are in power in most Third World states and who are progressive in terms of anti-imperialism but 'are reactionary to the extent that they would sooner make their peace with imperialism than surrender power to the masses and peasants'. This group uses international organizations to put pressure on imperialist states in order to extract concessions from them and appease the masses in their own countries. They see the UN as 'an opportunity to parley with their erstwhile imperial masters at a presumed level of equality' (p. 365). The second perspective is that of the 'really backward regimes' of the Third World, such as Taiwan and Jordan, 'for whom international organizations are of marginal significance for they prefer to deal with imperialism directly'. The third perspective identified by Tandon is that 'of the masses of the Third World' for whom international organizations are peripheral for as long as they 'continue to reflect the existing balance of class forces in favour of imperialism' (p. 378). Since the end of the 1960s forces representing this third group have become more prominent in world politics in the form of liberation groups such as the PLO, and whilst these have been interested in gaining recognition for themselves at the UN and the specialized agencies, they are not dependent on these organizations. Indeed, Tandon considered that, for the revolutionary struggles in South-East Asia and Africa 'international organizations are too peripheral to be of much significance' (p. 377).

Tandon provided an interesting history of the development of the anti-colonialist forces in the Third World since 1945 but his division into the three perspectives is too stark. Leaving aside the less important 'backward regimes', he has basically grouped the Third World leadership into the revolutionaries, who have little need for international organizations, and those who have slipped into reformism and have been duped into believing that they can change their dependence on industrialized nations through international organizations. This seems to understate the use of such organizations by revolutionary groups – especially the PLO and the Southern African liberation organizations – which have made substantial use of the UN, Arab League and OAU to sustain the political aspects of their efforts. It also overestimates the extent to which the Third World countries have any illusions through international organizations such as UNCTAD. Furthermore, the identification of 'good' revolutionaries and 'fallen' reformists is rather simplistic: the major sponsor of the UN's 'New Economic Order' which Tandon has condemned as the 'Old Economic Order, with a different Rhetoric' was the Algerian radical government of Boumedienne; the PLO itself is dependent on a number of 'bourgeois' Arab governments for financial and diplomatic support; and to Tandon's assertion that '[f]or national liberation movements guided by a proletarian ideology, such as those in China and Vietnam, international organizations were of no use' can be added the reservation 'until they came to power'. Whilst it took some twenty years before Communist China made use of such organizations, the unified communist state of Vietnam was quick to take up its position in the UN, to ask for aid through UN agencies as well as to become a member of the CMEA (Comecon).

Dependency School

Third World commentators on world politics have emphasized the nature of their area's political, economic and cultural relationship with the industrialized North. This is most often typified as being one of neo-colonialism – control of the Third World by the North by indirect means rather than by direct colonial rule – and one of economic dependency. International relations between states are subsumed to relations between classes world wide – between, on the one hand, the exploiting imperialist capitalists in the northern industrialised countries and their middle-class collaborators in the southern states and, on the other hand, the exploited masses, the proletariat, of the southern continents. The latter groups have been made economically dependent on the former so that they are, in the words of the Brazilian T. Dos Santos in a situation in which the economy of a certain group of countries is conditioned by the development and expansion of another economy to which their own is subjected. (Bodenheimer, 1971, p. 327)

The underdeveloped countries depend on the developed for their capital and expertise, they find key sectors of their economy controlled from outside, they act as a source of raw materials, as a cheap source of labour and as a market for manufacturers from Europe, Japan and North America. As their living standards were determined by the vicissitudes of the Northern-dominated 'world' market, the relationship was one of unequal exchange, the result of which was a world experiencing 'unequal development' with a developed, rich industrialized capitalist Northern centre and a poor, underdeveloped, agriculturally backward, exploited periphery in the South. The dependent South has been divided between the predominant underdeveloped areas and a few centres of development with their trade, cultural, traffic and political links to the developed North – the 'dependent development' outlined by F. H. Cardosa (1974), another Brazilian. Samir Amin (1977) rejected the prospect of an autonomous capitalist development in the Third World: the new bourgeoisie of Latin America, Africa and Asia were in alliance with capitalists from the North and the main source of finance for imported equipment was from the export of raw materials to the industrialised states. Amin (pp. 1–21) saw the call made for a New International Economic Order (NIEO) by Third World leaders at the UN, UNCTAD and the various North-South dialogues as an attempt to increase the price of their raw material exports, obtain more imported technology and thus to finance a new stage of development. He saw this as just placing the Third World more in the grip of the neo-colonialist system and instead recommended a more self-reliant development with mutual assistance between Third World states, a reduction in trade with the industrialized world and thus a loosening of dependence. Amin, like Tandon, had little faith in the present international organizations as tools for fashioning a more independent Third World. His suggestion of greater mutual assistance between Third World states implied something more sophisticated than a number of bilateral arrangements. As the present organizations used for intra-Third World co-operation – the OAU, the Arab League, ASEAN – are dominated by just those governments that accept the course condemned by Amin – the NIEO – then Amin's solution involves like-minded developing countries, or more likely, political changes leading to such indigenous international organizations.

Developmentalists

Other Third World writers have placed emphasis on greater use of existing institutions. Raul Prebisch, an Argentinian economist, has not only studied the question of economic dependency but his ideas have been used as the basis for the work of two major international organizations – the UN Economic Commission for Latin America (ECLA) and UNCTAD. In his study of British–Argentinian trading relations, Prebisch had identified the unequal terms of trade between the favoured industrialized state of the 'centre' and the less privileged non-industrialized 'periphery'. Prebisch, unlike the *dependencia* school of Amin, Dos Santos and Cardosa, believed that this inequality could be overcome by political action – by trade preferences favouring the periphery, by commodity agreements, by international aid and by more foreign investment in the periphery. It was these remedies that Prebisch encouraged when he was Executive Secretary of ECLA from 1955 to 1963 and Secretary-General of UNCTAD from 1964 to 1968. Indeed, the amount of aid the periphery needed in order to overcome their unfavourable trade balance became known in UNCTAD circles as the Prebisch Gap.

The distinguished African academic, Ali Mazrui, has written on the plight of that continent and its role in present-day international affairs. He sought to answer the question: 'Now that the Imperial Order is coming to an end, who is going to keep the peace in Africa?' and to examine the concept of *Pax Africana* – the African's ambition to be his own policeman. The policing and self-government of Africa depended on the notion of an African 'self' which Mazrui discussed in detail. He considered how this independence might be threatened by the political and cultural fragmentation of the continent and economically by dependence on Europe. He quoted Kwame Nkrumah, first president of Ghana, on the European Economic Community:

> The Treaty of Rome . . . marks the advent of *neo-colonialism* in Africa . . . and bears unquestionably the marks of French *neo-colonialism*. (1967, p. 93)

and concluded from this

> What Africans therefore needed was a central authority of their own to co-ordinate their economic and political defence against this threat. (p. 93)

Given this theme, it is not surprising that Mazrui set store by the OAU, but was realistic in his judgement:

> In relations between African states a modest step towards *Pax Africana* was taken when the Organization of African Unity set up its Commission of Mediation, Conciliation and Arbitration ... Another OAU Commission of relevance for *Pax Africana* is the Defence Commission. But the Defence Commission has so far been among the least effective of Pan-African institutions. Africa may indeed aspire to be her own policeman, but she does not seem ready as yet to pay the price for it. (p. 213)

Mazrui outlined the varied backgrounds of the leaders of newly independent Africa and their radical and revolutionary ideas, and it is perhaps surprising that the institutions they created for the continent were so conservative – with the possible exception of the OAU's National Liberation Committee. Mazrui noted that Africa still has the problem of how other powers respond to its behaviour and that foreign intrusion in Africa continued.

Radha Sinha's problem-oriented study *Food and Poverty* (1976) has an urgent message. Sinha, a former consultant of the FAO, produced an informed analysis of the world's food problem stressing in particular the maldistribution of food and other resources. Noting the proposals of UNCTAD with their multi-commodity approach and buffer stocks provisions, he commented: 'the greatest weakness of the UNCTAD scheme is its likely political unacceptability to the developed countries, particularly the USA' (p. 114). He identified a more aggressive attitude by Third World states, especially after the oil price rise of 1973/4 when the developing countries tried to maximize their own market powers by forming cartels such as the International Bauxite Association, the International Council of Copper Exporting Countries and the International Tin Agreement. He gave a qualified welcome to the Lomé Convention between the European Community and certain African, Pacific and Caribbean states. Writing in 1976 he commented:

> The recent change in the attitudes of the richer countries is largely due to the increasing militancy of the Third World countries. It is almost certain that the magnitude of future 'concessions' in the course of GATT and UNCTAD IV negotiations will depend mainly on the continued solidarity of the developing countries. (p. 116)

In his conclusion Sinha called for a fairer sharing of world resources and power if confrontation was to be avoided. He feared that the 'era of cooperation' between rich and poor countries had come to an end and that battle lines were being drawn. Instead he advocated 'major concessions from the richer countries on trade and aid issues' and also 'a major restructuring of the international organizations and negotiating machinery in order to provide a much greater say for the poorer countries in international trade, investment and monetary arrangements' (p. 132). GATT, IBRD and IMF have been the preserve of the rich with voting weighted in favour of the OECD countries and Sinha recommended that GATT and UNCTAD ought to be merged into an International Trade Organization (ITO) and the creation of a Third World permanent secretariat involved in all trade and aid negotiations. Though less radical than Amin, Sinha also recommended greater co-operation between developing countries and an end to their 'inferiority complex' with instead a sense of mutual self-esteem and trust being developed (ch. 10).

In all, Third World commentators have provided a varied and lively approach towards the problems of international organizations. Their emphasis has naturally been on the use of world institutions to change the economic condition of the southern continents. As this condition is unlikely to improve dramatically in the near future, further – and probably more radical – contributions on the role of international organizations in North–South relations can be expected from the Third World.

Summary

The four major schools dealt with in this chapter – the traditionalist, the revisionist, the Marxist and the Third World – and the variations they contain, did not exist in a historical vacuum. Ideas were formulated within the context of particular societies and in response to particular problems – the communications revolution of the nineteenth century, the First World War, the rise of Nazi Germany, the development of post-Second World War Europe, the processes of decolonization and detente. In some cases the views of those writings on international organizations have had an effect on events themselves, particularly on the attitudes of governments towards international organizations. An example is the work of Leonard Woolf whose suggestions concerning a world organization contributed to the detailed preparation for the League of Nations by the British Government. Likewise Hans Morganthau and E. H. Carr provided stimuli for informed US and British governmental thinking about international relations from the 1940s onwards. In other cases the general writings of persons such as Marx, Lenin, Mao Tse-tung and the *dependencia* school have affected the political climate within which governments conduct their policy, including that towards international organizations.

Other factors apart from their historical context have affected the views of the schools mentioned. They have different backgrounds in their ideology – Western, reformist, communist, Third World radical; in their level of analysis of international relations – state-centric, interest and transnational groups, class dominant; and this affects the type of international organization dominant in their studies – IGOs, INGOs – and their geographical area of interest – the North Atlantic, Western Europe, East Europe, Third World or global (see Table 3.1).

If writings on international organizations are affected by their authors' political and social surroundings, it may be possible to speculate about future developments in the subject. In the West, there seems little doubt that the 'complex interdependence' approach will expand as the political and economic interconnections throughout the world are perceived as being more nebulous and holistic. Harold K. Jacobsen's book *Networks of Interdependence: International Organizations and the Global Political System* (1979) is in this line. However, with the onset of a tougher, more consciously 'national interest' approach to world politics by the Reagan Administration in the USA, material more critical of specific international agencies and indeed of the whole concept of international organizations might be expected. Forerunners can be seen in Daniel Moynihan's apology for his behaviour as US delegate to the UNO and in the neo-realist writings of Robert Tucker. In Western Europe commentators seem likely to continue with their analyses of the strains and fractures in the institutions there (EC and NATO in particular) caused by persistent nationalism, economic recession and changes in the membership of the organizations. This interest in dis-integration may well spread to study of the Soviet bloc institutions if latent pressures in East Europe leads to East European countries pulling away from Soviet dominance in their economic and social life, if not in their politics and security.

There is a strong possibility that Third World publications will become increasingly disenchanted with existing international institutions as means of solving their problems. Their approach to UN institutions could become more openly cynical or hostile, reflecting their governments' attitudes. Greater emphasis could be placed on 'Third World Only' organizations, particularly if little comes out of the North–South dialogue.

As the Soviet Union becomes more enmeshed in the UN network,

Table 3.1   Literature on International Organizations: Four Major Views

View	Major contributor	Predominant area and period	Area of interest	Ideology	Level of analysis	Type of I.O. dominant
Traditionalist						
International lawyers	Jenks	N. Atlantic 1930s–50s	General	Western	Interstate	IGOs
World law school	Clark and Sohn	N. American 1940s–50s	General	Western Reformist	Interstate	IGOs
International government	Woolf	European 1910s–30s	General	Western Reformist	Interstate	IGOs
Realist	Morgenthau	N. Atlantic 1930s–60s	N. Atlantic	Western	Interstate	IGOs
Revisionist						
Functionalist	Mitrany	W. European 1940s–70s	General	Western liberal	Interest groups	INGO/IGOs
Neo-functionalist	Haas	N. Atlantic 1950s–60s	W. Europe	Western	Interest group	IGO/INGOs
Transactionist	Deutsch	N. American 1950s	N. Atlantic	Western	Transnational	INGOs/IGOs
Interdependence	Nye and Keohane	N. American 1960s–70s	General	Western	Transnational	IGOs/INGOs
Globalist	Ward	N. Atlantic 1970s	General	Western Reformist	Transnational	IGOs/INGOs
Marxist						
Marxism	Marx and Engels	Europe late 19th c.	General	Communist	Class	INGO
Marxism–Leninism	Lenin	E. Europe 1920s ff	General	Communist	Class	IGOs/INGOs
Neo-Marxist	Mandel	N. Atlantic 1960s	General	Communist	Class	INGOs/IGOs
Chinese Marxist	Mao Tse-tung	China 1950s–70s	General	Communist	Class	INGOs/IGOs
Third World						
Dependencia	Amin	Third World 1970s ff	Third World	Radical	Class	INGOs
Developmental	Prebisch	Third World 1970s ff	Third World	Radical	Core-periphery	IGOs/INGOs

so that present trend towards a closer study of international organizations within that country will continue. These works will become increasingly sympathetic towards organizations as their memberships slough off Western dominance and as Third World resolutions are adopted. If the US Government takes a negative attitude within international organizations such as the UNO and the specialized agencies, we may see Soviet commentators mirroring the dominating attitude of much US writing on these institutions in the late 1940s and 1950s when they were judged in Cold War terms.

Chinese academic interest in the study of the European Community has already been mentioned (p. 116) and this, plus concern with the UN and its agencies, will be apparent as long as the Chinese Government views the EC with enthusiasm and the UN with an interested reserve.

Perhaps the most lively thoughts with relevance to international organizations will come from the ecologists and the futurologists. These are respectively concerned with what is necessary rather than what is possible and with what is improbable as well as what is likely. As the next millennium looms, mankind must consider its own endangered planet, the co-existence of political, social and racial groups on a small globe and the ways in which groups – nations, states, companies, interest groups – can interact without destroying each other. The study of international organizations is just starting.

4

Role and Function of International Organizations

Chapter 1 placed international organizations in a historical context by demonstrating that this phenomenon had evolved during a definite period of international history starting in the mid-nineteenth century and flourishing in the period after the Second World War.

In Chapter 2 the aims and activities of international organizations were used as one way of classifying them. These aims and activities were primarily *internal* to the organizations – that is, they represented what their founders considered their tasks to be and what the organizations attempted to achieve during their existence.

The last chapter gave international organizations their intellectual backcloth showing both the philosophical foundations of certain organizations and how writers have approached the study of international organizations.

This chapter examines international organizations in the contemporary world. International organizations take their place in the political market place where the relationships between peoples, groups, nations, states and blocs can be observed. Here we seek to find out what role they play in this 'global market place': are they one of the many participants jostling in transactions with other groups, with political leaders and states' representatives? Are they the mere instruments of the other players, being used as tools to gain advantages or as means of communication between interlocutors? Or are they part of the scenery itself, plinths for speeches, forums for meetings, common grounds for gatherings?

Secondly, the functions of international organizations in international relations will be examined. How do they affect the functioning of the global market place? Do they allow those who frequent it to organize themselves more efficiently, to express their desires more forcefully or more clearly? Do they affect the running of the market place, or behaviour there? Can they determine who shall do business there, even to set standards for behaviour and perhaps enforce rules and regulations? Or can they affect the functioning of the market place by themselves trading in it or indirectly by providing information to those who buy and sell?

It should be clear that some organizations will fulfil limited roles and functions whilst others may cover a wide range. It should also be obvious that the role played by an international organization will affect the functions it performs in international relations. A mute messenger boy may have a less overt, a seemingly less important function in the running of the market place than an armed police-man. That is not to say that one day the messenger boy's duties may not include providing the crucial information for a life-and-death decision or that the work of the policeman might not be hamstrung by the actions of armed brigands or just by lack of public support.

Likening contemporary international relations to a global market place begs certain questions. What is the nature of the market place? Is it open with free contact between all who use it, man and best, large and small, whatever their background or intention? Or is it regulated with certain discrete areas having only carefully controlled relation-ships with others? Are the activities of individual citizens curtailed and just certain traders allowed to approach each other's territory? Or has it a loose structure with fairly random activities performed between groups who have little to do with each other outside their formal dealings?

Are, then, international relations part of a world *system* or a *network*? Those who identify a global political system consider that it

consists of numerous more or less autonomous actors interacting in patterned ways to influence one another. Their independent decisions and policies serve as stimuli for one another and induce or constrain the behavior of others. (Mansbach *et al.*, 1976, p. 5)

The emphasis here is placed on an overall pattern of interaction and response whereas a network suggests something more modest: contact and interconnections between individual entities which may not be used in a patterned fashion to influence each other. A network is less organized, less active and reactive, less enclosed than a system. The structure of world politics is clearly enclosed on the planet Earth (though this is beginning to change) but its level of organization and interaction depends on whether one sees the glass half full or half empty. Russett and Starr (1981) define a system as

> *a set of interacting elements.* When we speak of a global or regional system, we imply that the major elements or influences at different levels of analysis affect each other. (p. 17)

The crucial word here is 'major'. The two authors go on to identify a good analyst as one who can 'simplify a complex reality in a way that concentrates on the most important relationships and at least temporarily ignores the rest' (pp. 17–18). Following this advice, the term 'international system' – within which international organizations function – will be used in its fairly simple meaning suggesting that contemporary international relations take place within a defined area (which nevertheless is diffuse), wherein activities in one area are clearly seen to affect those elsewhere and the whole structure is seen to be interconnected, though to what extent may be disputed. It is clear that the whole set-up has no central authority, no directing power, no imposed pattern of behaviour.

It is perhaps the nebulous nature of the international political system that makes the task of assessing the role and function of international organizations within it so difficult. A number of warnings should be sounded.

The classification of international organizations in Chapter 2 showed that they range from those with general aims and activities and a wide membership to those with specific aims and a limited membership. It is therefore likely that a number of roles will be fulfilled by international organizations – some overlapping, some conflicting – making their function in international relations difficult to discern. International organizations cover such a broad spectrum that evidence about the activities of individual organizations, especially the more specific non-governmental organizations, is not readily available and the overall effect of their existence has to be estimated or summarized from the larger, better known institutions.

Secondly, the functional use of international organizations may be deduced from their aims and activities and the response of the membership to their existence. It is assumed that organizations are playing a role in international relations of some note, and importance is consequently attached to the work of the organizations. However, being short of laboratory conditions in international relations, it is not possible to compare 'reality' with a 'control' in which international affairs might be replicated in the absence of international organizations. Whilst it is possible to observe certain phenomena – such as war, trading and tourism – both before and after the creation of organizations affecting those activities, it is difficult to establish what factors have caused any changes. This is not to rule out such studies. Indeed, events over an extended period and studies with a large number of cases may suggest interesting associations between international organizations and certain behaviour in international relations; individual studies may demonstrate connections through 'detective work' – for example, a particular settlement of a dispute may have the 'fingerprints' of a UN mediator on it; and often negative evidence can be used to call in question common assumptions or to suggest further research.

Finally, an assessment of the role and function of international organizations in the international system is bound to be affected by the view of the nature of the system. It is generally accepted that the present international system has no controlling overall authority and is anarchic in the sense of being without government. How the present set-up may develop is disputed. Each interpretation can produce a different evaluation of international organizations' roles and functions. If the present system is seen as a necessary and continuing result of power politics, then any international institution will have a somewhat limited aspect and will only be able to ameliorate unwanted consequences of relations between sovereign states. If the contemporary system is interpreted in class terms, then the role of international organizations will be determined, in the eyes of the interpreter, by the requirements of the dominant class in the power structures behind the organizations. If, however, it is felt that the international system is developing very much in the way that political systems within states have, then present-day organizations can be seen in the role of potential instruments of world government.

International relations operate within an international system – 'a set of interacting elements' – where a bullet ringing out in Sarajevo can have major consequences for those living in South Africa, Siberia or Sydney and the activities of diplomats in New York or Geneva affects the future of a regime in Rhodesia, the survival of the Congolese state, the lives of political prisoners in South America or the use of the world's oceans, outer space or the Antarctic. In this system, rather as in the market place, relationships can cover a wide range of activities such as personal travel, trade, business, diplomacy, the exchange of information, propaganda, police actions, terrorism, and full-scale hostilities.

It is clear that international organizations' role and function have a part to play in the international system. Quantitative studies have demonstrated their *presence* and Chapter 2 showed their *range*. The *Yearbook of International Organizations* and works by Robert Angell (1965), Werner Feld (1971), David Singer and Michael

Wallace (1970), Kjell Skjelsbaek (1971) and G. P. Speeckaert (1957), have produced a welter of information on the growth of both IGOs and INGOS. As shown in Chapter 1, there was an exponential growth in the number of intergovernmental organizations in the century and a half after the Congress of Vienna, somewhat reflecting the expansion of the international system itself. Now that the system seems almost to have reached its limits in membership and coverage of the earth's surface, the *rate* of increase in the number of IGOs can be expected to fall – but the number of existing IGOs is likely to remain at approximately 300, at least until the end of the century. Jacobsen (1979, p. 52) shows that of the 289 IGOs accounted for in 1970, 276 had a specific purpose covering a field of activities such as health (WHO), education (UNESCO), agriculture (FAO), finance (IMF), trade (GATT) and fisheries (NEAFC). The number of INGOs has also seen an exponential rate of growth since 1815, to such an extent that they soon outstripped IGOs in quantity. There are now some 2,500 to 3,000, most of which have fairly specific aims (Speeckaert, 1957, p. xiii) and, unlike IGOs, the number of participants in INGOs (national NGOs, individuals) is still growing and their rate of increase may well continue: it has been estimated that with a modest growth of 5 per cent per annum there would be over 9,600 INGOs by the end of the century (*Yearbook of International Organization*, 1974, Tab. 4).

Roles of International Organizations

What roles do these considerable number of international organizations play in the montage of exchanges in the international system? Three major roles can be identified: those of instrument, arena and actor.

Instrument

Perhaps the most usual image of the role of international organizations is that of an instrument being used by its members for particular ends. This is particularly the case with IGOs where the members are sovereign states with power to limit independent action by international organizations. The former Executive Secretary of the UN's Economic Commission for Europe, Gunnar Myrdal, has outlined this role in a famous lecture from which it is worth quoting at some length:

> The basic fictitious notion about inter-governmental organizations, as conveyed by their constitutions, is that they are some-

thing more than their component parts: something above the national states ... [I]n the typical case international organizations are nothing else than instruments for the policies of individual governments, means for the diplomacy of a number of disparate and sovereign national states. When an inter-governmental organization is set up, this implies nothing more than that between the states a limited agreement has been reached upon an institutional form for multilateral conduct of state activity in a certain field. The organization becomes important for the pursuance of national policies precisely to the extent that such a multilateral co-ordination is the real and continuous aim of national governments. (1955, pp. 4–5)

Myrdal's intuition is supported by the empirical findings of a data-based study of IGO use by McCormick and Kihl who show that 'IGOs are used by nations primarily as selective instruments for gaining foreign policy objectives' (1979, p. 502). This view squarely relegates IGOs to the role of convenient tools for use by their member states. INGOs in an analogous position would merely reflect the requirements of the various trade unions, business organizations, political parties or church groups that were members. The consequences for the international organization are that it is likely to become fought over by the most powerful members eager to utilize it, and thus its chances of independent action are limited.

The United Nations in its first eight years of existence is often characterized as being an instrument of United States' diplomacy. The US Government could count on a majority consisting of the West European, Old Commonwealth and Latin American states in the General Assembly (thirty-four out of the original fifty-one members), on a majority in the Security Council only attenuated by the Soviet veto, and a secretary-general with clear pro-Western sympathies. During this period the USA used the United Nations to pillory the USSR over its activities in Eastern Europe; to help prevent Soviet incursions in Northern Iran; as a midwife for the birth of the two new states of Indonesia and Israel against, respectively, Dutch and Arab protests; to establish a multilateral force led by the United States to fight on behalf of South Korea against North Korea and Communist China; to extend the term of office of Secretary-General Trygve Lie against Soviet opposition; to exclude the new Communist Government in Peking from taking the China seat, and to have that Government condemned as an aggressor over the Korean War. The United States did not obtain all it wished for at the UN during this period: the Soviet Union vetoed a number of Security Council resolutions ranging from the admittance of Italy as a UN member to attempts to interfere in events in the Balkans. As Inis Claude (1964, p. 145) pointed out: 'From the Soviet standpoint, the veto power is an essential but regrettably limited and indecisive instrument of defense against Western utilization of the organization for anti-Communist purposes'. Indeed in 1950 when Soviet absence from the Security Council allowed the United States to mobilize United Nations' support for action in South Korea, the Soviet Government realized its mistake and sent back its representative to veto further Security Council action.

As well as these limitations experienced by the United States during the early period of the UN's existence, it soon became clear that the organization could not be used indefinitely as an appendage to US foreign policy machinery. The political shape of the world was changing with the emergence of the Soviet Union as a nuclear power and of the Third World non-aligned movement. Membership of the UN changed and by the mid-1950s the USA had lost its automatic majority in the General Assembly. The second Secretary-General, Dag Hammarskjold, was more his own man and was also aware of the fate of his predecessor. Even in the Security Council it was no longer only the Soviets who were defending themselves with the veto – in November 1956 Britain and France cast their first ones against resolutions concerning the Suez operation.

An organization cannot continue to be the instrument of policy of one dominant member when the membership is as varied as that of the UN. Whilst a large majority were satisfied with US activities in the UN – as seemed the case from 1945 to 1953 – then the United States Government could use this organization as a Cold War implement. This role of the UN could no longer be sustained once the membership of the General Assembly and the nature of the Cold War began to change. The USA did not cease its attempts to utilize the organization to further its foreign policy ends but it found that it was not alone in doing this successfully. The USSR, which up until the mid-1960s had merely defended its interests at the UN, began to take a more active approach. Furthermore, the Third World countries started to use the UN as an instrument for implementing their foreign policies, made more necessary by their not having a traditional network of diplomacy at their disposal. Indeed as early as 1956 Dag Hammarskjold described how through the machinery of the UN and other international organizations 'regularized multilateral negotiation has been added as a new tool for politicians, a new instrument for governments, a new technique of diplomacy' (Cordier and Foote, 1972, p. 661).

The use of international organizations as adjuncts to their members' policies affects their constitutions and development. The possibility of IGOs developing their own decision-making powers becomes, in Myrdal's words, 'a fictitious notion'. The UN's Economic Commission for Europe, of which Myrdal was Executive Secretary, was a classic example of an organization which only had modest institutions because of member states' unwillingness to lose control over their economic policies. Co-operative arrangements on specific research, co-ordination of national policies, multilateral agreements and limited delegated powers were accepted as they were 'nothing else and nothing more than a set of mutual promises of co-ordinated and synchronized national policy action' (Myrdal, 1955, p. 8). These limitations are reflected in the powers of the secretariat and in the decision-taking mechanisms.

The secretariat of an organization such as ECE represented the 'collective aspirations of the member governments' and herein lies both its strength and limitation. By earning the respect of member states, the secretariat can influence their thinking, act as honest broker and even find some matters increasingly delegated to them; for example, the secretariat of the ECE Coal Committee could prescribe changes, when conditions demanded, in the agreed quarterly allocations of coal (Myrdal, 1955, p. 23). Such powers are normally only 'technical', willingly delegated by governments and open to review by the members. The secretariat has to watch that it neither strays from its remit nor undermines the aims of member states – particularly powerful ones – as it will inevitably lose in a confrontation. Examples of individuals being ousted from secretarial posts of international organizations after having alienated one or a number of member states are Trygve Lie in the United Nations in 1953 (and Dag Hammarskjold had he not died in 1961), Etienne Hirsch of Euratom in 1962 and Theo van Boven of the UN's Human Rights Committee in 1982.

This sort of political interference of a secretariat should not be confused with the question of an international civil service. The League of Nations' first Secretary-General wrote that such a service would be one

in which men and women of various nationalities might unite in preparing and presenting to the members of the League an objective and common basis of discussion ... the Secretary-General would not only be the co-ordinating centre of the activities of the Secretariat, but its members would be responsible to him alone, and not to the Governments of the countries of which they were nationals...

but that such a secretariat would be entrusted 'with the execution of any decisions taken by the Governments' (Jordan, 1971, pp. 43–4). A secretariat based on those seconded from national missions is more open to direct interference and there is good evidence that since the 1960s the UN Secretariat has been increasingly subject to such pressures (Weiss, 1982, pp. 294–305). This can affect the efficiency of the organization and can also interfere with its ability to carry out policy agreed by the collectivity of members and thus represents an attempt by some states to have 'two bites at the cherry': having not quite obtained all they want in plenary meetings they can then direct 'their' members of the secretariat to implement (or not implement) policy in such a way as to favour their interests. It seems that a growing number of states agree with Mr Krushchev's statement cited by Walter Lippmann, 'that there can be no such thing as an impartial civil servant in this deeply divided world' and that, therefore, members of an international civil service can legitimately be used to further the demands of their home state. Governments of such states do not seem to be diverted from such action by it being contrary, in the case of the UN, to the requirements in Article 100 of the Charter that

> In the performance of their duties the Secretary-General and the staff will not seek or receive instructions from any government...

and

> Each Member of the United Nations undertakes to respect the exclusively international character of the responsibilities of Secretary-General and the staff and not to seek to influence them in the discharge of their responsibilities.

The way that decisions are taken in many international organizations can also demonstrate their use 'for the pursuance of national policies'. It is noticeable that, as well as limiting the powers of any secretariat, the constitutions of most international organizations do not allow for decisions, at least major ones, to be taken that may bind members that have voted against them. This is not the case in the United Nations but is the rule in most IGOs. In the case of the UN General Assembly resolutions only have the strength of recommendations, and Security Council resolutions, which can be passed by a majority of nine out of the fifteen members and can be mandatory, are subject to veto by any one of the permanent members. The use of the veto has severely limited the number of cases where states have found that the UNO, far from helping in the pursuance of their national policies, has over-ridden their wishes and even acted against them. In these rare cases – South Africa and Israel come to mind – these states still use the UN machinery to persuade Western states, especially the USA, to prevent really effective action against them by use of the veto. Thus the UN has produced verbally strong resolutions but little harmful action against Israel and South Africa in addition to that already organized by the Arab League and the OAU.

Organizations with a more limited membership often have decision-taking mechanisms which reflect their being at the service of the membership. Whilst the unanimity principle is the best assurance for a member that its interests will not be traduced by the decisions of the organization, it has its limitations. A vote at every stage of a complicated process of decision-taking would soon paralyze an institution if complete unanimity were needed at all times. Gunnar Myrdal claimed that in the ECE's technical agencies votes were not taken, non-substantive issues were cleared in advance by the secretariat for unanimous decisions 'while the efforts in deliberations on substantive questions were directed towards reaching a maximum agreement between a maximum number of governments' (Myrdal, 1955, p. 19). Furthermore it was not necessary for all to agree on a programme: 'one or several governments should not hinder two or more other governments from using the organization to reach a settlement among themselves'. This has also been the case in the Organization for Economic Co-operation and Development where those voting for decisions are bound by them whilst those abstaining are not.

These apparent deviations from the rule of unanimity do not undermine a member's ability to use an international organization as an instrument of policy. Instead they demonstrate that in any political process the participants have to calculate the extent to which they are in a 'zero-sum game'. If they believe that gains made by any other member are going to be to their detriment, then they will insist on tight constitutional control of the international organization, exercising their right of veto over any move that does not benefit them. If they believe that co-operation can produce new benefits which would otherwise remain unexploited and that all, or most, members can take advantage of these, then it is logical to allow the institutions of the organization some scope for action. Likewise a long-term view may persuade a member to suffer apparent losses by not preventing decisions detrimental to its interests in the expectation that larger gains will be made when other decisions are taken. To describe international organizations as functioning as instruments of their membership does not mean that each and every decision made must be explicable in terms of serving the interests of each and every member. An instrument demonstrates its purpose if it shows its utility over a period of time to those that have brought it into service. Their satisfaction should not be jaded when another makes use of the instrument, provided it is not turned into a weapon against them.

Arena

A second image of the role of international organizations is that of their being arenas or forums within which action takes place. In this case, the organizations provide meeting places for members to come together to discuss, argue, co-operate or disagree. Arenas in themselves are neutral – they can be used for a play, a circus or a fight. Stanley Hoffmann (1970, pp. 398–9), examining the various roles of the UNO, writes of this aspect:

> As an arena and a stake it has been useful to each of the competing groups eager to get not only a forum for their views but also diplomatic reinforcement for their policies, in the Cold War as well as in the wars for decolonization.

Conor Cruise O'Brien's view of the UN is that '[i]ts Council Chambers and Assembly Hall are stages set for a continuous dramatisation of world history' (1968, p. 9). A more down-to-earth approach is advanced by Yeselson and Gaglione in a book the title of which suggests that the UNO plays more the role of an instrument: *A Dangerous Place – The United Nations as a Weapon in World Politics*. Despite this, the UN is described as 'an arena for combat' (p. 3). More traditionally, international organizations have provided their members with the opportunity of advancing their own viewpoints and suggestions in a more open and public forum than that provided by bilateral diplomacy. It is not surprising to find that a study of forty-one academic publications written during the 1970–7 period showed that 78 per cent portrayed the UN as an arena (Dixon, 1981, p. 51).

During the 1970s the United Nations and its agencies were used by Third World countries to air their views on the subject of a New International Economic Order (NIEO). The old order had been based on the negotiations carried out at Bretton Woods, 1944–6, when the victorious Allies – though with opposition from the Soviet Bloc – created a multilateral structure for the post-Second World War economy. This system was based on American economic strength, the dollar as the lynchpin currency and an agreement to liberalize markets and the exchange of currencies, so that eventually a free market could be created for the Western world and its dependencies. By the start of the 1970s this system was collapsing. A large number of newly dependent countries found the Bretton Woods system and its associated organizations – the IBRD, IMF and GATT – unsympathetic to their economic aspirations and they resented the dominance of OECD countries in these institutions and in the world economy generally. The United States was no longer in the superior position it had been in 1945 – other economic centres had emerged in West Europe and Asia which, whilst not as powerful as the USA, sapped some of its economic strength. The dollar had been severely weakened by constant US balance of trade deficits, inflation and growing fears about its link to gold. From 1971 to 1973 the dollar-based currency system of Bretton Woods gave way: the US dollar ceased to be backed by gold and was devalued in price. At the end of 1973, after the Arab–Israeli Yom Kippur War, the Middle Eastern oil producers persuaded their colleagues in OPEC to increase petroleum prices substantially – fourfold from October 1973 to the summer of 1974 – thereby delivering another blow to the already reeling Western industrialized states. The West still held control of the world's financial and trading institutions and the rules of the economic game were those drawn up largely by the USA and Britain at Bretton Woods.

The new Third World states had already been calling for a new set of economic priorities and by 1964 they had established the UN Conference on Trade and Development (UNCTAD) as a forum at which they could articulate their trade and economic demands outside the pre-defined discussion of the Bretton Woods organizations. As a result of UNCTAD meetings the Third World had formed the Group of 77 (G77) – a bloc whose interests were those of the African, Asian and Latin American developing states. On political questions G77 was mirrored by the meeting of ministers from the non-aligned countries which again were most of the states of the Southern continents. By the end of the 1960s the Third World had enough forums within which to put forward their ideas and demands, but when the richer industrialized states were present – at the Bretton Woods institutions, in ECOSOC, at UNCTAD meetings – the poorer states could exercise little or no bargaining power, only persuasion. As Sidney Weintraub (1977, p. 97) commented: 'Each group of countries will wish to negotiate issues of importance to it in the institutions that it dominates'. The difference is outlined by Robert Gregg (1981, pp. 54–5) as such: the South preferred the UN General Assembly, and to some extent UNCTAD, because of its 'universality, its egalitarian/majoritarian decision-making rules and practices, and its political character'; the North, the developed economies, preferred a more pluralistic system of forums with regard for the specialized institutions such as IMF, IBRD and GATT.

The search by the developing states for a NIEO surfaced in the 1970s at the Third United Nations Conference on Trade and Development (UNCTAD III) in 1972, the 1973 Algiers Summit of Non-Aligned States and a preparatory committee of the developing countries which produced a draft Declaration and Programme of Action for the Establishment of a NIEO ready for the UN General Assembly's Sixth Special Session on raw materials and development. The four basic points advanced were: 1. Permanent sovereignty over natural resources; 2. The right to establish commodity producers' associations by developing states; 3. The indexation of commodity export prices linking them to the cost of imports from industrialized countries; 4. International control of multinational corporations. The Sixth Special Session was not a noticeable success. Its product, the Charter of Economic Rights and Duties of States, was adopted at the following regular General Assembly session, much against the opposition of the developed countries, sixteen of which either abstained or voted against. Later in 1974 the French Government called for a meeting of a small number of states representative of developed and developing countries and in early 1975 both the OPEC ministerial meeting at Algiers and the Dakar Conference of Developing Countries accepted the idea. During 1975 a preparatory conference for the 'North–South' Paris meeting showed that, despite any reservations, the OPEC states were willing to back Third World demands against the developed world. Further preparations for dealing with economic questions in a wider framework were made at the meetings of the UN Industrial Development Organization and of the non-aligned countries, both held in Lima, Peru, in March 1975; the Commonwealth Ministerial gathering at Kingston, Jamaica, in May 1975; an OECD meeting and an ECOSOC preparatory session in the summer of that year.

The Seventh Special Session of the UN General Assembly (summer 1975) dealt with development and international economic co-operation and produced – by unanimity – what the US Ambassador to the United Nations described as 'the broadest development program in the history of the United Nations and, for that matter, in the history of the world' (Moynihan, 1979, p. 139).

The agreement reached between developed and underdeveloped states at the Seventh Special Session provided some solid achievements and guidelines for further negotiations. The USA agreed to a system of compensatory financing in the world commodity market which was intended to safeguard against the economic effects of market disruption on the developing states; the Generalized System of Preferences allowed by the Western countries for goods exported from the less developed states was to be continued; aid targets were confirmed and promises made to expand the resources and the flexibility of the World Bank Group and the UN Development Programme; the transfer of technology to the Third World was to be made easier. Many of the more difficult problems – the future market structure for raw materials and commodities, indexation schemes, the removal of trade barriers to developing states' exports, an international investment trust scheme, the problem of the debt burden of the Third World, a code of conduct for technology transfers – were postponed to be discussed at UNCTAD IV in Nairobi, 1976. Progress in these later discussions was laborious and somewhat uncertain. Furthermore, the gathering of a number of developed, developing and OPEC states in Paris in 1975–7 at the Conference on International Economic Co-operation proved less than successful, and by the end of the decade much of the initiative created at the Seventh Special Session had been dissipated. The independent commission of 'wise men' which produced the Brandt Report in 1980 helped to raise expectations that rich and poor could find common interest in a new economic world plan, but the Reagan Administration's hard line at the subsequent North–South summit in Cancun (1981) put an end to any speculation that the United States would support a rescue programme for the economically beleaguered Third World.

The NIEO has been dealt with in a number of international organizations acting as forums at which proponents, detractors and the half-convinced can propose, discuss and formulate solutions. Some of these organizations, such as the World Bank Group, were also used as means to implement some of the solutions but most were primarily arenas for debate and negotiation. The confluence of the collapse of the Western-based Bretton Woods monetary system, the political uncertainty of US leadership after the Watergate scandal and withdrawal from Vietnam, the increased desperation of indebted underdeveloped states and the growth in the bargaining power of the oil-producing countries, presented the chance in the mid-1970s for serious negotiations over a wide range of socio-economic issues. The Seventh Special Session of the UN General Assembly demonstrated that the UNO could provide the right context for such a massive task.

This second image of the role of an international organization can also be seen reflected in the working of its institutions. In the case of the negotiations for a NIEO it was essential that the process should be inclusive of as many states as possible, that any new rules should be agreed by the widest range of states, that both principle and detail should be open to informed discussion and negotiation, and that the process should have a time limit, though unfinished business might be delegated to associated bodies. A Special Session of the United Nations General Assembly fitted these requirements well. It had to finish before the new plenary session of the General Assembly met, but matters could be handed on to other UN agencies and associated institutions such as the World Bank Group and UNCTAD IV. The preparatory work of UNCTAD III, of the non-aligned states, of the OECD countries and at ECOSOC meant that a variety of topics ranging from the general principles of world trade down to the details of patent law could be encompassed. The Secretariat of the UN was needed in this case to fulfil the vital role of servicing the meetings, preparing documents, advising and conciliating. Although the UNCTAD Secretariat had done much to prepare material on trade and development issues, it was 'never able to perform for the Group of 77 the functions which the OECD Secretariat has performed for Group B [the Western states] (not to mention the superior resources which many of the Western market economy states have at their disposal back in their capitals)'. However, '[t]he trade-union mentality of the UNCTAD Secretariat has seriously compromised its ability to play the role of honest broker in the NIEO negotiations, and has contributed to the weakening of UNCTAD's role in these negotiations relative to the UN in New York' (Gregg, 1981, p. 63).

The aim of the Seventh Special Session was not to force through radical resolutions against the wishes of the richer industrialized states but to gain acceptance of the process of revising the existing economic order – something that could only be done with the rich countries' consent or, at least, lack of resistance. With this in mind, the negotiations at the Session tended to be between the OECD states, led by the USA, and G77, led by the Algerian Foreign Minister who was also President of the General Assembly, Abdelazziz Bouteflika. The European Community and the industrialized countries sympathizing with the developing states – Sweden, Norway, Finland and the Netherlands – formed two other groups actively participating in the debate (Dolman, 1979, p. 62). On the whole the Soviet Bloc tended to remain on the sidelines, claiming that the socialist countries were not responsible for the plight of the Group of 77 and could not be expected to make recompense, as should the West. These groupings and the desire not to cause the breakdown of the Session led to its relatively successful conclusion despite the wide range of topics and the participation of some 140 delegations. The process was facilitated by the absence of voting. Rather than rely on the weight of majority votes, G77 accepted that consensus with the West had to be sought. In the words of the first Secretary-General of UNCTAD, Raoul Prebisch, 'There is obviously no immediate practical purpose in adopting recommendations by a simple majority of the developing countries but without the favourable votes of the developed countries, when the execution of those recommendations depends on their acceptance by the latter' (Cassan, 1974, p. 456). This tactic meant not only giving way on certain important issues – at least for the time being – but also formulating resolutions acceptable to all. The US delegation helped in this by using the G77 working paper as the basis for negotiation (Gosovic and Ruggie, 1976, p. 322).

The system of blocs, formalized in UNCTAD and seen in the Seventh Special Session, and the use of consensus, meant that on this occasion the General Assembly could offer an effective forum for a wide range of states to discuss the process of revising the world economic order. The forum itself was neutral: the previous year the Sixth Special Session had ended in failure as the major contenders were not ready for mutual compromise. The forum of the UNO may have added authority to the agreement but did not guarantee its future sanctity – indeed political events conspired against continuing success.

In its role as a forum, the UN General Assembly was in this case fulfilling a requirement often sought of international organizations. When members of organizations want to negotiate, agree or publicly disagree, they can of course do so on a bi- or multilateral basis. They can arrange an *ad hoc* meeting for their purpose. First they would have to agree on the time, place, the protocol, even the shape of the table around which all would sit. They would have to agree the agenda, the method of voting, the rules of conduct of the negotiations and the status of any conclusions reached by the negotiations. What better than having an acceptable meeting place, set of rules and conventions, together with ancillary services? Whether it be the members of the International Olympic Committee planning the next Olympics, delegates of the International Red Cross discussing activities in war zones, The Council of Ministers of the European Community coming together to air their views on a trade agreement or the 150 plus members of the UN General Assembly gathering in New York to discuss a new world economic order, all have decided that an existing international organization provides them with a forum which otherwise would have to be created from the start.

Actor

The third role attributed to international organizations in the international system is that of independent actor. The crucial word here is 'independent'. If it means that international organizations – or at least some of them – can act on the world scene without being significantly affected by outside forces, then very few, if any, fulfil that criterion. Neither do many 'independent' sovereign states. If it is used to mean autonomous in the sense Karl Deutsch uses it, that the organization's 'responses are not predicated, even from the most thorough knowledge of the environment' and that 'it possesses a stable and coherent decision-making machinery within its boundaries' (1966, p. 7), then a number of international organizations clearly fit this description. Arnold Wolfers (1962, p. 23) considered that there was, even in the early 1960s, ample evidence to show that a number of non-state entities, including international organizations, were able to affect the course of world events:

> When this happens, these entities become actors in the international arena and competitors of the nation–state. Their ability to operate as international or transnational actors may be traced to the fact that men identify themselves and their interests with corporate bodies other than nation–states.

Wolfers goes on to claim that the 'actor capacity' of an international institution depends on 'the resolutions, recommendations, or orders emanating from its organs' compelling 'some or all member governments to act differently from the way in which they would otherwise act' (1962, p. 22). This leads to Inis Claude's dictum that '[a]n international organization is most clearly an actor when it is most distinctly an "it", an entity distinguishable from its member states' (1971, p. 13). Thus the oft-asserted contentions that 'the UN should do something' or that 'OPEC has increased petroleum prices' show the popular form of attributing an organization with the flesh and bones of an existence somewhat apart from that of its membership.

How far can this be taken? Clearly almost all organizations are dependent for their existence on their membership – this is as true for the UNO as for a trade union, a religious order or a scout troop. Some have such a weak institutional form that they are little more than the collective wills and activities of the members – for example the South African–Botswana–Lesotho–Swaziland Customs Union. However, many international organizations have institutional frameworks that allow them to achieve more than would be the case if their members acted separately or only co-operated on an *ad hoc* basis. It can be claimed that this shows up these organizations as instruments, being used by the members to obtain their requirements on the international scene. That is undeniable, but the very existence of an organization and, in some cases, the strength of their institutions mean that those representing the institution can make their own decisions, can act contrary to the wishes of some members and can affect the actions of other members. Also the presence of these international organizations collectively and individually has an effect on the international system and some of them are more active than some of the weaker sovereign states.

Many well-known INGOs display a strong corporate identity showing the organization to be stronger than the sum of its membership, and also act effectively on the world stage. The International Committee of the Red Cross has provided relief assistance in war and disaster zones, has generally cared for many suffering people whom governments have been unable or unwilling to help, and has also provided discreet mediation services in international disputes, for example in the Lebanon and in Korea. On a more limited scale, Amnesty International has organized extensive pressure to help prisoners of conscience of whatever political hue and has sometimes been more effective than individual governments or the UN's Human Rights Committee. Other INGOs such as the International Confederation of Free Trade Unions, the World Confederation of Labour, the International Organization of Standardization, the International Chamber of Commerce, the International Co-operative Alliance and the World Federation of United Nations Associations have pursued their aims through national contacts and by a network of relationships with the leading IGOs in their functional areas, such as ECOSOC, ILO, UNESCO, and FAO (*Yearbook of International Organizations*, 1974, p. S25). Many of these organizations possess 'stable and coherent machinery' within their own institutions and their activities compel governments to act differently than they would otherwise. The extent to which they themselves are significantly affected by outside forces depends on organization and circumstances but it is safe to say that, in the international system of the early 1980s, the International Committee of the Red Cross is more of an independent actor than, say, Nauru or Swaziland.

Estimating the degree of independent actor capacity of IGOs in the international system presents a further problem. As these organizations are established by intergovernmental agreement can they have a role separate from that willed by their membership? Can they be anything more than instruments of or forums for those member states?

It can be justifiably claimed that certain international organizations, by the sovereign will of their founders, have been given a separate capacity to act on the international scene and that this is reflected in their institutions. The International Court of Justice and the European Coal and Steel Community are two examples. The structure of the ICJ prevents any interference in its work by the signatories to its articles and the judges appointed by the members of the UNO may be representative of certain streams of law throughout the world but they are not the delegates of their state of origin. Their decisions are taken independently, not after instructions from their home base and each case is adjudged by the standards of international law not by an amalgam of national laws.

The European Coal and Steel Community, set up by the Treaty of Paris in 1951, established a High Authority which could act independently of the member governments. Its members, although appointed by the six ECSC states, were to act independently of national governments and in the interests of the Community as a whole. They had wide powers to affect the production and trading conditions for coal and steel in the Community, powers that were not open to veto by the representatives of the governments (as was the case for the European Economic Community) and were directly applicable to industries within the Community. The ECSC's Court could rule on cases concerning Community questions and its decisions could be applicable to other Community institutions, to individuals, businesses and member governments. Thus it had authority superior to that of national courts on Community matters.

Both in the case of the ICJ and that of the ECSC it can be claimed that not only is any 'independent' actor capacity dependent for its existence on the desires of the member governments but also the very substance of that capacity – implementation – is reliant on the authorities and agencies of the members. President Jackson of the USA said of the Chief Justice of the Supreme Court who had rules against his policy: 'John Marshall has made his decision: let him enforce it'. If the presidents and prime ministers of the signatory states of the ICJ or ECSC ever say likewise those institutions would face an even greater task, especially as their authority has not the standing that the US Supreme Court had after some five decades of existence.

Once life has been breathed into an intergovernmental organization and once it has started to build up a bureaucracy, a *modus operandi* and a role not totally dependent on the acceptance of its every act by all its membership, then it becomes politically more difficult for a member state effectively to stop that IGO's activities. To prevent unwanted action by the international organization risks alienating other states as well as ending any benefits that the IGO may provide. This gives organizations with a wide range of members and activities and well-developed central services a certain degree of autonomy in their actions. The United Nations Organization offers the greatest possibility here, even in the crucial area of the search for peace.

UN peacekeeping operations demonstrate the ability of an international organization to perform on the world stage with a certain degree of independence and with an effectiveness not always matched by state actors. They also show the limitations on international organizations – even the UN – as actors.

The UN's peacekeeping role is not mentioned in the Charter by which the original member states established the organization, neither has it been the subject of any amendment to that Charter. What can be found in the UN Charter is Chapter VI (Articles 33–8) on the Pacific Settlement of Disputes and Chapter VII (Articles 39–51) on Action with Respect to Threats to the Peace, Breaches of the Peace, and Acts of Aggression. Chapter VI first of all requires states party to a dispute to settle it

> by negotiation, enquiry, mediation, conciliation, arbitration, judicial settlement, resort to regional agencies or arrangements, or other peaceful means of their own choice

with the possibility that the Security Council may call upon the parties to end their differences by such means (Article 33). Indeed the Security Council may investigate disputes to see whether they threaten international peace and security (Article 34), it can recommend solutions to the dispute (Article 36) and states can bring disputes to the Security Council or the General Assembly for peaceful settlement (Articles 35, 37 and 38).

Chapter VII is quite distinct from the pacific settlement of disputes covered by Chapter VI. Article 39 states

> The Security Council shall determine the existence of any threat to the peace, breach of the peace, or act of aggression and shall make recommendations, or decide what measures shall be taken in accordance with Articles 41 and 42, to maintain or restore international peace and security.

Article 41 covers a number of non-warlike sanctions that the Security Council can ask UN members to employ 'to give effect to its decisions'. If these prove inadequate then Article 42 provides for 'such action by air, sea, or land forces as may be necessary to maintain or restore international peace and security'. These actions could include 'demonstrations, blockade, and other operations by air, sea, or land forces of Members of the United Nations'. Furthermore Article 47 created a Military Staff Committee consisting of the chiefs of staff of the permanent members of the Security Council (or their representatives) meeting together to decide on how best to provide the military requirements for the maintenance of international peace and security – forces, armaments, strategic plans, command and control. The Committee was soon plagued with Great Power disagreement and became practically defunct in 1947. In the case of the North Korean invasion of South Korea in June 1950, it was possible to utilize Chapter VII because the Soviet delegation withdrew from the Security Council in protest against the exclusion of the Communist Chinese from that body. The subsequent military operation by UN troops in Korea was scarcely of the sort that could be envisaged from a reading of Chapter VII – it was an American led and dominated force given UN legitimacy by the Security Council in the Soviet's absence. Such an occasion proved unlikely to recur: Chapter VII continued to be a victim of the Cold War.

It was during the Cold War in the 1950s that the peacekeeping operations of the UN emerged. In the late 1940s the UN Security Council and General Assembly had authorized peace-observation missions in Greece (UNSCOB), Palestine (UNTSO), Kashmir (UNMOGIP) and Indonesia (UNCI), and the League of Nations even carried out a type of peacekeeping operation in the Saar referendum of 1935 (Fabian, 1971, pp. 136–40). The first major military operation was that of the UN Emergency Force interposed between Egypt and Israel to allow the withdrawal of British and French troops that had supported Israeli action against Egypt in the Suez Crisis of November 1956. Since then similar operations have been undertaken in the Congo (ONUC), Cyprus (UNFICYP), again in Sinai (UNEF II), the Golan Heights between Israel and Syria (UNDOF) and the Lebanon (UNIFIL).

These activities, undertaken in different parts of the world and in varying political circumstances, have some basic elements in common. Peacekeeping is not peace enforcement envisaged under Chapter VII of the Charter. Forces are present with the consent of host governments and are not supposed to interfere in domestic politics; on the whole they are lightly armed for self-defence purposes only; they are made up of troops mainly from small or non-aligned states, only exceptionally accepting contributions from the permanent member of the Security Council; and they are assembled on an *ad hoc* basis for each operation. Their task is not to enforce a particular settlement but to prevent the spread of an already existing conflict. Thus they are not necessarily part of a peaceful settlement under Article VI: they exist to supervise or observe a ceasefire, a disengagement or the status quo, though their presence may eventually contribute to the peaceful solution of a dispute. It is noticeable that when peacekeeping operations have attempted to enforce particular political solutions they have run into trouble. This was the case in the Congo operation of 1960–4, and with UNEF II a peaceful settlement process – the Camp David Agreement between Egypt and Israel – led to the disbanding of the force as the process was not approved of by a substantial majority of the UN members.

The whole concept of peacekeeping has been tied up with the 'preventive diplomacy' ideas of the UN's second Secretary-General,

Dag Hammarskjold. Hammarskjold considered it part of the task of the UN secretariat to help stabilize areas of conflict so that parties might be brought together (Cordier and Foote, 1972, p. 694). This was particularly necessary in those parts of the world from which the European colonial powers were withdrawing, lest the USA and USSR be drawn into a simmering dispute.

Peacekeeping emerged in the peculiar historic conditions of the period from the end of the Second World War up to the 1980s, when East–West confrontation cast a shadow over the process of decolonization and allowed the institutions of the UN, particularly the secretariat, to take an active role. With the establishment of UNEF in 1956–7, the General Assembly gave Hammarskjold a remarkably free hand: 'The Secretary-General made it clear that the composition of the Force was a matter for him to decide' (Higgins, 1969, p. 300). Although he had two advisory committees (one political, one military) of secretariat members and troop-donor states, Hammarskjold was determined to keep the reins in his hands: '. . . ultimate decisions rest with the Secretary-General, as the executive in charge of carrying out the operation' (Hammarskjold, cited in Verrier, 1981, p. 21). This was confirmed in a negative way when U Thant, at the behest of President Nasser of Egypt, withdrew UNEF in 1967 without reference to the General Assembly or the Security Council of the UN. Similar independent views were held by the two Secretaries-General on their role in the Congo and ONUC and the outcome was by no means happy (Higgins, 1980; O'Brien, 1962; Verrier, 1981). Since then the control of peacekeeping operations has been exercized more strictly by the Security Council and the involvement of U Thant and Waldheim in UNIFICYP, UNEF II, UNDOF and UNIFIL tended to be that of stage managers rather than executive directors.

To what extent can the United Nations Organization in the form of the secretariat be said to have displayed the capacity of being an independent actor in its peacekeeping activities? There are three touchstones by which this capacity can be gauged: the existence of control of the institution by the UN membership; the ability of the institution to take its own decisions; the likely outcome had UN peacekeeping facilities not been available.

Existence of Control

In the case of UN peacekeeping, the institution that attempted independent action was the secretariat, attempts at control by the membership of the UNO being expressed either through the General Assembly or by the Security Council or unilaterally by individual members. In the end, the ultimate control on any secretary-general is refusal to re-appoint him to office – something that the Soviet Union threatened with Trygve Lie because of his support of the UN operation in Korea. Short of that action, refusal to co-operate can be just as deadly as the secretary-general, in Hammarskjold's words, 'commands only the influence that the Member Governments of the United Nations are willing to give his office . . .' (Cordier and Foote, 1972, p. 285). This was said scarcely a year after his taking office to replace Lie who, on having his term extended, found himself faced by a Soviet boycott and decided to resign. Hammarskjold's actions with respect to the establishment of UNEF in 1956 were taken at the behest of the General Assembly after such plans had been vetoed by France and Britain in the Security Council. In the end those two powers were willing to co-operate with the Secretary-General and there was little concern by member states over the initiative and independence of action shown by the Secretary-General in setting up UNEF. Although the United Nations Operation in the Congo (ONUC) was created by a Security Council resolution, this was after Hammarskjold had exercised his right under Article 99 to bring to the attention of the Council any matter – in this case the political situation in the Congo – 'which in his opinion may threaten international peace and security' and the whole operation was run more by the inspiration of the Secretary-General than to the letter of Security Council or General Assembly resolutions which were anyhow often contradictory. This did not stop the USSR from trying to place pressure on Hammarskjold when they felt that his activities in the Congo were working contrary to Soviet interests. The USSR went so far as to suggest the abolition of the post of the secretary-general and its replacement by a 'troika' of three secretaries-general, one from the West, one from the Soviet Bloc and one from the Third World. With Hammarskjold's death, his replacement by U Thant and the relatively speedy end to ONUC, the pressures on the institution of the secretary-general were eased. The lesson had been learnt and when the next UN peacekeeping operation was established in Cyprus, the powers given to the secretary-general were severely curtailed and a much closer control exercised by the Security Council.

Independent Decisions

To what extent has the secretary-general acted independently over peacekeeping? As suggested above, Hammarskjold exercised a good deal of initiative in both UNEF and ONUC. This was in line with his view of the office of secretary-general and the authority established under Chapter XV of the Charter ('The Secretariat'). Early on in his period of office he told a press gathering:

> The right of initiative given to the Secretary-General in the Charter for situations of emergency is important especially because this right implies a recognition of his responsibility for action for peace . . . irrespective of the views and wishes of the various Member Governments. (Cordier and Foote, 1972, p. 285)

Part of the basis for such a role was the assumption that the secretary-general has at his disposal an international civil service – one which serves the Organization, whose members do not take instructions from the governments of their home states and which the member governments do not try to control (Article 100). Hammarskjold had to contend with another remnant of Lie's period in office – the attempt by the US Government to remove certain American citizens working in the UN secretariat because of their suspected communist sympathies. Whilst Hammarskjold overcame that crisis there are indications that since the growth in UN membership in the 1960s the staff of the secretariat have become more susceptible to pressure from home and that many of them are only seconded from their own civil service (Weiss, 1982, pp. 294–305). With an international civil service in the sense established by Article 100; with the philosophy that the institutions should serve 'the Organization', the Charter or even the spirit of the Charter rather than national views; and with international events requiring non-Great Power activity of a sort that the non-aligned states were not able to carry out, the role of the secretary-general could indeed be that of a fairly independent actor on the world stage. Once these conditions changed – the secretariat's personnel became more partisan, the Hammarskjoldian philosophy of the role of the secretary-general was challenged and was no longer asserted with such vigour, and international conditions changed – then the independence of the UN institutions, including the secretariat, was curtailed. By the late 1960s the two superpowers were showing greater willingness to become involved in Third World disputes and the non-aligned countries themselves were organizing their own forms of managing conflict, whether through the UN or through regional agencies such as the Organization of African Unity and the Arab League, so leaving less to the good offices of the secretary-general of the United Nations. To this extent the United Nations Organization and its institutions such as the secretariat, like most sovereign states, could not be said to be actors independent of world events.

Without Peacekeeping Facilities

A third test of the extent of the actor capacity of the UN's institutions, especially in the field of peacekeeping, is to estimate whether events would have been substantially different without them. If one imagined a UN with a secretariat similar to that under Drummond, the first Secretary-General of the League of Nations, then the UNEF and ONUC operations would certainly have been different. Whether there would have been any international intervention in the Congo is doubtful, though the Western allies might have been induced to take action similar to that by Belgium on the breakdown of law and order in the country. Some form of international operation in the Suez–Sinai area might have been mounted in 1956–7 though the multilateral diplomacy needed to organize it could have postponed its inception. The two models available for copying are those of the Saar referendum of 1935 where Britain played a dominant role as the League's agent, the secretariat scarcely being of any importance (Fabian, 1971, pp. 137–41) and of Chanak in 1922 when an Allied force kept the Turkish army out of a neutral zone due mainly to the determination of the local commander backed up by the diplomacy of the Great Powers (Verrier, 1981, p. xvii). Agents such as the International Red Cross, the Swiss, the Swedes or regional organizations could replace the UN in some peacekeeping activities, but the acceptability of such agents would have to be negotiated case by case. This was done when Western observers took over the role of UNEF II in Sinai in order to observe the implementation of the last stages of the Camp David Israel–Egypt agreement in 1982.

With the use of other agents or joint forces of a small number of states for peacekeeping operations, the independent role of the UN and its secretariat would decrease. Likewise a lack of UN involvement in peacekeeping would either have led to further interventions in the Third World by the superpowers or the continuation of local conflicts or *ad hoc* and possibly less successful attempts to introduce third party supervision into trouble spots. In this sense the UN's peacekeeping operations and the crucial role played in them by the secretariat have demonstrated the capacity of the organization and its institutions seriously to affect world problems. It is noticeable that this capacity has been less prominent since the 1970s with the Western force replacing UNEF II in Sinai, the Syrian (Arab League) peacekeeping force, and later the Israelis, overshadowing the work of UNIFIL in the Lebanon, the Commonwealth and the OAU providing troops and observers in many of Africa's troubled areas from Uganda to Chad to Zimbabwe, and joint forces intervening in Zaire (once the Congo, ONUC's stomping ground) and the New Hebrides (Vanuatu).

The three roles that international organizations can perform – instrument, arena and actor – are not mutually exclusive. As can be seen, the United Nations has played, and does play, each role in international relations. The importance of each has changed over the years with the instrument element being dominant in the late 1940s and early 1950s, the actor capacity becoming of greater importance in Hammarskjold's term as Secretary-General and the role as a forum developing since the 1960s with the increase in membership and the new demands of the Third World.

On a smaller scale other international organizations, both governmental ones and INGOs, may find themselves taking on two or three roles. The European Community, for example, has been in the past an instrument by which the French Government could regulate the peaceful economic and political development of the Federal Republic of Germany and at the same time obtain German support for French agriculture, whilst the Federal Republic used it to gain access to the markets of other members and to obtain a place in the comity of nations after the defeat of the Second World War. The Community has also provided a forum within which a number of political problems ranging from aid to the Third World to international terrorism could be discussed by the member governments and, in some cases, common policies adopted. Finally, the institutions of the Community, in particular the Commission and, before it, the High Authority of the European Coal and Steel Community, have shown a propensity to act independent of the member states. The World Council of Churches, as an INGO, has also played the three roles though perhaps in different proportions. It has been used by some members to promote their ideas in certain areas – for example, the African and more radical European churches giving support to liberation movements; it has certainly provided an arena within which a whole range of views have been expressed; and its secretariat has occasionally acted without first hearing the expressed wishes of the membership, though this has rarely been done in such a way as to annoy the majority of members.

Some useful generalizations about the three roles of international organizations can be made.

If the constitutions of the organizations create strong institutions insulated from interference by the membership and with powerful resources – such as the ECSC of the 1950s – then it is more likely that they will perform the role of a relatively independent actor. If the members have constitutional safeguards which allow them to prevent the growth of strong institutions – as had been the case in the European Free Trade Association – then the organization is only

likely to function either as a forum for the membership as a whole or
as a tool for the furtherance of the policy of some members.

If an international organization has a membership dominated by
one powerful member, that organization is susceptible to being used
as a hegemonic instrument – rather as the USSR has used the Warsaw
Treaty Organization. Organizations whose members are of about the
same weight, EFTA after 1973 being an example, will be more
egalitarian by nature and thereby act as a meeting-place for equals.

Extent of membership may condition the ability of an international organization to accept certain roles. Whilst it would seem
that IGOs with a limited membership can play any of the three roles,
those organizations with near universal membership will find it
increasingly difficult to remain the instrument of a small group of
members or to be an active independent actor on the world stage.
This is the case with the UNO and a number of associated agencies. A
wide membership has ruled out domination over a period of time by
the USA, USSR or even Third World cabals. Whilst the growth in
membership in the 1950s and 1960s helped the central institutions to
take on a more active, independent role, now that the new members
are organized into their own groupings – G77 and the non-aligned
movement – the idea of a secretariat exercising too wide a discretion
of judgement has become almost as unacceptable to them as to the
Soviet and Western blocs. By their nature the universal institutions
will become forums within which a range of views will be expressed.

Functions of International Organizations

To return to the metaphor of the market place with which this
chapter opened, it can be seen that international organizations can
indeed play the role of instruments being used by those who bargain
in this place – as servants carrying messages, changing money to order
or acting as bodyguards; they can also be likened to that part of the
market place where the occupants meet to discuss, trade and settle
disputes – the forum; and they may also be given the likeness of a
participant in the market place, perhaps as powerful and as able to
mould events as some of the other traders and customers. All these
demonstrate possible roles of international organizations in international relations. How then might international organizations, in
whatever role, affect the working of the world market place, that is,
present-day international relations? This section will examine the
functions that international organizations may perform in the international system.

To answer such a question, some consideration must be given to the difficult problem of just how an international system works. An estimation of how international organizations affect the functioning of this system can then be attempted.

To function, any system needs resources in order to transform inputs into that system into outputs. This is what Almond and Powell call its *conversion function*. It also needs to *maintain and adapt* itself. Furthermore its relations with its surroundings have to be considered. This 'behaviour of the system as a unit in its relations to other social systems and the environment' represents its *capabilities* (1966, pp. 28–9).

In terms of our world market place how does this work? The market place consists 'of numerous more or less autonomous actors interacting in patterned ways to influence one another' – in other words, it is a system (Mansbach *et al.*, 1976, p. 5). The buyers and sellers trade, bargain, do business, threaten, cajole, form associations and groupings. From these people within the market place, certain demands are made on and support given to the system that is the market place – *inputs*. These supports and demands are **articulated** ('the streets should be cleaned', 'no trading on Sunday', 'we need better policing', 'someone should check weights and measures') and **aggregated** ('the street traders demand . . .', 'consumers want . . .', 'money changers request . . .'). The system itself has certain *resources* which often reflect its ability to maintain and adapt itself and its capabilities. For example, there may be the ethics of the market place established over the years – general **norms** that are commonplace and associated with the system of the market place: 'cheating customers is bad for business', 'dirty streets drive away trade'. Furthermore the system, to survive, needs new blood and so there may be an established method of **recruiting**, say, new stallholders. To live with change, the system may also provide that novices, as well as traditional traders, are well and truly inducted into the ways of the market – they are **socialized**. A system that has demands made on it – inputs – and which because of its resources is fairly resilient over time, responding to its environment, maintaining and adapting itself, will also produce *outputs* in the form of authoritative decisions that can be implemented. This can be done by **rule-making** ('By law: littering the streets is an offence'), **rule application** ('I arrest you for littering the pavement') and **rule adjudication** ('You are fined two days' wages for littering the streets'). Outputs may also be in the form of **information** (a public notice board in the market place) or certain **operations** (street cleaning) which are not directly connected to the process of rule-making, application and adjudication.

The international political system functions in a way not unlike our world market place imagined above. The participants in the system (governments, MNCs, IGOs, INGOs, individuals) are making constant demands on the set-up – that it should bring peace, redistribute wealth, increase wealth, satisfy religious or cultural requirements – and these demands are aggregated by states, groups, individuals acting together bilaterally, multilaterally, *ad hoc*, at conferences or in organizations. Despite appearances to the contrary, the system does have resources, however brittle they may be. There are certain generally accepted norms – agreements should be kept, genocide and slavery are bad; the system has recruited new actors – not only newly independent states but also the growing number of non-state actors that have appeared on the scene in the last hundred years; and a process of socialization exists by which states and non-state actors learn to consider not just their own requirements but those of the system as well. The international political system produces authoritative decisions that can be implemented, though this is not always done. Decisions may be made by the various actors meeting in small groups or in a large plenary session or they may be arrived at more formally. Efforts are also made to supervise such rules – to apply them and then adjudicate. Furthermore the system has a network of political communications and it offers some other services.

How then do international organizations, in their various roles as instruments, forums and actors, affect this functioning of the international political system?

Articulation and Aggregation

International organizations can perform the task of *interest articulation and aggregation* in international affairs just as national associations of like-minded people do within a national political system. Within a sovereign state a national union of miners brings together all those working in the coal-mining industry in order to voice their demands on the employers – better wages and working conditions – and on the political system – a more advanced welfare state, better retirement arrangements, compensation for coal-related illnesses – and to aggregate the interest of each individual miner, each pit, each region, each skill or job into a national voice. Sometimes groups may disagree with what is being said on their behalf by the national organization, and if this disenchantment is consistent enough they may dissociate themselves from the national leadership and form their own association.

Within a national political system the authoritative allocation of values – the decisions as to who gets what, when and how – is nominally conducted by a central authority – the government – with a number of institutions available through which these decisions may be affected by, say, trade unions, employers' associations, veterans' leagues, youth movements, religious bodies and political parties. The international system is not so structured: it lacks a central body to allocate values, let alone resources. Quite clearly this does not stop values, and resources, being allocated and this process is not totally one of states imposing their values (whether economic or political or even religious and cultural) on others and seizing resources for themselves. Much of this allocation is still done by agreement, however reluctantly, and this is usually preceded by a process of discussion and negotiation. International organizations, being one of the institutionalized forms of contact between the active participants in the international system, are forums for such discussion and negotiation. Like the institutions of government on a national level, they provide groups having common interests with a focus of activity. International organizations in fact operate in three ways in this context: they can be instruments for interest articulation and aggregation (rather like the national union of mineworkers in the national example), or they can be forums in which those interests are articulated, or they can articulate interests separate from those of members.

Many INGOs are instruments of interest articulation and aggregation on an international plane. Examples of this are the World Zionist Congress which brings together the supporters of the state of Israel and Zionism and is used to voice the demands of these groups at the international level; the International Chamber of Shipping which aggregates shipowners' interests; and the Campaign for a World Constituent Assembly which acts as a voice for world governmentalists. An example of an INGO acting as a forum for interest articulation would be that of the World Council of Churches where the participants form groups and temporary coalitions on particular issues such as human rights, world poverty and disarmament. They can also be actors in the articulation and aggregation process: the Salvation Army is one such INGO which puts forward its own views and demands on the international system, for example in the World Council of Churches before it parted ways with that organization over the financing of liberation movements.

Certain IGOs with a tightly-knit membership and closely-defined aims may act as instruments of interest articulation and aggregation. This was probably the case with OPEC which behaved rather like an oil exporters' 'trade union' in the middle and end of the 1970s.

On the whole IGOs tend to be stages for interest articulation and aggregation with the various contending sections forming into 'blocs' or 'groups'. The United Nations Conference on Trade and Development (UNCTAD) – which now has regular meetings and a permanent secretariat – has even formalized members into groups which, it is assumed, have aggregate interests to articulate in matters of trade and development: the Western industrialized states, the Soviet Bloc countries, the Third World (G77) and a few independents such as China. The International Labour Organization provides an example of interests being aggregated not just in blocs of countries but across national divisions. Each member state's delegation to the General Conference is divided into three autonomous sections, two members representing the government, one the employers and one the work-people (Article 3 (1) of the Constitution of the ILO). The chance arises for representatives of the employees to combine together and those of the employers to unite, with the governmental representatives playing an important intermediary role. However this threefold division is not always so obvious, as in many states employers' and employees' associations are not free from government direction.

When considering the resources of the domestic political system it can be seen that various organizations – political parties, trade unions, religious associations, pressure groups – help to maintain and adapt the system. They promote certain norms, recruit new participants into the system and take part in the process of socialization by which others are encouraged to consider the needs of the system as well as their own requirements. Whether these resources are sufficient to keep a domestic political system functioning, let alone allowing it to adapt to changing conditions, will depend on the various values promoted, the membership recruited and the efficacy of socialization. A deeply divided political system with ideological differences over accepted norms, where new members are not being recruited to take part in the politics of the system and where individual members look after their own concerns to the detriment of any collective need, will not be a strong system.

Norms

International organizations have made a considerable contribution as instruments, forums and actors to the normative activities of the international political system. Some of the earlier INGOs in the nine-teenth century were concerned with establishing world-wide certain values that were already accepted in the more economically-advanced West European and North American states – the rejection of slavery (the Anti-Slavery Society), control of the effects of war (the International Committee of the Red Cross), protection of less sophisticated peoples (Aborigines Protection Society). The establishment of norms in international relations has now become a complex process to which a wide range of IGOs as well as INGOs contribute.

The UN Charter itself provides a set of values for the international system in its preamble where 'we the people' reaffirmed their 'faith in fundamental human rights', 'in the equal rights of men and women and of nations large and small' and determined 'to promote social progress and better standards of life in larger freedom'. Furthermore Chapter I, Purposes and Principles, outlines the concern with the suppression of acts of aggression, the support of the principles of international law, peaceful settlement and international co-operation. A specific proclamation can be found in the Universal Declaration of Human Rights, adopted by the UN General Assembly in December 1948 'as a common standard of achievement for all peoples and all nations' and which includes reference to personal human rights, social and economic rights as well as 'the development of friendly relations between nations'. In the field of justice and social welfare a network of a number of IGOs under the auspices of the UN family has been established and underpinned by a system of consultation of and support by the INGOs. These have formalized already existing sets of norms – for example in the UN Convention for the Suppression of the Traffic in Persons (1949) – or have amended existing conventions (the 1926 Slavery Convention was amended in 1953) or articulated relatively new normative values in their conventions against genocide and apartheid.

In the field of economic affairs, international organizations have helped establish norms of behaviour. Again the UN and its associated agencies have played a leading role in both encouraging and reflecting the setting of standards for the functioning of the world economy. After the experience of the interwar depression, it was not surprising that the Bretton Woods meeting of 1944 set up institutions which stressed the universality of the economic system and the need to utilize the globe's resources. With the coming to independence of former colonial countries since 1947, emphasis has shifted towards the development of these new states and their right to control their own resources – a right reflected in the 1974 Charter of Economic Rights and Duties of States which proclaimed

> Every state has and shall freely exercise full permanent sovereignty, including possession, use and disposal, over all its wealth, natural resources and economic activities. (Article 2)

Meetings of UNCTAD, the UN Industrial Development Organization (UNIDO) and the Sixth and Seventh Special Sessions of the UN General Assembly elaborated on these statements to the extent that UN evocations on the world economy are now quite different from those advanced at Bretton Woods in 1944 – the emphasis being less on expanding trade and more on the disposal of economic benefits. Another shift over the past decades has been the concern with the qualitative side of the world economy: the framework has been established for population policies at the World Population Conferences, and for ecological policies in the Declaration on the Human Environment.

In the field of international security, standards are also accepted which have been the work of the UNO and other international organizations. Harold Jacobsen divides the normative activities of international organizations in such areas into five categories: refining principles against the use of force; delegitimizing Western colonialism; pronouncing on specific situations; urging disarmament and arms control; exhorting states to arm. Examples of the first category include requirements prohibiting intervention in the affairs of independent states as outlined in the charters of the OAS, the OAU and the Arab League, as well as the 1965 General Assembly declaration on the Inadmissibility of Intervention in the Domestic Affairs of States and the Protection of their Independence and Sovereignty. Delegitimizing Western colonialism can be found not only in the statements of INGOs such as the Afro–Asian Peoples' Solidarity Organization but also in the output of the General Assembly following on Resolution 1514 in December 1960 on the Granting of Independence to Colonial Countries and Peoples. International organizations have also been used in the process of 'collective legitimization' to approve or disapprove of specific actions by particular countries – the UN on Portuguese colonialism or Israel's activities, the OAS against Cuba and in support of US action, NATO condemning the USSR action in Hungary, Czechoslovakia, Poland and Afghanistan. A wide range of INGOs and IGOs have also dealt with the question of armaments – how to abolish them or control them. Ranging from the Quaker (Society of Friends) pacifist groups to the UN Committee on Disarmament, international organizations have been prominent in this question. It is, however, fair to say that on such a problem, dealing as it does with the core area of national security, states have been more willing to negotiate agreements either bilaterally (Strategic Arms Limitation Talks between the USA and the USSR) or multilaterally outside the major UN forums (the Treaty Banning Nuclear Weapon Tests in the Atmosphere, in Outer Space, and Under Water, 1963). The exhortation to arm is expressed by organizations that offer selective collective defence, such as NATO and WTO, with part of the agreement by the members being an agreement on the norm of a certain level of armed force.

International organizations have played an important part in the world's institutions which have helped create norms in international relations, though it should be noted that a number of these values are fairly weak and many are also contradictory.

Recruitment

International organizations can have an important function in the *recruitment* of participants in the international political system. The fact that IGOs consist almost exclusively of representatives of sovereign states gives a further incentive to non-self-governing territories to achieve their independence. This allows them to represent their own interests in a range of IGOs and brings those organizations closer to universality of membership. In theory membership of an IGO may require a little more than that the prospective state be sovereign. For example, the UN Charter allows membership

> to all peace-loving states which accept the obligations contained in the present Charter and, in the judgment of the Organization, are able and willing to carry out these obligations. (Article 3 (1))

It may appear that this paragraph and Article 6, which allows for the expulsion from the UN of a state that has persistently violated the Principle of the Charter, encourage states joining the international political system, as manifested in the United Nations Organization, to recognize a certain minimal standard of behaviour. However, exclusion from the UN has almost always been on political grounds through the veto of a permanent member of the Security Council and members of the Organization have been remarkably lax in excluding or expelling states on the grounds cited under Articles 3 (1) and 6. Furthermore it is generally accepted that it is governments rather than states that are peace-loving or not, and the usual way of condemnation of warlike activities has been the non-seating of governmental representatives. This was the case in the UN with the Communist Chinese Government after 1949 (especially after its involvement in the Korean War) and the Heng Samrin regime established in Kampuchea (Cambodia) by the Vietnamese in 1979. The irony of the latter case was that a majority of members rejected the Vietnamese-backed regime because it had been established by an invasion of Kampuchea but they were prepared to accept the indigenous Pol Pot Government (which the Vietnamese had evicted) despite its genocidal record. This illustrates the tension between making universal organizations such as the UN truly global forums covering all countries and the need to uphold certain accepted norms, particularly when this is being done by existing UN members using the organization as an instrument for the furtherance of their policy – the USA in the case of China, South-East Asian states and China in the case of Kampuchea.

INGOs have increasingly recruited new participants to the international political system. By gathering together groups and individuals for a particular purpose, whether supporting world government, promoting trade union activity, furthering commercial interests or spreading religious beliefs, they have mobilized what must be regarded as the fastest growing and widest based group of participants in the current international political system. They have brought into the old nineteenth-century state-centred system new actors. They provide the underpinning for a more close-knit international system and for the intergovernmental organizations. This is recognized by the observer and consultative status granted to many INGOs by the leading IGOs such as the UN Economic and Social Council, ILO, FAO, UNESCO and UNCTAD (*Yearbook of International Organizations*, 1974, p. S25).

Socialization

Socialization is carried out within the nation state by a number of agencies. Its aim is to instil in the individual loyalty to the system within which he or she is living and to gain acceptance of the prevailing values of that system and its institutions. Schools, churches and youth clubs can all be used as agents of socialization. In newly independent states the armed forces may be the main instrument of socialization inculcating loyalty to the country, its flag, anthem and president instead of a feeling of identification with a smaller group such as a regional nation, a tribe or the family. Whilst a government may have a number of instruments of socialization available to it – compulsory schooling, military service, state-run youth groups, political parties – it is rarely without competition. This may be in the form of more traditional socialization – through the family or the tribe – the values of which clash with those of the government, or they may be organizations such as trade unions preaching workers' solidarity or a church teaching Christian values in opposition to the belief system of the state. The effect of the existence of such groups that have undergone their own socialization quite different from that of the ruling elite can be destabilizing. Communist-ruled Poland provides an example: throughout the 1970s the government there was unable to impose its will on a people who had on the whole resisted the agents of socialization provided by the Communist Party but had accepted those of the Catholic Church.

As there is no world government, the forces of socialization at an international level can be expected to be weaker than those within the state. The process of socialization works at two levels internationally. Agents of socialization may work across frontiers affecting directly individuals and groups in a number of countries. Multinational corporations have taken a powerful lead here. Barnet and Muller (1975, p. 13) quote Aurelio Peccei, a Fiat director, as claiming that the global corporation 'is the most powerful agent for the internationalization of human society' and another director as describing such corporations as 'agents of change, socially, economically and culturally' (p. 31). INGOs may not have the wealth, expertise and manpower of transnational corporations but they too can seek to affect peoples' systems of belief and patterns of behaviour by a process of socialization. The International Olympic Committee attempts to further the ideals of Baron de Coubertin amongst the world's athletes whilst the Boys Brigade and the Scout movement spread similar values to the youth of many countries. Among the IGOs the European Community probably has the most sophisticated instruments of socialization. Through Community institutions such as the Commission, the Economic and Social Committee, the Parliament and the Court of Justice, a 'Community spirit' can be fostered among the various interest groups dealing with the Communities and among the citizens of the member countries. These institutions are by no means as strong as the national ones but neither are they necessarily in direct competition with the nation state for citizen loyalty: the idea still exists that one can be a good Community citizen and a good Frenchman, Dane or Irishman. Although many interest groups tend to use Community institutions to further their own ends and are not especially interested in the 'message', the extent of Community feeling fostered among the people of the original six EEC member states is noticeable. Surveys have shown a degree of Community identification yet to be experienced in the newer members such as the United Kingdom, Denmark and Greece. A process of socialization brought about by a mixture of informal contacts, non-institutionalized formal contacts, INGOs and IGOs is apparent in the Nordic area where it has led to 'the establishment of increasingly integrated Nordic societal conditions in most spheres of life' (Nielsson, 1978, p. 306).

Secondly, the process of socialization can take place between states acting at the international level and between their representatives. In other words, over a period of time states' governments can become 'socialized' to act in a certain way that is acceptable to the rest of the international community or to adopt a certain common value system. A classic example was that of the new Bolshevik Russian Government which after renouncing 'bourgeois' diplomacy in 1917 soon found itself an outcast in international society and eventually started to re-adopt most of the norms of accepted diplomacy in order that it might obtain the benefits of international commerce and of the security provided for by bilateral treaties and, eventually, membership of the League of Nations.

Organizations such as the League of Nations and the United Nations are voluntary by nature – states are not compelled to become members or stay members – so the sanctions against asocial behaviour are few. The League attempted to socialize members into following set procedures for the settlement of disputes (as laid down in Articles 12–16) with sanctions against any 'outlaws'. During the 1930s it became clear that states could behave unsocially towards countries outside the European pale – in Manchuria or Abyssinia for example – with only ineffectual recourse to or punishment by other League members. When it suited the others they were prepared to stigmatize the Soviet Union by expulsion from the League for its invasion of Finland in 1939.

The members of the UNO seem even more tolerant than their pre-war predecessors. Both because there is no longer agreement over what should constitute social behaviour internationally now that the standards of European diplomacy and international law have been challenged by the Soviet Bloc and the Third World countries and because UN members rate universal membership so highly, there has been a great reluctance to condemn other states, let alone expel them from the UN for asocial activities. Israel after its takeover of Jerusalem and the Golan Heights and its invasion of Lebanon, apartheid South Africa, Idi Amin's Uganda, Pol Pot's Kampuchea, Iran after United States embassy staff had been taken hostage in 1979, the Soviet Union after its invasion of Afghanistan and Argentina after its occupation of the Falkland Islands in April 1982, all remained UN members.

Despite this unwillingness to use sanctions – whether moral or actual – against the asocial, international organizations have not been totally ineffective in the socialization process. A study by R. L. Butterworth in 1978 of the UNO , the OAS, the OAU, the Arab League and the Council of Europe concluded that

> The institutionalization of shared norms and perceptions will enhance the force of national reputation and organizational precedent in effecting interstate cooperation ... Habits of co-operation will enhance the importance of policies that simulate compliant behaviour through consensus, rather than coercion ...

The organizations contribute by encouraging members to act in a co-operative way and, in particular, not to undermine the norms that they share with other members: the stress is on 'establishing dependable and enduring patterns of behaviour'. The study attributes to the OAS, the UNO and the OAU a degree of success in registering and contributing to moderation by its members, whilst the League of Arab States and the Council of Europe have had less success (ch. 8). This seems to give some credence to the idea that states can be socialized into a particular pattern of behaviour by membership of an international organization.

Rule-Making

The function of *rule-making* in international organization is more obvious than that of socialization. Unlike the domestic political system, the international system has no central formal rule-making institution such as a government or a parliament. It should be noted that even in the domestic system there are often a number of subsidiary rule-making institutions apart from the most obvious governmental ones. Local or regional governments often have such powers delegated to them and a number of bodies ranging from the civil service to trade unions and private associations make rules for the internal running of their organizations. It is not surprising that the sources of rules are more diverse in the international field with the absence of world government: they may be based on the acceptance of past practice or on *ad hoc* arrangements or they may be founded in bilateral legal agreements between states or they may emanate from international organizations.

Paul Tharp (1971, p. 5) lists the traditional 'confederal' principles on which most international organizations have based their rule-making:

1 The rules are formulated by unanimous or near-unanimous consensus of members.
2 Members have the practical option of leaving an organization and ending their assent to the existing rules.
3 Even within the bounds of membership, a state can assert the right to interpret unilaterally rules to which it has consented.
4 The 'executive–bureaucratic' structure of the organization has little or no power to formulate (and implement) rules.
5 Delegates to the organizations' rule-making bodies are instructed by their governments and do not act as independent representatives.

6   The international organization 'has no direct relationship with private citizens of the member states'.

This leaves the formulation of rules – and their acceptance – in the hands of an organization's member states and downgrades any possible autonomous role by the institutions of the organization itself. Even so, the function of providing a focus for the setting of rules is an important one, regardless of the technical process used by the organization. Some are almost exclusively dedicated to rule-making (or, in some cases, rule-changing) whether they be the specialist organization such as the International Building Classification Committee or the wide-ranging Third United Nations Conference on the Law of the Sea. Other institutions have an element of rule-making in their work: the United Nations General Assembly sometimes performs this task by adopting resolutions or conventions on questions such as diplomatic practice, highjacking or relations with South Africa. Few organizations, including INGOs, have no rule-making capacity for the simple reason that the membership has to agree on rules for the running of the organization itself. Indeed sometimes it is just these rules that can cause greatest trouble: this was the case in 1965 when the French Government boycotted meetings of the Council of Ministers of the EEC, ostensibly over the new regulations for the Common Agricultural Policy but in fact over the questions of majority decisions in the Council and the role of the Commission of the Community.

The European Community provides the most advanced model of another type of institution when judged on the criteria of rule-making: that which has advanced beyond the 'confederal' model mentioned by Tharp and which can make its own rules independent of the wishes of the member states. This represents a move towards a more 'federal' model with a central rule-making institution which the various parts (member states) are obliged to obey. As yet the Community has not advanced so far and only certain of its institutions can be called supranational (that is, existing above rather than between states). The Community Court clearly makes rules by its judgements which can be applicable throughout the Community and the Commission pours out administrative rules, especially in connection with the Common Agricultural Policy. Furthermore both these bodies can have direct dealings with private citizens, interest groups and firms in each of the member states. However the major rule-setting institution is still the Council of Ministers which is dominated by member states' representation and leans towards the 'confederal' description.

Rule Application

What has been said here about the formulation of rules in such organizations as the European Community touches also on the function of *rule application*. In the domestic political system rule application is undertaken mostly by government agencies – and *in extremis* by the police, militia, or armed forces. In the international political system rule application is left mainly to sovereign states as there is no central world authority with agents to undertake the task.

Under certain circumstances international organizations take on aspects of applying generally accepted rules. Their supervision has been the task of organizations such as the Trusteeship Council, which concerns itself with the keeping of the conditions of the International Trusteeship System (Chapter XII of the UN Charter), the Committee on Information on Non-Self Governing Territories which attempted a similar monitoring task for colonial areas under Article 73e of the UN Charter and the 'Committee of 24' which replaced the Committee on Information in 1961 and attempted a more vigorous implementation of the anti-colonial Declaration on the Granting of Independence to Colonial Countries and Peoples (Resolution 1514 (XV)). As the 'Committee of 24' received little co-operation from colonizing states such as the United Kingdom, France, Portugal and Spain, its effectiveness was somewhat curtailed. IGOs have been more active in the application of agreed rules in the field of nuclear energy – the International Atomic Energy Agency has wide powers which allow it to keep track of the spread and use of fissionable materials. INGOs have participated in the monitoring of international rule application by governments. The three major international trade union groupings – the International Confederation of Free Trade Unions, the World Confederation of Labour and the World Federation of Trade Unions – have actively fed complaints into the ILO's Committee on Freedom of Association which then investigates the cases, a process that may lead to moral pressure being placed on states breaking ILO conventions. The International Committee of the Red Cross supervises the application of the rules of war and conflict in many parts of the world. Amnesty International and the various international pressure groups of indigenous peoples, aboriginal rights and human rights participate in the implementation of the UN Universal Declaration of Human Rights. Again their most telling means of 'enforcement' is publicity and moral pressures – methods which are, after all, used in rule application in domestic society.

What is lacking in international rule application is a means of enforcement when pleading, persuasion and pressure fail. Chapter

VII of the UN Charter contains the instrumental potential for enforcing decisions in the case of 'any threat to the peace, breach of the peace, or act of aggression' but, as mentioned previously (pp. 144–7) this section can rarely be used in a period of superpower conflict. Should the two superpowers agree that a certain settlement should be 'enforced', then an international organization such as the UN can act either as the instrument for this policy or at least as a forum within which a bargain might be struck. The Security Council agreed from 1965 to 1968 that economic sanctions against the illegal white minority regime in Rhodesia should be enforced and this task was partly delegated to the British navy whose 'Beira run' off the coast of Mozambique checked sanction-breaking imports of petroleum headed for Rhodesia. After the Yom Kippur War between Israel and Egypt plus Syria in October 1973, the two superpowers agreed on a particular ceasefire and were prepared to see the United Nations re-establish UNEF under Security Council control – and with some NATO and Warsaw Pact contribution – for the purpose of ensuring the disengagement around the Suez Canal.

International organizations as instruments or forums for rule application fit into the more traditional 'confederal' principles outlined by Tharp. As with rule-making, the European Community may claim to be less 'confederal' and more 'federal'. It is part of the task of the Commission to make sure that the laws of the Community are applied within the member countries and the Commission may take a law-breaker to the European Court if necessary. To a great extent the actual enforcement of Community law is undertaken by the agents of the member governments – the local authorities, the ministries, the boards and agencies – as if it were purely domestic law. Indeed the member states have incorporated Community law into their own domestic legal framework and have accepted the authority of the Community Court. The EC has mobilized its member states to perform the task of rule application for it. Problems arise, however, when the deliberate policy of a member state is contrary to Community policy and that state insists on applying *its* policy, for example a subsidy to agriculture not agreed by the EC. Here enforcement of Community policy rests either on the final sanction of the state realizing that it will lose other benefits if it insists on breaking the rules and alienating the other EC members or on the state's government bowing to the judgement of the Court or on a political agreement to change the rules so that they become more acceptable to the renegade state. The latter can happen within sovereign states – governments change legislation which has been openly broken by powerful groups such as trade unions or multinational corporations but for a government – or for the European Community – to do this too often weakens both confidence in its political system and its credibility as an applier of rules.

Rule Adjudication

Within the state *rule adjudication* is normally carried out by the judiciary – law courts, arbitration panels, tribunals and so forth. The process is closely associated with that of rule-making as courts can by their judgements develop or interpret the law in such a way that new standards are set. However, the prime aim is to pronounce on existing law and the judicial institutions are normally not involved in the political process of law-making. The process of rule adjudication at the international level lacks the extensive institutions and compulsory nature of that at nation state level. As with rule-making, there is a great deal of rule adjudication that arises from the existence of international organizations – that associated with their internal running – but a more important function is played by certain institutions whose task it is to adjudicate between the competing claims of states. The most noticeable of these institutions are the International Court of Justic (ICJ) – the Permanent Court of International Justice (PCIJ) in the interwar period – and the Permanent Court of Arbitration. Using Tharp's criteria mentioned above, these organizations exhibit a 'confederal' nature meaning that, on the whole, states have to consent to disputes being heard by them. Some of the more geographically-confined judicial institutions, such as the Court of the European Community or that of the Council of Europe, are less permissive by nature. In some cases organizations that do not have courts or panels or arbitrators still carry out a rule-adjudication function. The European Free Trade Association (EFTA) has a complaints procedure by which the Council of Ministers – minus the state which is the subject of the complaint – judge whether the free trade area rules have been frustrated.

Because of the lack of a universally accepted and comprehensive corpus of international law and the permissive nature of enforcement of any laws, the process of rule adjudication at the international level is more difficult than at the national level and there is more frequent resort to political settlement in order that rules may be accepted. It is noticeable that the politically open industrialized Western democracies have tended to make greatest use of the PCIJ and ICJ (Rochester, 1974, pp. 31–6) probably because the sort of established international law on which those courts depended was that formulated by the trading nations of Western Europe and North America. It is difficult to foresee a thriving future for such courts outside those based on some form of cultural unity and political agreement as in

Western Europe, though even these have not been without their problems.

Information

International organizations also perform certain activities within the international political system which are useful but are not directly involved in the conversion function of the system or in its maintenance and adaptation. They are invaluable in *communication and information*. The more traditional approach towards transmitting ideas and messages in the system was through national governments with the help of their diplomatic services. The growth in international organizations together with the increased and easier use of the media of communications has meant that sovereign states can no longer pretend to be dominant in the exchange of international information. The creation of global organizations such as the UN and its associated agencies has produced a forum for governments – the part of the market place where they can issue and receive information. The UN and its agencies act as providers of information as attested by the vast amount of printed material they produce, in particular statistical data. The World Weather Watch of the World Meteorological Organization provides valuable information as do the scientific services of the World Health Organization and the Food and Agriculture Organization. Some INGOs perform similar roles of providing a particular public with the knowledge it seeks whether it be the specialist work of the International League against Rheumatism or the more widespread work of the Boy Scouts World Bureau. Such organizations perform these functions in a dual role of forums within which members may meet and exchange ideas and actors which present their own output of information. The European Community comes into the latter category with its vast information network issuing not only official documents in eight languages but also journals such as *Europe* in the United Kingdom with its twelve associated editions in other countries – for example, *EF-avisen* in Denmark, *Communidad europea* in Spain and *Community Report* in Ireland.

Operations

Finally, international organizations undertake a number of *operational* functions much in the same way as governments. These may be banking (International Bank for Reconstruction and Development, the Bank for International Settlements), providing aid (UN agencies), helping refugees (UN High Commission for Refugees), dealing with commodities (the European Community in its Common Agricultural and Common External Tariff policies) and running technical services (INTELSAT). These activities are ones not covered by other headings such as rule application and may include the UN peace observation corps. The INGOs also make a contribution – especially in the aid area with well-known names such as the International Red Cross, Caritas and War on Want prominent.

Conclusion

It can be seen that international organizations – IGOs and INGOs – play important roles and undertake particular functions in the world market place. It is difficult to imagine the contemporary world without them. In such a case sovereign states would contact each other by the traditional means of diplomacy, at most conference diplomacy. National groupings and individuals might well have contact with those sharing common interests in other parts of the world but this relationship would not be formalized into a continuous structure with members from several states. Forums for discussion and exchange would be less frequent and would be one-off occasions with no certainty of any continuity. Governments and groupings trying to further their own ends internationally would have fewer instruments to use. Those tools available would be national ones, thereby avoiding the pressure for compromise, the socialization process that comes with membership of an organization which one does not totally control. There would be no international organization acting in an independent role, no bodies willing to take up the tasks refused by sovereign states and national groups.

The international political system would still function, but less effectively. Demands by national groupings would be articulated and aggregated on a more *ad hoc* basis and the resources of the system would be less visible and probably more unevenly distributed. More than now they would tend to be the resources – the norms, values, the protégés – of dominant regional powers or of a prevailing superpower. The outputs of the system would be more irregular and rule-making, application and adjudication more dependent on national decisions than at the moment. Information, communication and operational activities would also be in national or private hands.

The number of international organizations has grown precisely because they have a function which cannot be fulfilled by national states and groupings. In their roles as instruments, forums and actors they perform functions that help to keep the international political system working. To what extent they may be able to help it adapt to new circumstances will be discussed in the next chapter.

5

International Organizations – the Future

At the end of the historical account in Chapter 1, the dynamic element in international organizations was introduced. These institutions form part of the present international system built up since the end of the Napoleonic Wars. A world with a different configuration of states – or indeed with no sovereign states as we know them – would present a different prospect than the present post-colonial, nuclear, superpower-dominated polity.

Some of the works cited in Chapter 3 give an indication of how future developments may affect international organizations. The approach of the realist school confines international organizations to a very restricted future with the only developments being those allowed for by the member states in pursuit of their national interests. The functionalist view of the future stresses international organizations serving humankind across state frontiers. Their aspiration is to make the old nation state redundant. The neo-functionalists have attenuated this view of the future by accepting regional-based functional organizations and by emphasizing the importance of their having a political authority that can actively sap away the strength of sovereign state governments. On the other hand the 'one-world' globalists hope for the development of institutions that will serve the needs of the planet rather than the demands of a small elite of a minority species – mankind. Marxist writers see a progressive advancement towards a communist world in which there are no oppressors and no oppressed, no want, no war, no divisions into classes or states. By definition interstate organizations would also have withered away though it is conceivable that world-wide interest organizations would continue, linking together those who play chess, football or even baseball in the free time provided by the communist millennium. Third World writers who stand outside the Marxist mainstream have tended either to recommend that international organizations should develop symbiotic North–South relations in order to create a fairer, more secure world (the reformist approach) or to suggest that they should act as instruments against imperialist exploitation and for co-operation between Third World states (the more revolutionary approach).

These viewpoints tend to prescribe how international organizations should develop in the sort of world the authors hope to see in the future. These prescriptions, dependent on change in the international political system, have consequences for the types of international organizations that might exist (if any) and their roles and functions. Should this book be re-written after the triumph of functionalism or the achievement of world communist society, then Chapters 2 and 4 would have a completely different content. In the case of the arrival of communism, such an effort would be considered superfluous, a mere rummaging in the dustbin of history.

Believers in an ideology – Marxism, free market competition, Islam, Christianity – tend to accept the inevitability of its complete triumph. Indeed one of these viewpoints – or one of the many others – may eventually prevail, sweeping all before it, or mankind may first destroy itself and the planet. Until that time, we seem to face a future with a variety of belief systems, each with significant support, co-existing in this world. At the moment, this plurality is reflected in the international political system. However, the present balance of forces within this system may change as may the nature of the system itself. The rest of this chapter will extrapolate the present trends in the position of international organizations and will evaluate an alternative development.

The Probable Future

It has been previously stated (p. 31) that the growth in the number of IGOs is likely to decline and their number remain at approximately 300, whilst the number of INGOs (at present about 3,000) could well grow to 9,600 by the turn of the century, even given a modest rate of increase. Such an extension of present trends does not allow for the demise of IGOs and INGOs and sheer numbers alone offer little information about the aims and activities of these organizations or about their continued role and function in the international system. It is perhaps unreasonable to assume that international organizations will develop until the end of this century in approximately the same way as since the mid-1960s, but such a supposition is nevertheless a good starting point. For the sake of clarity, this overview will divide international governmental organizations into those dealing with questions of international peace and security, and those covering economic and social questions.

IGOs dealing with Peace and Security

The major IGO at present concerned with international peace and security is the UN, in particular the Security Council. Current threats to world peace are manifold and enduring: superpower conflict reflected in the arms race; the precarious balance of the two major nuclear arsenals and the proliferation of weapons of mass destruction to non-superpower states; the extension of Soviet–US confrontation into the Third World; indigenous Third World disputes; intra-state and trans-border conflict.

During the 1950s and 1960s the UN was prominent in at least freezing many Third World disputes and trying to prevent the superpowers from being drawn into post-colonial conflicts in Palestine, Kashmir, Suez, Cyprus, Congo, Yemen, Western Iran, Laos and Lebanon. Since the mid-1950s the superpowers have continued to deal directly with each other over strategic matters, although the spirit of detente of the late 1960s and early 1970s had retreated by the end of the 1970s. During the 1970s and early 1980s the superpowers have become increasingly directly involved in Third World conflicts – the Soviet Union supporting Vietnam in its conflicts with surrounding countries after US troops had left Indochina; Soviet activity in Afghanistan, Angola, Ethiopia, Mozambique and South Yemen; the United States involvement in Chile, El Salvador and Iran; and the deeper commitment of both in the intricacies of the Middle East. There has also been an increased propensity by Third World countries to ignore the resolutions of the United Nations – Israel over Jerusalem, the West Bank, the Golan Heights and Lebanon; Iran in the case of US embassy hostages in 1979–81; Iraq and Iran in their Gulf War; and Argentina's invasion of the Falklands.

Fear of losing control could lead to further attempts by the superpowers to bolster their position in the Third World: the USA in Central America, the Caribbean and, possibly, the Middle East; the USSR in Central Asia and parts of Africa. A wider range of Third World conflicts might be expected in Africa, the Middle East, Latin America and the Pacific Basin, making a greater demand on peacekeeping operations and 'good offices'. Whilst the UN may still be the major centre for necessary diplomatic activity, it is possible that *ad hoc* peacekeepers and observers (such as the Western multilateral force used in Beirut to oversee the Palestinian evacuation in August

1982) and the more limited membership international organizations such as the OAU, the OAS, the Commonwealth of Nations and ASEAN, might play an increased role. In turn, such tasks would place more stress on the fabric of these organizations, leading to internal dissension and even deadlock. Meanwhile the two superpowers would continue their bilateral negotiations concerning weapons and force levels. Whilst any results of such negotiations may receive UN blessing, the Organization is unlikely to contribute much to their achievement. The disappointment of the Second UN Special Session on Disarmament in 1982 showed once again that the path to control and limitation of arms does not pass through the discussion chambers of the United Nations. At the same time this will not stop the various organs of the UN from making declaratory statements on questions of international peace and security and drawing up conventions on particular aspects of the subject. This can be seen as a continuation of rhetoric in the absence of ability to act independently. Under such conditions, the UN will be of decreasing use even as a forum for the discussion of threats to international peace and security, once countries realize the fruitlessness of taking disputes to the Security Council or General Assembly.

IGOs Dealing with Economic and Social Questions

The present IGOs dealing with economic and social questions, broadly defined, are currently faced with an uphill task. The size of economic and social problems has grown purely because the Earth's population has mushroomed since the Second World War, increasing by about a billion from 1945 to 3·4 billion in 1965 and then by another billion up to 1980. This in itself has created a problem of feeding, housing and educating an extra 2 billion people since 1945 on the same basis as the original $2\frac{1}{2}$ billion. However, the situation is not so simple. The growth in world population has taken place in those areas with the least utilized resources – the world has just been adding to its numbers of poor, underfed, diseased, unhoused and illiterate. At the same time a shift of population from the land to the city has taken place, adding to urban congestion, most noticeably in the Third World. Too often resources have been misused, maldistributed or eroded away.

The post-war institutions established to deal with social and economic problems – the UN and its specialized agencies, the Bretton Woods system, regional agencies – have found increasing difficulties in carrying out their tasks. Growing challenges have been met by reduced budgets, inefficient bureaucracies and greater national interference. Another phenomenon has been the series of megaconferences and joint organizations established by the UN to deal with certain social and economic problems: the UN World Population Conferences followed by the UN Fund for Population Activities; the 1972 UN Conference on the Human Environment leading to the Environment Programme Secretariat being established in Nairobi; the UN Conferences on Desertification; the World Food Programme; the 1975 UN 'Women's Conference'; the 1982 Vienna meeting on ageing; and the longest running one of all – the Third UN Conference on the Law of the Sea. In some cases the number of IGOs dealing with a particular subject has grown surprisingly: by 1972 eight specialized agencies and regional UN agencies, as well as the EC, NATO, OECD and the Council of Europe, were dealing with environmental questions in Europe (Johnson, 1972, pp. 124–34). Organizations dealing with a limited topic such as whaling have multiplied as the number of whales has declined.

A continuation of present trends in economic and social IGOs seems to point to larger bureaucracies, more politicized and less effective organizations, and conferences forever defining problems and setting rules but without the wherewithal to enforce decisions. As the Titanic sinks, the orchestra is quarrelling over which music should be played.

A Better Alternative?

Humanity's future may be a continuation of these disorders projected into the next century on a grander scale. Stubborn or weak governments being overwhelmed by lack of resources and widespread challenges do not produce a sound foundation on which IGOs may develop their functions in the international system (as outlined on pp. 152–4 above), let alone become the basis for a truly global governance of world issues.

Modest reforms undertaken by governments and IGOs alike could transform the scene into one of hope. 'The Brandt Report' (Independent Commission on International Development Issues, 1980) outlined the economic and social problems being faced by the world and recommended a common action programme. This included greater assistance to the least developed states, agrarian reform and international food security for the undernourished part of the globe, aid for population and resource management policies, a diversion of resources from armaments into development, a strengthening of the infrastructure of developing states, stabilization and expansion of the commodity market, conservation of energy, control of transnationals, reform of the world monetary system and a more generous transfer of resources to the Third World to alleviate poverty (pp.

282–92). The Report chose, on the whole, to utilize existing institutions including international organizations to carry out such reforms. Emphasis was placed on replenishing the IMF, the IDA and the Regional Development Banks; on using the UN Development Programme, the International Fund for Agricultural Development, the UN Fund for Population Activities and the UN Revolving Fund for Natural Resource Exploration; on strengthening UN Regional Economic Commissions; and on establishing more effective international commodity agreements.

'The Palme Report' (Independent Commission on Disarmament and Security Issues, 1982) examined current questions of peace and security and concluded that

> [a] doctrine of common security must replace the present expedient of deterrence through armaments. International peace must rest on a commitment to joint survival rather than a threat of mutual destruction. (p. 139)

The Commission – consisting of diplomats and statesmen – recommended a programme of arms control and disarmament, cutting qualitative arms competition, building confidence between states, strengthening the UN security system, encouraging regional approaches to security and ensuring economic security.

Institutional aspects are prominent in this move toward a more secure and peaceful world. Reference is made to 'the need to strengthen the security role of the United Nations' with the Security Council encouraging the Secretary-General to bring to its immediate attention threats to international peace and security, as he is entitled to do under Article 99 of the UN Charter (pp. 161–2). Also recommended is the adoption by the Security Council of collective security measures with fact-finding missions, military observer teams and UN forces to deter aggression, all facilitated by a 'concordat' between the permanent members of the Council (pp. 162–4). The Military Staff Committee, foreseen in Article 43 of the Charter, would be reactivated to supervise standby forces, ready for enforcement action (p. 165). UN peacekeeping operations would be strengthened and regional approaches used to complement global UN action (pp. 167–71).

The changes recommended by the Brandt and Palme reports are scarcely revolutionary and, when seen in a time scale of ten to twenty years, are not 'unrealistic' in the sense that they would be no more substantial than many of the social and economic upheavals that have occurred over the past twenty years – the process of decolonization, the massive expenditure on armaments, the rise of the oil-producing states and the newly industrialized countries.

Faced by a future world of greater peace and security – as recommended in the Brandt and Palme reports – or the bleak prospect of a decline into economic depression, social tension and possible military destruction, prudence, let alone common sense, suggests that governments choose the former path. Yet this is by no means certain. The meeting of heads of state and government convened to discuss the Brandt Report's ideas – the Cancun Summit of 1981 – provided no new impetus in the field of global economic reform. The 1982 Second UN Special Session on Disarmament was a failure.

This need not be the end of the story. Governments should exist to serve their people and sometimes the people realize this. It is noticeable that the governments of the small democratic states of Scandinavia and the Low Countries have been amongst the most responsive to the issues of development and arms control and disarmament, primarily because of the home-grown pressure groups on these subjects. In the past, international non-governmental organizations have acted as catalysts for action on a wider basis than that by just one or two governments. For example, the global nature of environmental problems received its earliest recognition by the scientific INGOs and these, together with environmentalist pressure groups, were prominent at the 1972 UN Conference on the Human Environment. Since then, research and action on the environment has been undertaken by a mix of government agencies, IGOs and INGOs (Allen, 1980; Boardman, 1981; Johnson, 1972; Smith, 1972). National and international NGOs have played important roles in bringing to world attention the consequences of apartheid, the question of human rights and women's issues, amongst others (Willetts, 1982). They have been active in teaching, ministering and healing throughout the world; they have supported trade union, business and professional activities across frontiers; and they have proselytized on subjects as diverse as new languages, planned parenthood and world government.

Before the Second World War, the ideas of an economically united Europe and of a decolonized Africa and Asia were those of small pressure groups which, more often than not, worked across the frontiers of the governments that ignored or derided them. The war then unleashed social and political forces that allowed their time to come. The conditions prevailing in the closing years of the twentieth century offer many opportunities to modern-day INGOs. Such pressure groups 'may not have great military or economic resources but they can communicate political ideas' (Willetts, 1982, p. 196).

With this power to mould people's minds and strengthen their will-power, the international non-governmental organizations have the potential to transform that which seems unlikely into a programme governments and IGOs can accept as possible. The history of international organizations, with its modest beginnings in the nineteenth century, might then enter a golden age.

List of Abbreviations

ASEAN	Association of South East Asian Nations
BINGOS	Business international non-governmental organizations
CMEA (also Comecon)	Council for Mutual Economic Assistance
ECE	Economic Commission for Europe (of the UN)
ECLA	Economic Commission for Latin America (of the UN)
ECOSOC	Economic and Social Council (of the UN)
EFTA	European Free Trade Association
GATT	General Agreement on Tariffs and Trade
IBRD	International Bank for Reconstruction and Development
ICES	International Council for the Exploration of the Sea
IDA	International Development Association
IEA	International Energy Agency
IFC	International Finance Corporation
IGO	Intergovernmental organization
ILO	International Labour Organization
IMF	International Monetary Fund
INGO	International non-governmental organization
INTELSAT	International Telecommunications Satellite Organization
ITO	International Trade Organization
ITU	International Telecommunication Union (formerly International Telegraph Union)
IUCN	International Union for the Conservation of Nature and Natural Resources
IULA	International Union of Local Authorities
IWC	International Whaling Commission
MNC	Multinational corporation
NATO	North Atlantic Treaty Organization
NEAFC	North East Atlantic Fisheries Commission
NIEO	New International Economic Order
OAS	Organization of American States
OAU	Organization of African Unity
OECD	Organization of Economic Co-operation and Development
ONUC	Operation des Nations Unies au Congo (United Nations Operation in the Congo)
OPEC	Organization of Petroleum Exporting Countries
PLO	Palestine Liberation Organization
TNC	Transnational Corporation
UIA	Union of International Associations
UNCHE	United Nations Conference on the Human Environment
UNCI	United Nations Commission for Indonesia
UNCLOS	United Nations Conference on the Law of the Sea

UNCTAD	United Nations Conference on Trade and Development
UNDOF	United Nations Disengagement and Observer Force
UNEF	United Nations Emergency Force
UNESCO	United Nations Educational, Scientific and Cultural Organization
UNFICYP	United Nations Force in Cyprus
UNICEF	United Nations Children's Fund
UNIDO	United Nations Industrial Development Organization
UNIFIL	United Nations Interim Force in Lebanon
UNSCOB	United Nations Special Committee on the Balkans
UNTSO	United Nations Truce Supervisory Organization
UNMOGIP	United Nations Military Observer Group in India and Pakistan
UPU	Universal Postal Union
WEU	Western European Union
WHO	World Health Organization
WMO	World Meteorological Organization
WTO	Warsaw Treaty Organization ('Warsaw Pact')

Bibliography

Allen, R. (1980), *How to Save the World: Strategy for World Conservation* (London: Kogan Page).

Almond, G. and Powell, G. B. (1966), *Comparative Politics: A Developmental Approach* (Boston: Little, Brown).

Amin, S. (1977), 'Self reliance and the New International Economic Order', *Monthly Review*, vol. 29, no. 3, pp. 1–21.

Angell, R. (1965), 'An analysis of trends in international organizations', *Peace Research Society (International) Papers*, vol. 3, pp. 185–95.

Archer, C. and Main, J. (1980) *Scotland's Voice in International Affairs* (London: Hurst).

Atherton, A. L. (1976), *International Organizations: A Guide to Information Sources* (Detroit: Gale Research).

Baldwin, D. A. (1980), 'International interdependence: the evolution of a concept' (Mimeographed paper for British International Studies Association, Lancaster University, December 1980).

Barnet, R. J. and Muller, R. E. (1975), *Global Reach: The Power of the Multinational Corporations* (London: Cape).

Barros, J. (1979), *Office without Power: Secretary-General Sir Eric Drummond 1919–1933* (Oxford: Clarendon Press).

Bennett, A. Le R. (1977), *International Organizations: Principles and Issues* (Englewood Cliffs, NJ: Prentice-Hall).

Berki, R. N. (1971), 'On Marxian thought and the problem of international relations', *World Politics*, vol. 24, no. 1, pp. 80–105.

Black, C. E., and Falk, R. A. (eds) (1969), *The Future of the International Legal Order, Vol. I Trends and Patterns* (Princeton: Princeton University Press).

Black, C. E., and Falk, R. A. (eds) (1972), *The Future of the International Legal Order, Vol. IV The Structure of the International Environment* (Princeton: Princeton University Press).

Boardman, R. (1981), *International Organization and the Conservation of Nature* (London: Macmillan).

Bodenheimer, S. (1971), 'Dependency and imperialism', *Politics and Society*, vol. 1, no. 3, pp. 327–57.

Bowett, D. W. (1970), *The Law of International Institutions*, 2nd edn (London: Stevens & Sons).

Bozeman, A. (1960), *Politics and Culture in International History* (Princeton, NJ: Princeton University Press).

Brierly, J. L. (1946), 'The covenant and the charter', *British Yearbook of International Law*, vol. 23, pp. 83–94.

Brown, J. S. (1909), *The Hague Peace Conference of 1899 and 1907: Vol. 2* (Baltimore: Johns Hopkins Press).

Brucan, S. (1977), 'Power and conflict', *International Social Science Journal*, vol. 29, no. 1, pp. 94–114.

Bull, H. (1966), 'The Grotian conception of international society', in Butterfield and Wight (eds) (1966).

Bull, H. (1972), 'The theory of international politics 1919–1969', in Porter (ed.) (1972).

Burton, J. (1972), World Society (Cambridge: CUP).

Butterfield, H. and Wight, M. (eds) (1966), Diplomatic Investigations (London: Allen & Unwin).

Butterworth, R. L. (1978), Moderation from Management: International Organizations and Peace (Pittsburgh: University Center for International Studies).

Cantori, L. J. and Spiegel, S. L. (1970), The International Politics of Regions: A Comparative Approach (Englewood Cliffs, NJ: Prentice-Hall).

Cardosa, F. H. (1974), 'Notas sobre el estado actual de los estudios sobre dependencia', in Sierra (1974), pp. 325–56.

Carr, E. H. (1939), The Twenty Years Crisis 1919–1939, 1st edn (London: Macmillan).

Carr, E. H. (1945), Nationalism and After (London: Macmillan).

Carr, E. H. (1946), The Twenty Years Crisis 1919–1939, 2nd edn (London: Macmillan).

Cassan, H. (1974), 'Le consensus dans la pratique des Nations Unies', Annuaire Français de Droit International, vol. 20, pp. 456–85.

Cecil, Viscount (1941), A Great Experiment (London: Cape).

Chamberlain, J. P. (1955), 'International organziation', in Jessup et al. (1955).

Chen, K. C. (ed.) (1979), China and the Three Worlds (London: Macmillan).

Clark, G. and Sohn, L. B. (1966), World Peace Through World Law: Two Alternative Plans, 3rd edn (Cambridge, Mass.: Harvard University Press).

Claude, I. L. (1964), Swords into Plowshares, 3rd edn (London: University of London Press).

Claude, I. L. (1968), 'International organization: the process and the institutions', in Sills (1968), pp. 33–40.

Claude, I. L. (1971), Swords into Plowshares, 4th edn (New York: Random House).

Cocks, P. (1980), 'Towards a Marxist theory of European integration', International Organization, vol. 34, no. 1, pp. 1–40.

Cordier, A. W. and Foote, W. (eds) (1972), Public Papers of the Secretaries-General of the United Nations. Vol. 2: Dag Hammarskjold 1953–1956 (London and New York: Columbia University Press).

de Russett, A. (1950), Strengthening the Framework of Peace (London: Royal Institute of International Affairs).

Deutsch, K. (1966), 'External influences in the internal behavior of states', in Farrell (1966).

Deutsch, K. et al. (1957), Political Community and the North Atlantic Area (Princeton: Princeton University Press).

Dixon, W. J. (1981), 'The emerging image of UN politics', World Politics, vol. 34, no. 1, pp. 47–61.

Dolman, A. (1979), 'The like-minded countries and the New International Order: past, present and future prospects', Cooperation and Conflict, vol. 14, nos 2–3, pp. 57–85.

Duverger, M. (1972), *The Study of Politics* (London: Nelson).

Eagleton, C. (1948), *International Government*, revised edn (New York: Ronald).

Etzioni, A. (1964), 'Atlantic Union, the southern continents, and the United Nations', in Fisher (1964).

Fabian, L. L. (1971), 'International administration of peace-keeping operations', in Jordan (1971).

Falk, R. A. (1969), 'The interplay of Westphalia and charter conceptions of international legal order', in Black and Falk (eds) (1969).

Farrell, R. B. (ed.) (1966), *Approaches to Comparative and International Politics* (New York: Free Press).

Feld, W. (1971), 'Non-governmental entities and the international system: a preliminary quantitative overview', *Orbis*, vol. 15, pp. 879–922.

Feuer, L. S. (ed.) (1969), *Marx and Engels. Basic Writings on Politics and Philosophy* (London: Collins, The Fontana Library).

Fisher, R. (ed.) (1964), *International Conflict and Behavioural Science* (New York: Basic Books).

Gerbet, P. (1977), 'Rise and development', *International Social Science Journal*, vol. 29, no. 1, pp. 7–27.

Gladwyn, Lord (Sir Gladwyn Jebb) (1953) 'The free world and the United Nations', *Foreign Affairs*, vol. 31, no. 3, pp. 382–91.

Gladwyn, Lord (Sir Gladwyn Jebb) (1966), 'World order and the nation state – a regional approach', *Daedalus*, vol. 95, no. 2, pp. 694–703.

Goodrich, L. M., Hambro, E. and Simons, A. (1969), *Charter of the United Nations: Commentary and Documents*, 3rd edn (New York: Columbia University Press).

Gosovic, B. and Ruggie, J. G. (1976), 'On the creation of a new international economic order', *International Organization*, vol. 30, no. 2, pp. 309–45.

Gregg, R. W. (1981), 'Negotiating a New International Economic Order: the issue of venue', in Jütte and Gross-Jütte (1981).

Haas, E. B. (1958), *The Uniting of Europe: Political, Social and Economic Forces, 1950–1957*, 1st edn (Stanford, Calif.: Stanford University Press).

Haas, E. B. (1961), 'International integration: the European and the universal process', *International Organization*, vol. 25, pp. 336–92.

Haas, E. B. (1964), *Beyond the Nation State* (Stanford, Calif.: Stanford University Press).

Haas, E. B. (1968), *The Uniting of Europe: Political, Social and Economic Forces, 1950–1957*, 2nd edn (Stanford, Calif.: Stanford University Press).

Haas, E. B. (1970), 'The study of regional integration: reflections on the joy and anguish of pretheorizing', *International Organization*, vol. 24, no. 2, pp. 607–46.

Haas, E. B. (1975), *The Obsolescence of Regional Integration Theory* (Berkeley, Calif.: Institute of International Studies).

Haas, E. B. (1976), 'Turbulent fields and the theory of regional integration', *International Organization*, vol. 30, no. 2, pp. 173–212.

Haas, E. B. and Rowe, E. T. (1973), 'Regional organizations in the United Nations: is there externalization?' *International Studies Quarterly*, vol. 17, no. 1, pp. 3–54.

Haas, E. B. and Schmitter, P. C. (1964), 'Economics and differential patterns of political integration', *International Organization*, vol. 18, no. 4, pp. 705–37.

Haas, M. (1971), *International Organization: An Interdisciplinary Bibliography* (Stanford, Calif.: Hoover Institute).

Hankey, Lord (1946), *Diplomacy by Conference. Studies in Public Affairs 1920–1946* (London: Ernest Benn).

Henig, R. B. (ed.) (1973), *The League of Nations* (Edinburgh: Oliver and Boyd).

Higgins, R. (1969), *United Nations Peacekeeping 1946–1967: Documents and Commentary. Vol. 1 – The Middle East* (London: OUP).

Higgins, R. (1980), *United Nations Peacekeeping 1946–1967: Documents and Commentary. Vol. 3 – Africa* (London: OUP).

Hinsley, F. H. (1967), *Power and the Pursuit of Peace* (Cambridge: CUP).

Hoffmann, S. (1970), 'International organization and the international system', *International Organization*, vol. 24, pp. 389–413.

Hudson, M. O. (1944), *International Tribunals, Past and Future* (Washington, DC: Carnegie Endowment for International Peace and Brookings Institutions).

Independent Commission on Disarmament and Security Issues (1982), *Common Security. A Programme for Disarmament* ('Palme Report') (London: Pan).

Independent Commission on International Development Issues (1980), *North–South: A Programme for Survival* ('Brandt Report') (London: Pan).

Jacobsen, H. K. (1979), *Networks of Interdependence: International Organizations and the Global Political System* (New York/Westminster MD: Alfred A. Knopf/Random House).

James, R. R. (1971), 'The evolving concept of the international civil service', in Jordan (1971).

Jenkins, R. (1971), *Exploitation* (London: Paladin).

Jenks, C. W. (1945a), 'Some constitutional problems of international organizations', *British Yearbook of International Law*, vol. 22, pp. 11–72.

Jenks, C. W. (1945b), *The Headquarters of International Institutions. A Study of their Location and Status* (London: Royal Institute of International Affairs).

Jenks, C. W. (1962a), 'The significance for international law of the tripartite character of the International Labour Organization', *Transactions of the Grotius Society*, vol. 22, pp. 45–81.

Jenks, C. W. (1962b), 'Some legal aspects of the financing of international institutions', *Transactions of the Grotius Society*, vol. 28, pp. 87–132.

Jessup, P. C., Lande, A., Lissitzyn, O. J. and Chamberlain, J. P. (1955), *International Organization* (New York: Carnegie Endowment for International Peace).

Johnson, B. (1972), 'The United Nations institutional response to Stockholm: a case study in the international politics of institutional change', in Kay and Skolnikoff (1972).

Jordan, R. S. (ed.) (1971), *International Administration: Its Evolution and Contemporary Applications* (New York: OUP).

Judge, A. J. N. (1978), 'International institutions: diversity, borderline cases, functional substitutes and possible alternatives', in Taylor and Groom (1978).

Jütte, R. and Gross-Jütte, A. (eds) (1981), *The Future of International Organization* (London: Frances Pinter).

Kaiser, K. (1968), 'The interaction of regional subsystems. Some preliminary notes on recurrent patterns and the role of superpowers', *World Politics*, vol. 21, no. 1, pp. 84–107.

Kay, D. A. (ed.) (1977), *The Changing United Nations* (New York: The Academy of Political Science).

Kay, D. A. and Skolnikoff, E. B. (eds) (1972), *World Eco-Crisis: International Organisations in Response* (Wisconsin: University of Wisconsin Press).

Kelsen, H. (1950), *The Law of the United Nations* (London: Stevens and Sons).

Keohane, R. O. and Nye, J. S. (1971), *Transnational Relations and World Politics* (Cambridge, Mass.: Harvard University Press).

Keohane, R. O. and Nye, J. S. (1977), *Power and Interdependence: World Politics in Transition* (Boston, Mass.: Little Brown).

Keynes, J. M. (1919), *The Economic Consequences of the Peace* (London: Macmillan).

Kindleberger, C. P. (ed.) (1970), *The International Corporation* (Cambridge, Mass.: MIT Press).

Klepacki, Z. L. (1973), *The Organs of International Organisations* (Alphen aan den Rijn: Sijthoff and Noordhoff).

Kubalkova, V. and Cruickshank, A. A. (1980), *Marxism–Leninism and Theory of International Relations* (London: Routledge & Kegan Paul).

Lauterpacht, E. (ed.) (1970), *International Law, Being the Collected Papers of Hersch Lauterpacht*, Vol. 1 (Cambridge: CUP).

Lauterpacht, Sir H. (1934), *The Development of International Law by the Permanent Court of International Justice* (London: Longman).

Lenin, V. I. (1966), *Imperialism. The Highest Stage of Capitalism* (Moscow: Progress Publishers).

Lenin, V. I. (1970), *On the Foreign Policy of the Soviet State* (Moscow: Progress Publishers).

Lindberg, L. N. (1963), *The Political Dynamics of European Economic Integration* (Stanford, Calif.: Stanford University Press).

Lindberg, L. N. (1966), 'Integration as a source of stress on the European Community system', *International Organization*, vol. 20, pp. 223–65.

Lindberg, L. N. and Scheingold, S. A. (1970), *Europe's Would-Be Polity* (Englewood Cliffs, NJ: Prentice-Hall).

Little, R. and McKinlay, R. D. (1978), 'Linkage–responsiveness and the modern state: an alternative view of interdependence', *British Journal of International Studies*, vol. 4, no. 3, pp. 209–25.

Luard, E. (1977), *International Agencies – Emerging Framework of Interdependence* (London: Macmillan).

McCormick, J. M. and Kihl, Y. W. (1979), 'Intergovernmental organizations and foreign policy behavior: some empirical findings', *American Political Science Review*, vol. 73, no. 2, pp. 494–504.

Mandel, E. (1970a), 'The laws of uneven development', *New Left Review*, no. 59, pp. 20–35.

Mandel, E. (1970b), *Europe Versus America? Contradictions of Imperialism* (London: New Left Books).

Mansbach, R. W., Ferguson, Y. H. and Lampert, D. E. (1976), *The Web of World Politics* (Englewood Cliffs, NJ: Prentice-Hall).

Marx, K. and Engels, F. (1965), *Manifesto of the Communist Party* (Moscow: Progress Publishers).

Mazrui, A. (1967), *Towards a Pax Africana: A Study of Ideology and Ambition* (London: Weidenfeld & Nicolson).

Michalek, S. J. (1971), 'The League of Nations and the United Nations in world politics: a plea for comparative research and universal international organizations', *International Studies Quarterly*, vol. 15, pp. 387–441.

Mitrany, D. (1965), 'The prospect of integration: federal and functional', *Journal of Common Market Studies*, vol. 4, no. 2, pp. 119–49.

Mitrany, D. (1966), *A Working Peace System* (Chicago: Quadrangle Books).

Mitrany, D. (1975), *The Functional Theory of Politics* (London: Martin Robertson).

Morgenthau, H. J. (1960), *Politics among Nations. The Struggle for Power and Peace* (New York: Alfred A. Knopf).

Morgenthau, H. J. (1970), *Truth and Power: Essays of a Decade 1960–70* (London: Pall Mall Press).

Morozov, G. (1977), 'The socialist conception', *International Social Science Journal*, vol. 29, no. 1, pp. 28–45.

Moynihan, D. (1979), *A Dangerous Place* (London: Secker & Warburg).

Myrdal, G. (1955), 'Realities and Illusions in regard to inter-governmental organisations', in *Hobhouse Memorial Lecture 1955* (London: OUP), pp. 3–28.

Nicolson, Sir H. (1969), *Diplomacy*, 3rd edn (London: OUP).

Niebuhr, R. (1936), *Moral Man and Immoral Society. A Study in Ethics and Politics* (New York: Charles Scribner's Sons).

Niebuhr, R. (1948), 'The illusion of world government', *Foreign Affairs*, vol. 27, pp. 379–88.

Nielsson, G. P. (1978), 'The parallel national action process: Scandinavian experiences', in Taylor and Groom (1978).

Northedge, F. S. (1976), *The International Political System* (London: Faber).

Nye, J. (1970), 'Comparing common markets: a revised neo-functionalist model', *International Organization*, vol. 24, no. 4, pp. 796–835.

Nye, J. S. (1972), 'Regional institutions', in Black and Falk (1972).

O'Brien, C. C. (1962), *To Katanga and Back* (London: Hutchinson).

O'Brien, C. C. and Topolski, F. (1968), *The UN – Sacred Drama* (London: Hutchinson).

O'Leary, G. (1980), *The Shaping of Chinese Foreign Policy* (London: Croom Helm).

Osakwe, C. (1972), *Participation of the Soviet Union in Universal International Organizations* (Leiden: A. W. Sijthoff).

Padelford, N. J. (1954), 'Regional organization and the United Nations', *International Organization*, vol. 8, no. 1, pp. 203–16.

Padelford, N. J. (1955), 'Recent developments in regional organizations', *Proceedings of the American Society of International Law*, 1955.
Peaslee, A. J. (1974), *International Governmental Organizations – Constitutional Documents. Part 1*, 3rd edn (The Hague: Martinus Nijhoff).
Peaslee, A. J. (1975), *International Governmental Organizations – Constitutional Documents. Part 2*, 3rd edn (The Hague: Martinus Nijhoff).
Pentland, C. (1976), 'International organizations', in Rosenau *et al.* (1976).
Pheelan, E. T. (1949), *Yes and Albert Thomas* (London: Crescent Press).
Plano, J. C. and Riggs, R. E. (1967), *Forging World Order* (London: Collier-Macmillan).
Porter, B. (ed.) (1972), *The Aberystwyth Papers: International Politics 1919–1969* (Oxford: OUP).
Reuter, P. (1958), *International Institutions* (London: Allen & Unwin).
Rochester, J. M. (1974), *International Institutions and World Order: The International System as a Prismatic Polity* (Beverly Hills and London: Sage Professional Papers in International Studies).
Rosecrance, R., Alexander, A., Koehler, W., Kroll, J., Laqueuer, S. and Stoeker, J. (1977), 'Whither interdependence?', *International Organization*, vol. 31, pp. 425–72.
Rosenau, J. N., Thompson, K. W. and Boyd, G. (eds) (1976), *World Politics – An Introduction* (New York: The Free Press).
Royal Institute of International Affairs (RIIA) (1946), *United Nations Documents 1941–1945* (London: Royal Institute of International Affairs).
Russell, R. and Muther, J. E. (1958), *A History of the United Nations Charter. The Role of the United States 1940–1945* (Washington, DC: The Brookings Institution).
Russett, B. M. (1967), *International Regions and the International System: A Study in Political Ecology* (Chicago: Rand McNally).
Russett, B. M. and Starr, H. (1981), *World Politics: The Menu for Choice* (San Francisco, Calif.: W. H. Freeman).
Schermers, H. G. (1972), *International Institutional Law*. Vol. 1 – *Structure* (Leiden: A. W. Sijthoff).
Schwarzenberger, G. (1941), *Power Politics* (London: Cape).
Selznick, P. (1957), *Leadership in Administration* (New York: Harper & Row).
Sierra, J. (ed.) (1974), *Desarrollo Latinoamericano: Ensayos Criticos* (Mexico City: Fondo de Cultura Economica).
Sills, D. (ed.) (1968), *International Encyclopedia of the Social Sciences*, Vol. 8 (New York: Macmillan and Free Press).
Singer, D. and Wallace, M. (1970), 'Intergovernmental organization and the preservation of peace, 1918–1964', *International Organization*, vol. 24, no. 3, pp. 520–47.
Sinha, R. (1976), *Food and Poverty: The Political Economy of Confrontation* (London: Croom Helm).
Skjelsbaek, K. (1971), 'The growth of international non-governmental organisation in the twentieth century', *International Organization*, vol. 25, no. 3, pp. 420–42.
Smith, J. E. (1972), 'The role of special purpose and non-governmental organizations in the environmental crisis', in Kay and Skolnikoff (1972).

Smith, M., Little, R. and Shackleton, M. (eds) (1981), *Perspectives in World Politics* (London: Croom Helm).

Society for Anglo-Chinese Understanding (SACU) (1979), *China's World View* (London: Anglo-Chinese Cultural Institute).

Speeckaert, G. P. (1957), 'The 1,978 international organizations founded since the Congress of Vienna: a chronological list', *Documents for the Study of International Nongovernmental Relations*, no. 7 (Brussels: Union of International Associations).

Sterling, R. W. (1974), *Macropolitics: International Relations in a Global Society* (New York: Alfred A. Knopf).

Sullivan, M. P. (1978), 'Competing frameworks and the study of contemporary international politics', *Millennium: Journal of International Studies*, vol. 7, no. 2, pp. 93–110.

Symonds, R. (1971), 'Functional agencies and international administration', in Jordan (1971).

Tandon, Y. (1978), 'The interpretation of international institutions from a Third World perspective' in Taylor and Groom (1978).

Taylor, P. and Groom, A. J. R. (eds) (1978), *International Organisation: A Conceptual Approach* (London: Frances Pinter).

Tharp, P. A. (ed.) (1971), *Regional International Organisations: Structures and Functions* (London: St Martin's Press).

Vasquez, J. A. (1979), 'Colouring it Morgenthau: new evidence for an old thesis on quantitative international politics', *British Journal of International Studies*, vol. 5, no. 3, pp. 210–28.

Verrier, A. (1981), *International Peacekeeping* (Harmondsworth: Penguin).

Virally, M. (1977), 'Definition and classification: a legal approach', *International Social Science Journal*, vol. 29, no. 1, pp. 58–72.

Wagner, R. H. (1974), 'Dissolving the state: three recent perspectives on international relations', *International Organization*, vol. 28, no. 2, pp. 435-66.

Wallace, M. and Singer, D. (1970), 'Intergovernmental organization in the global system 1815–1964', *International Organization*, vol. 24, no. 2, pp. 239–87.

Waltz, K. (1970), 'The myth of national interdependence', in Kindleberger (1970).

Ward, B. and Dubos, R. (1972), *Only One Earth. The Care and Maintenance of a Small Planet* (Harmondsworth: Penguin).

Weintraub, S. (1977), 'The role of the United Nations in economic negotiations', in Kay (1977).

Weiss, T. (1982), 'International bureaucracy: myth and reality of the international civil service', *International Affairs*, vol. 58, no. 2, pp. 286–306.

Wells, L. J. (1971), 'The multinational business enterprise: what kind of international organization?' in Keohane and Nye (1971), pp. 97–114.

Willetts, P. (ed.) (1982), *Pressure Groups in the Global System* (London: Frances Pinter).

Wolfers, A. (1962), 'The actors in international politics', in *Discord and Collaboration*, ed. A. Wolfers (Baltimore: Johns Hopkins Press).

Woolf, L. (1916), *International Government*, 2nd edn (London: Allen & Unwin).

Wright, Q. (1965), *A Study of War*, 2nd edn (Chicago: University of Chicago Press).

Yalem, R. (1965), *Regionalism and World Order* (Washington, DC: Public Affairs Press).

Yalem, R. (1966), 'The study of international organization, 1920–65; a study of the literature', *Background*, vol. 10, no. 1.

Yearbook of International Organizations (1974), 15th edn (Brussels: Union of International Associations).

Yearbook of International Organizations (1976/7), 16th edn (Brussels: Union of International Associations).

Yearbook of International Organizations (1981), 19th edn (Brussels: Union of International Associations).

Yeselson, A. and Gaglione, A. (1974), *A Dangerous Place – The United Nations as a Weapon in World Politics* (New York: Grossman).

Zimmern, Sir A. (1939), *The League of Nations and the Rule of Law*, 2nd edn (London: Macmillan).

Index